Contents

Part III: Writing

Part IV: Delivery

Foreword

I started to learn how to rap just watching the older dudes do it in the park. I had to be about 9, 10 years old when I first started hearing hip-hop music being played out in the parks, out in the neighborhoods. I saw the DJ on the two turntables scratching, and I saw dudes on the microphone just really keeping the party amped and charged up—just being masters of ceremony, where the word "MC" comes from, just keeping the party alive.

When I first heard some of them spitting back then, as a kid, I was just fascinated by it. I started repeating what I would hear the older guys saying, and that was my first brush with just beginning to learn how to rap.

Being from the era that I'm from, you had to really stand your ground as far as this lyric shit, and that's why that era bred rappers like a Big Daddy Kane, a KRS-One, a Rakim, a Chuck D. . . . These dudes, they moved you—they moved you from the soul. Their rapping capability and ability—these dudes were phenomenal.

I'm a student of the Grandmaster Caz's, the Melle Mels, the Kool Moe Dees, Silver Fox from Fantasy 3, and a lot of others, so when people took to me, they were really taking to a part of each of those rappers, because that's where G Rap was branded from. These were the dudes that influenced G Rap to rap the way he raps or to even just have the motivation to want to stand out from everybody else and not only be different but be the best at what I do—it was inspired by those rappers.

So I think you definitely have to study some of the people that are considered to be legends, and great lyricists, and great rappers—study and do your homework and brush up on your history. You gotta know what it is to be a great MC in order to do it—you gotta hear it, you gotta feel it.

KOOL G RAP

Kool G Rap is a legendary MC whose complex rhyme style and vivid street imagery have influenced a whole generation of MCs. From Eminem showing his respect to G Rap in his Grammy acceptance speech to Jay-Z citing G Rap's greatness in his song "Encore" ("hearing me rap is like hearing G Rap in his prime") to being named as a major influence by the majority of the rappers interviewed for this book, Kool G Rap's standing as one of the most influential and skilled MCs of all time is indisputable.

Introduction

*Always continue to learn—reading is a great way to intake
information—and never think you're the best. You always
have something to learn from someone.*

◄ MURS ►

How to Rap teaches you the art and science of MCing through
the words and lyrics of some of the most influential and respected
MCs of all time, from all areas of hip-hop. Over a hundred MCs
were interviewed exclusively for this book, including pioneers
and contemporary MCs, mainstream and underground rappers
(there is a complete list of all the interviewed artists on p. 315). As
many different types of artists as possible were included, to draw
on their individual strengths—explaining everything from writing
deep political lyrics to crafting chart-topping choruses.

All the techniques, methods, and suggestions come directly
from the artists themselves, so that you can learn in the same way
that all rappers have learned—from other rappers. As Tech N9ne
says, "Study MCs, see what they do, then make your own—that's
how everybody started." All the artists interviewed for *How to Rap*
told a similar story of how they learned their craft by listening to
other MCs, analyzing those artists' work, and constantly expanding their range of skills.

Rah Digga

I studied KRS-One, Rakim. . . . Kool G Rap from the Juice Crew kind of set the standards for me as far as what was considered a dope verse and dope rhyming, so I basically just mimicked him. I just kind of analyzed their styles, like, OK, Kool G Rap uses a lot of similes and metaphors, and I just made sure I did that a lot.

The words of the interviewed artists will guide you step by step through the art form, breaking down the different elements of the craft. The fundamental elements of MCing divide *How to Rap* into the following parts: "Content," "Flow," "Writing," and "Delivery." By exploring the key components individually, you can focus on and master each one.

Bishop Lamont

If you want to be someone great and someone who will be remembered, you have to master that field, and that means mastering every aspect and every style that there is. You take 2Pac—he mastered every element, every aspect—[and] Biggie under the same circumstances, of mastering all the hemispheres of the music.

How to Rap also provides valuable insight into the history of MCing, exposing you to many of the pivotal figures in hip-hop, their music, and their influences, and to the notable styles within the genre. And knowing this history helps you become a great MC by building on the decades of work and innovation of other MCs. Myka 9 of Freestyle Fellowship notes that "today's MCs are building on a foundation that has already been established," and Guerilla Black adds, "Study, really pay attention to what's going on—it'll teach you a lot. That's one thing about Eminem: Eminem listened to everything and that's what made him one of the greats."

will.i.am, Black Eyed Peas

Study, know all of the facts. Know where Nas got his style from, know Jay-Z, where he came from—go get the Jaz [Jaz-O], go buy "Hawaiian Sophie" [a Jaz-O single featuring Jay-Z]. Go learn where Biggie got his style from, and once you realize he was influenced by people like Black Moon, and you like Black Moon and you like Heltah Skeltah [both of supergroup Boot Camp Clik], then you can find out where Black Moon got their style from, and then you go learn about Stetsasonic— "Talkin' All That Jazz"—and De La Soul and Jungle Brothers. Debbie Harry, Blondie and Fab Five Freddy—that's the first Pharrell and Gwen Stefani, that's the first will.i.am and Fergie in Blondie and Fab Five Freddy. If you like Missy Elliot then you know she got her shit from Roxanne Shanté and [others], if you like Lil Jon, they got their style from Luke and 2 Live Crew . . . you like 2 Live Crew, they got their style from blah blah blah . . . and then you got a history. So if you want to be an MC, you've got to know where shit comes from, you gotta know different styles, you gotta know different patterns, you gotta know different coasts. You gotta know Geto Boys, you gotta know why T.I. is T.I., where did T.I. get his style from—I could break T.I. down, T.I. is dope, but everybody get their style from somebody. That's what makes a good MC, a person that knows and that can be a chameleon—chameleon MCs are cats that can do all the styles.

How to Rap covers a wide range of the techniques used by many artists. Although different MCs have different opinions and different ways of doing things, every viewpoint and technique has been included to give a complete picture. In fact, the majority of MCs don't have a set formula they use all the time— they use different combinations of the techniques found in *How to Rap*.

III Bill

There's no set process [for me]—there's a hundred different ways to skin a cat and I use all one hundred and beyond. A lot of different things influence me to write rhymes, a lot of different ways I end up writing them—there's no specific ritual. I don't think there's any artist that's gonna tell you there is one specific way they create every single time—there might be, but I doubt it. It's just not gonna work that way, especially if you're a touring artist [who's] always in the mix of different situations at any given time.

There is no single "correct" way to do anything—the right way is whatever works best for you and your music. As you pick and choose from among the huge range of techniques and methods found in this book, you will develop your own style.

MCs, Emcees, Rappers, Lyricists, Artists

The terms *MC* (sometimes spelled *emcee*), *rapper*, *lyricist*, and *artist* appear many times in *How to Rap*. Sometimes distinctions are made among these terms—for example, *MC* may be used to imply a high level of live performance skill, while *lyricist* may be used to describe an artist with particularly intricate lyrics. However, the majority of the people interviewed for this book used these terms interchangeably, so to avoid confusion, *How to Rap* makes no distinction between the terms—they all refer to someone who raps.

Shock G, Digital Underground

The origin of why rappers are called "MCs" in the first place comes from the phrase *Master of Ceremonies*—thus the *MC* prefix to so many rappers' names, especially in the [early days of hip-hop].

◀ ▌ ▶

Content

Content Topics

*Honestly, nothing is nothing without content, because
a lot of [rappers] be flowing but they ain't saying shit.
I kick stories, I kick conscious shit, I kick braggadocio
shit, freestyles. . . . I kick everything.*

◄ 2Mex, The Visionaries ►

The content of a hip-hop song (sometimes called the *subject matter*) includes every subject you talk about in your lyrics. It is what you're actually rapping about, rather than the rhythms and rhymes you're using (the *flow*), or how you're using your voice to perform, or "spit," those rhythms and rhymes (the *delivery*). Hip-hop artists tackle a huge range of content in their music—anything you can think of can become the subject of a hip-hop track.

will.i.am, Black Eyed Peas

[Topics come] from anything and everything. Sometimes I rap about stuff from clubs. Sometimes I rap about the world. It just comes—whatever inspires me.

Some MCs like to stick to the topics they're most familiar with, while others cover a wide variety of subjects. MURS, for example, says, "I can write about anything. A challenge to me is you saying, 'MURS, you're in a room with a paperclip and a stripper—make a song about it.'" Content will always vary from artist to artist.

Evidence, Dilated Peoples

That's the dynamic of our group. We speak on a lot of different topics because as MCs we're real different kinds of people.

Rock, Heltah Skeltah

There have always been simple rappers, and there have always been complex rappers . . . there have always been party rappers, there have always been gangsta rappers. There have always been a lot of different types of rap, and there still are a lot of different types of rap.

The content can give you a direction to take a song in—Paris says, "I'll have a list of topics that I want to cover [and] after I'm sure I've covered everything, I'll start composing the actual tracks." Most MCs like to have strong content, because it helps them express themselves better as artists, rather than just rhyming for the sake of rhyming. They agree that what you're saying is just as important as the way you're saying it with your flow and delivery.

MC Shan

If I just wanted to pull out a rhyming dictionary and make something just to make words rhyme, I could do that, but I be having thought behind the things I say.

Lord Jamar, Brand Nubian

At the end of the day, subject matter is the thing that would really be the meat of what you're doing. A flow is a flow—I can hum a flow right now—[but] the substance to the flow is what's being said. What really makes a flow dope is what's being said within the flow, not just the flow itself.

Many listeners like to hear something being said in a hip-hop track, so having strong content is a great way to draw people to your music. If listeners know that you have great subject matter, they will be more willing to listen to what you're saying and will pay more attention to it. Entertaining content will always draw people in.

Lateef, Latyrx

The subject matter, the content, is gonna be how it is that people are able to relate to what it is that you're saying. There are a lot of MCs that I can think of that do subject matter really, really well. Eminem does subject matter really well, where the song is not about the same shit, and it's fucking crazy. . . . The subject matter is so out there that you're really entertained.

Good content also makes your lyrics deeper, which can keep people interested in your music. Instead of just listening to it a few times because it sounds good, they'll keep coming back to it because they know they can get more out of it. Chuck D of Public Enemy notes that a good flow can make up for a lack of subject matter, "but always short term. After a while it's gonna be like, OK, where do we go from here?"

Real-Life Content

The majority of MCs like to write from real-life experience—either autobiographical lyrics about things they have actually gone through or lyrics at least generally inspired by situations they've encountered.

Havoc, Mobb Deep

[My lyrics come from] life experiences, things I go through, things I see my people go through, stuff like that—everyday life.

Big Pooh, Little Brother

[I like writing about] things I'm going through at the time, things that I went through when I was younger—those are the best, because those are things I went through firsthand, the things I'm going through firsthand, and there's no better way to start off writing than explaining or writing about something you went through firsthand.

Life is a great source of material. Lyrics are readily available if you can simply rap about what has happened to you at some point in your life.

Tech N9ne

I go out there and I live it—I write my life and then I put it on paper. I don't believe in writer's block, because the cure for writer's block to me is to go out and have something happen to your ass. I'm always having something happening to me.

Termanology

It's like poetry, man. Every time you got a feeling, you mad at your girlfriend, you're gonna write a rhyme about it. Cops just beat you up and arrested you, you gonna write a rhyme about it. It's definitely autobiographical.

MC Serch

Write about yourself. The best way to become a great MC, I feel, is to make your ordinary story, about how you grew up, extraordinary. And if you can bring your story about where you were raised, on what block and what your mama did, and all of that, I think when you do that, and you do it in a way that makes people wanna listen and care, you're on your way to being a great MC.

Connecting with Listeners

Lyrics that deal with real life are a great way to connect with listeners, as people can easily relate to what you are saying if they have been through something similar. Many of the most admired artists use this technique.

Big Daddy Kane

I think when you look at artists like Melle Mel, Chuck D, 2Pac Shakur, when you look at artists like these cats, it's the type of thing where what they're talking about is something that you've experienced, something that you're probably having a problem with. [Like] a bad part of your life, something that you hate having to deal with, and they just touched upon it in song and you felt it, because this is something that's been messing with you mentally. You felt it and it touched you that way—it hits your heart.

Brother J, X Clan

Look at Eminem. Eminem represented for all of the "white trash," as they say, with the trailer park and all of the other stuff. He took that whole American community, everybody who related with that, and he went from [there] to being a number-one artist—he's going down like Elvis in rap, homie. That's a dream now. He took a whole audience with him. That's real—you can't hate on that. [And] you think about 50 Cent, who represented the same elements for every cat hustling a mixtape, trying to get a buzz on in a city of millions of people, and overcoming that to getting a deal.

Even if listeners have not gone through the exact same experience, they will find it easier to relate to the content if they know that the artist has actually experienced it, and if the artist is able to express all the emotion of that experience in his or her lyrics.

Brother Ali

I always want to make music that's really powerful and personal and real, and that when you hear it, you can feel the feeling that I'm going through. And so the only way that I really know to definitely ensure that is to [write] stuff about my life. Even if I'm writing things that aren't necessarily *my* story, it's somebody very close to me, or something that I've seen or that I've been involved in. So it's all from real-life things, and then basically at that point the idea is to just tell you what you need to know to understand where this feeling is coming from.

Expressing Yourself

Writing from real-life experience is also a good way to express yourself as an artist and deal with topics that are important to you.

Remy Ma

[Ideas come from] different places. A lot of times it's things that you go through, things that you're feeling, whatever is on your mind that particular day or that particular time period.

Gift of Gab, Blackalicious

[I write about] who I am, who I'd like to be, how the world is, how I'd like the world to be, my victories, my struggles—everything. I'm just telling my story. I think being any kind of artist, you gotta tell your story, you gotta get off your chest the things that you think about on the daily.

Fictional Content

Although many MCs write content that is exclusively based on real life, there are also plenty of MCs who feel that there is a place in hip-hop for fictional content. They believe that because MCing is an art form, you shouldn't have to limit your imagination and the scope of your music.

O.C., Diggin' in the Crates

KRS[-One] said it best—he said, "Poetry is the language of imagination" [on the track "Poetry" from Boogie Down Productions' album *Criminal Minded*]. I always try to use my imagination, so I usually try to just draw from my imagination on some Steven Spielberg shit.

Fictional content can make lyrics very vivid and entertaining, as you are limited only by what you can think of, rather than having to stick to what actually happened in real life.

Andy Cat, Ugly Duckling

A lot of rap is autobiographical—it's talking about where you're from, and your life, and all of that, but I got news for you, [many classic hip-hop artists,] they used to make it all up. They weren't going out killing people every night—it's called creativity. I'll be listening with a friend to some track, and be like, "Dude, why do they think anybody cares about what they do every single day that they hang out, smoke weed, watch movies?" Make some stuff up, man.

Different types of songs may call for different amounts of fiction or reality. For example, a lot of battle-oriented songs (see chapter 2, p. 25) use fictionalized, fantastical content to get the point across and entertain the listener.

Vinnie Paz, Jedi Mind Tricks

When you're just doing some battle shit, and when you're saying you're going to chop someone's head off, it's not necessarily very realistic. So it's really whatever the song calls for. I think if you want to be picky you can critique everyone—if all [someone] talks about is their life and reality then you can critique them for favoring that too much, and if someone's whole shit's just constantly over-imaginative, then you would critique them for never really showing a part of who they are. So to me it's each individual's choice for what they want people to know about them.

Many MCs use both reality *and* fiction in their content. As Bishop Lamont says, "I like to combine both, because that's what the world is. As much as there is black and white, there is a gray area, and all things should be represented, and that gives it the spice."

Controversial Content

Often, hip-hop lyrics focus on topics that can be controversial, such as violence, sex, drugs, alcohol, power, and money. These forces are sometimes said to have a negative impact on society, but artistically speaking they are inherently attention-grabbing subjects—which is why numerous classic hip-hop albums have revolved around them and will continue to do so.

MURS

No one saw gangsta rap coming. They told them they were crazy: *You're gonna curse on a record and it's gonna get played? Yeah, right!* And now everything on the radio [is like that]. They changed the world [and] you couldn't have told anyone. . . . And I think that's the beauty of hip-hop—you'll never see it coming, whatever it is.

Devin the Dude

To each his own—that's what makes rap so incredible, man. There's so many different kinds of raps and styles and everything, and some people feel that their life is not peaches and cream and it's hard on the streets and the world is tough and they feel that they should kinda reflect that in their music.

Many artists argue that the negative topics covered in hip-hop lyrics simply reflect those elements that are present in society. One such artist is Lord Jamar of Brand Nubian—a group that is actually noted for its positive, socially conscious lyrics.

Lord Jamar, Brand Nubian

I guess hip-hop represents society in general and America, the best and worst of it. You're not going to change things in hip-hop if you don't change things in the world. Anything you find in hip-hop, you're going to find in society, especially this American society.

But some MCs also warn that if you're going to cover controversial topics, you should be ready to explain your reasons for doing so.

Crooked I

You might have to sharpen your blade mentally, because when somebody challenges you and says why the hell are you rapping about this and that and this, you want to be able to have a conversation with them and explain exactly why you're rapping about this and that and the other thing.

Quality and Creativity

Many of the best MCs have covered controversial subjects at some point in their careers and have found that they can inspire great creativity.

Fredro Starr, Onyx

Back in the day, what me and Sticky [Fingaz] used to do is see who could write the most fucked-up shit, like who could write the worst shit. It was fun doing that, coming up with the wildest, most outrageous shit, so it'd stand out.

But these artists put a high level of craft and attention to detail into writing about controversial subject matter. That's what separates the classic hip-hop albums from the mediocre ones. If you decide to cover these topics, then you should make an effort to do it in an entertaining, original way.

Sheek Louch, D-Block/The LOX

Even if you're going to talk about guns every second, or drugs every second, I need you to word it [well]. Give me something—bring it to life a little more.

Sean Price, Heltah Skeltah

You're talking to Sean Price. [With] my subject matter, I'm not trying to save the world. I be smacking the shit out of people in my rhymes, I be drop-kicking people. I know what I'm writing when I write it, though, so it might be some crazy shit, but I know I'm writing the crazy shit, and I want to write the best crazy shit I can write.

Balancing the Negative and the Positive

Life has both positive and negative aspects. Because artists are often influenced by the things they do and witness—the good as well as the bad—this range of experiences is reflected in their content.

Ill Bill

Whatever is going on around me influences me, positive or negative.

David Banner

My environment, stuff that I see around me, things that I'm doing—it was hard for me to write balling songs when I wasn't balling. I wrote more about pain, I wrote more about the environment which I came out of, I wrote more about struggle.

Some artists make a deliberate effort to include every side of life in their music.

Buckshot, Black Moon

It is trying to [do] the best that I can do, create something spiritual. I try to take the yin and yang approach, which is the balance. Negative and positive is a part of life, so when I write, I write from that perspective—I write from the yin and yang.

Reality/Fantasy

Controversial topics can reflect the harsh realities of life, or they can encourage listeners to fantasize about doing things they can't do in real life. On the one hand, the reality of struggle and pain can have a profound effect on the listener. A large part of 2Pac's appeal was the way that the listener could relate to his struggles.

Guerilla Black

2Pac spoke about the common struggle every day in his rhymes—he was never above the average street dude. He always made you feel like he was on the corner with you smoking that last dime bag of weed, with corrupt cops looking for you, and your enemy threatening your life, and how are we gonna survive, and will we die tonight. That's how Pac made you feel—with 2Pac, you feel like grabbing a pistol and going against the government.

David Banner

It's about touching somebody's emotions—the best music is always music that people feel. The one common denominator that all people have and the only thing that links all men and women together is pain, and that's because of death—everybody's gonna die, I don't give a fuck how much money you got.

On the other hand, controversial content can let the listener revel in a fantasy lifestyle along with the artist. The music of the Notorious B.I.G. could have this effect.

Guerilla Black

Whenever B.I.G. would start rapping about the good life, it was like he brought you and sat you at his ever table of luxury and let you eat caviar and drink champagne and let you ride around—he made you feel like you were in a Phantom when you weren't. He made you glorify those things, the upper echelon. Even when you didn't have it, you felt like you were there with him—with B.I.G. he made you feel like you just won a million dollars.

Conscious Content

A number of MCs like to focus on conscious content, content that is generally positive or calls for some sort of change or advancement. It often deals with political or social issues, or explores subjects such as relationships in ways that are insightful rather than exploitative. This kind of content can sometimes be difficult to write.

Vast Aire, Cannibal Ox

I could brag all day, but when I'm trying to make a point about religion, or George Bush, or a girl that hurt me—that's when the rhyme really has to come together well.

Conscious content has long been a big part of hip-hop lyricism, and it remains an important element to this day.

Myka 9, Freestyle Fellowship

In the early, early '80s—late '70s, early '80s—you had cats like [Grandmaster] Caz and Melle Mel that were putting messages in the music and coming with real lyrics.

Brother J, X Clan

Conscious music is forever fresh, homie. It's never something that is like, "Oh, that was good for yesterday." There's always something you can get from it—there's always someone you can pass it on to and can learn something.

Conscious content often deals with political issues, usually involving the government, economics, or just social conditions in general. To write political content, an artist must have a good knowledge of current events. Vinnie Paz of Jedi Mind Tricks says, "I just try to stay on top of what's going on, not [just relying on] the traditional means that the American public have for information."

As for conscious content about relationships, the subject is covered extensively in most musical genres, and hip-hop is no exception. However, because it has been done so many times before, it can be hard to do it well.

Imani, The Pharcyde

You can always get inspired by a pretty woman—there'll never be enough songs about a fine woman or a scenario or a situation with a woman—so I try to stay away from those situations because it's not easy to write about. But you always find yourself getting caught up writing about a woman.

Vast Aire, Cannibal Ox

[With one of my songs about relationships,] "The F-Word," I

just went into myself and dug deep and was like, I'm gonna write about dating women that used to be your friend and dating a girl, or trying to date a girl, that doesn't want to date you because y'all are friends. So I just took it from those angles and used my real experiences. When [Cannibal Ox producer] El-P made the beat, I told El-P, I said, "Yo, El, I'm writing a girl joint to this," and he was just like, word.

The conscious content of a song doesn't have to be explicitly presented. It can be subtly woven into the lyrics.

Imani, The Pharcyde

I feel like at times we have our way of letting people know where we stand on certain issues without even really speaking on certain things. Like we'll put smoke out there because the whole thing is, where there's smoke, there's fire, so sometimes you can say something without even saying it.

Harnessing the Power of Hip-Hop

Hip-hop's popularity and global reach make it a very powerful medium with which to spread messages and influence people. As a result, a lot of artists feel that they carry a great responsibility for delivering conscious content in their songs—they know they can have a major impact on the world, and they don't want to squander the platform they've been given.

Lord Jamar, Brand Nubian

Hip-hop is one of the most influential genres in the world, and we're selling all kinds of merchandise for people with hip-hop when we can be selling ideas to help change things for the better in the world—using this [genre] for what it could be really for: to make change.

Akir

It might just be my sensibilities or my stance on life, but there's so much going on around us that I feel needs to be touched on, and the fact that we're currently in a state of emergency in terms of hip-hop as well, it makes me feel like if somebody's really giving me the opportunity to say something to them, to inspire their life or inform them, then why would I waste that opportunity?

Brother J, X Clan

We have the opportunity to take what we've learned from our teachers and our ancestors and put it into a major media forum. Hip-hop music is a powerful, powerful beast. It relates worldwide—everything is hip-hop. So for us to have the honor to do that here and the honor to put the message of freedom out, that's where our vibe comes from.

On the other hand, some MCs include conscious content simply to express themselves and their views, rather than to try to prompt social change.

Brother Ali

Even my political songs and stuff, they're all personal—I'm not doing them to raise awareness. If that does happen, then that's cool, that's great, but I'm not making these songs with the idea that I'm gonna change the world with these songs—I'm gonna express myself with these songs.

Substance

Conscious content often has what is described as substance—meaning the content is long lasting, important, and profound, with more relevance and "real meaning" than other content. Vast

Aire of Cannibal Ox defines it by saying, "I'll be dead and gone and people will be playing me and loving me and understanding the time I lived in—that's substance." Cormega puts it another way: "Substance will always, always carry you."

To increase the substance of your content, it is helpful to study other songs that are relevant and profound.

Wise Intelligent, Poor Righteous Teachers

Listen to more intelligent music every day. That'll help you. . . . Money is definitely necessary, but it's not good for the soul to go without knowledge, so money is nothing without knowledge, because knowledge is what fuels the purpose.

Exposure

Conscious content doesn't always get as much exposure as other types of content in hip-hop. Several artists feel that more pressure should be put on the people in charge of pushing and breaking records to support conscious hip-hop, so that there is more balance in what is played.

Tash, Tha Alkaholiks

The radio stations just need to let people that really, really love this shit get on—give a chance to send a positive message along with the booty-shaking songs, play both of them. Don't not play "Slap That Booty" or whatever, but in the same breath, play my boy Talib Kweli—play both.

will.i.am, Black Eyed Peas

I think MCs should rap about whatever is on their mind . . . [but] what I think should happen is companies that put out records should invest in subjects that have meaning to inspire artists to rap about bigger subjects. There's a lot of rappers out there that rap about meaningful things, it's just that you don't hear them on the radio. You have to push radio to play that—radio has to start playing more of that stuff.

Although artists don't necessarily think they should be *made* to write about these kinds of topics, in recent years some MCs have seen a rise in the demand for politically aware music—not from the people in charge but from listeners.

Immortal Technique

I don't think we should force people to [write about more political topics]—I think people should do what they feel. I think right now, in this climate that we're in, the audience is becoming more demanding of the artist himself.

Club/Party Content

Hip-hop lyrics frequently focus on being in the club, partying, and having a good time in general. Although party content isn't usually as highly regarded as other kinds of subject matter, it has always been a part of hip-hop, with its own important role to play.

Immortal Technique

Hip-hop in itself used to be a combination of both the knowledge of self [and] hard-core street rhymes, and then there was the party music too. Hip-hop was born in an era of social turmoil and real economically miserable conditions for the black and Latino people living in the hood in America, so in the same way that slaves used to sing songs on a plantation about being somewhere else—that's the party songs that we used to have.

Tash, Tha Alkaholiks

It's in the eye of the beholder, man, whoever is listening to it. If you want substance, check out that Strong Arm Steady album, check out that Common, check out that Talib Kweli. If you want to party, turn on that Tash from Tha Alkaholiks, turn on that good Redman, Method Man, turn on the good party music. There's so many different facets of rap—there's so many different levels, and personalities, and subject matters. I get on the microphone and I rap about what I like. I rap about having fun, getting busy. MCing—it started with a party atmosphere: let's party, let's get back to the basics, everybody put a smile on their face, have fun.

Party content is still difficult to do well, and there is an art to it. As will.i.am of Black Eyed Peas notes, the same care and level of craft goes into creating a club-based song as into any other song: "The making of the song 'My Humps' is just as important as 'Where Is the Love'—the same quality control and paying attention to detail takes place."

Highlighting Flow

Party content is often a good way to show off an impressive flow (see chapter 4, p. 63). There usually isn't any complicated or profound subject matter to divert the listener's attention away from the rhythm and rhyme—so the flow becomes the main attraction.

Mighty Casey

If I'm doing a party song, I'll try and write to the beat, [because] the flow is more important on a party song.

Stressmatic, The Federation

If it's just like a party song, a club song, I'd say the flow [is more important], and how it makes you feel, because when you're in the club you're not really tripping off the subject matter of the song. . . . You're kind of tripping off the beat and how the rapper flows to the beat.

Club tracks often require a fun vibe during the writing and recording processes, so that the right atmosphere is there when the song is played in a club or party setting. Nelly, who has written a number of successful club tracks, including the hit singles "Hot in Herre" and "Shake Ya Tailfeather," describes writing the track "Party People": "It was fun—if you listen to that track, that track's a monster, and I like to switch the flows up a lot, man, so I thought it was great."

2

Content Forms

As far as writing goes, there's many different forms.
◄ Myka 9, Freestyle Fellowship ►

Content forms are the basic ways of structuring the content of a song. A song's form is not its topic but the overall method it uses to present that topic. For example, an MC could focus on politics as a topic but then present that topic in the form of a story or a battle rap. Having varied content forms allows you to present familiar subjects in a new light, helping you stand out from other MCs and be more original.

Hell Rell, Dipset

The music and the subject matter is constantly changing, so I always challenge myself, like, "OK, what am I saying differently from every other artist?"—and that's what makes an artist dope and hot: originality. Like the forefathers of hip-hop thrived on originality—if you were a biter, or somebody who copied another person's style, you had a real black cloud over you, [so] I just try to keep it original.

Rampage, Flipmode Squad

I want to hear a record that's hot, but I also wanna hear different concepts—I like the artist to take me there, so I can see your point of view.

The Lady of Rage

I don't wanna hear the same old thing, I wanna hear something that's gonna blow my mind! [Did] you put some thought in there, did you take the time, did you really sit down and think about that? I just like different, thought-provoking stuff—I'm a lyricist, so I like lyrics. Lyricists and MCs, that's their main thing—who's saying the dopest shit, not the simplest shit.

Knowing how to use different content forms can also add variation to your music and make you a much more versatile MC. By approaching the same topics from different angles, with lyrics that range from simple to complex, you increase your ability to connect with many different types of listeners.

Pharoahe Monch

With me a lot of times, it is a concerted effort to do a dense piece of work—and I guess that's not for everybody. Everybody doesn't go into a gallery and look at art the same way, and over the years I have painted more simple portraits. I just enjoy not being boxed in as a portrait painter or an abstract artist. You have works like "Who Stole My Last Piece of Chicken?" and "Fudge Pudge" and "My Life" and "Oh No," and you also have works like "Agent Orange" and "Hypnotical Gases" and "Rape" and "Trilogy," which are a little more complicated and take more time for the listener to retrieve. But the beauty about that is that you listen to the album for a month and put it down, and [then you] pick it up again and you hear something new.

Braggadocio/Battling Form

Bragging and boasting, known as braggadocio content, have always been an important part of hip-hop lyrics and are an art form all in themselves. This type of content, combined with put-downs, insults, and disses against real or imaginary opponents, makes up the form known as battle rhyming.

Dray, Das EFX

I'm still from [that] era—I came from the era of bragging [and] boasting. Our stuff was more of "Ooh, did you hear what he said?" type of lyrics. That's what we were going for.

Big Daddy Kane

As an MC from the '80s, really your mentality is battle format, so when you're writing a rhyme, the majority of the time you're writing a bragging and boasting rhyme about yourself being the nicest MC. Really what your focus was, was to have a hot rhyme in case you gotta battle someone, so that was your main focus, not really making a rhyme for a song.

Braggadocio

Braggadocio rhymes can take a number of different forms, from simply saying that you're the best MC ever to getting deeper and wittier with the boasting.

Myka 9, Freestyle Fellowship

Through the '80s, you had Kool Moe Dee, Ultramagnetic MC's, the early days of LL Cool J, Rakim, KRS-One, where they were very, very technical, where they were talking about physics and talking about metaphysics and things like that.

An example of this is in Eric B. & Rakim's "No Omega":

I'm the Alpha, with no Omega,
Beginning without the end, so play the . . .

Here, Rakim describes himself as the first letter of the Greek alphabet (Alpha) and then says there is "no Omega," which is the last letter of the same alphabet. So he is saying he can flow forever because he begins but doesn't end—but he says it in a technically inventive way.

Different artists have their own ideas about what inspires the braggadocio form, from the competitive nature of hip-hop to the struggles of young black men in America.

Guerilla Black

Every MC, he feels like he's the best, and I guess you have to have the arrogance and the bravado to feel like that, to be able to be in this game, because the competition is real hot out there.

Esoteric

A lot of my stuff stems from old-school hip-hop, braggadocio ethic, where my shit is better than yours and that's the bottom line. I was raised playing basketball and everything, a very competitive sport, and I kinda looked at hip-hop in the same way.

MURS

When you're a young, black male in America, you feel powerless—you feel like you don't have a voice, you're disenfranchised—so when you get the microphone, you wanna just pump yourself up. I think that's where all of the bravado comes from, where all the braggadocio comes from.

Braggadocio, like most content forms, can be mixed with other techniques.

Paris

Most material back in the day was centered around the MC and bragging about "greatness" and "skills," [so] I had some of that in my material along with my social commentary.

Vursatyl, Lifesavas

On my first record I probably spent more time talking about how dope I am. As you grow, you want to use that vehicle to talk about other things besides bragging and boasting, though I think bragging and boasting has its place, and I think hip-hop should always keep that.

Battling

Battle raps appear on a lot of records, but they are also often recited or freestyled off the top of the artists' heads in live battles, where MCs will perform on the same stage to see who has the better verses.

40 Cal, Dipset

A battle is straight like fighting. I think about it like this—if what I'm doing right now is just straight NBA games as far as making tracks and putting them out, putting out albums, then battling would be like the three-point and the dunking contests. That's how I compare it—when I'm battling, I'm just doing extracurricular shit, that's the three-point contest and the dunking contest. If you watch basketball, a lot of people who [win those contests], they're not always the nicest [best all-around] people in the NBA, but they're nice at that particular craft.

Many artists make battle rhymes one of their main forms of content. Some consider them a key component of being considered a great MC, because they are often written purely to impress people technically.

Esoteric

Pretty much my favorite thing to do is battle-oriented lyrics. A lot of the battle-oriented tracks come from the beat—if I get a really murderous beat, I'm gonna try to come up with some murderous rhymes. It doesn't really have to stay on a particular theme as long as I'm letting you know I'm not to be fucked with, the other MCs are gonna get decapitated, things like that.

Big Daddy Kane

If you're looking to be accepted as the nicest MC, then I guess your battle rhymes are gonna make you come across that way, because they're like, "Yo, did you hear what he said? Oh my goodness," because they're listening to the rhymes that you're saying, like as far as how nice you are or the incredible stuff you're saying.

Knowing a variety of different ways of rhyming is a big part of battle raps. Your goal is to outdo the person you're battling.

Akil the MC, Jurassic 5

The whole basis of being an MC is kind of like competitive in its nature. He shoot a three pointer, you want to come back and make a three pointer, [but] make a three pointer with a left hand. It's still a three pointer, but you want to try to outdo them or at least equal them.

Knowing a wide variety of MCs and their styles is also important if you want to be good at writing battle raps.

will.i.am, Black Eyed Peas

[If you know the history of different MCs,] you know how to approach a person if a person wants to battle you. If a person battles you and they're coming with [a certain style], it's like, OK, I know where this [guy] is getting that shit from, he's got a little 2Pac in him. I'm gonna fuck this [guy] up, with some 2Pac, and I'ma add 2Pac and mix 2Pac with Chuck D, and I hit them—boom—and I hit them from every single angle.

Battle rhymes can be aimed at a specific person, or they can be written just with general insults. The writing process may be different depending on which option you choose.

Royce Da 5'9"

It's only difficult to write battle rhymes when it's somebody dissing you that you don't really know nothing about, because then you're wondering, what do I say about them? So if it was like a diss track, I probably wouldn't do it if I didn't know enough about the person. As far as just regular spitting rhymes that's not about anybody in [particular], but that can apply to people, I kind of started off doing those, so that's always gonna be there. What makes it a different process is the mind frame that I'm in coming to the table, like knowing that I gotta come up with just regular spitting battle-sounding rhymes, I'll come in that mind frame.

A lot of MCs gain experience and confidence by writing battle rhymes and learning how to battle other MCs. Papoose notes, "Basically I feel like hip-hop is all about confidence, and I gained that confidence when I was younger because I used to battle a lot as a kid."

Conceptual Form

With the conceptual content form, you come up with a concept and write the lyrics around it—you have one idea or theme that joins all of the lyrics together. For example, Lil Wayne's "Dr. Carter" has the concept of Wayne playing the role of a doctor who has to save "patients" who have no style, confidence, or respect for the game, among other things, and this concept directs all three verses and links them together. Gift of Gab of Blackalicious and Papoose have both written concept songs in which the concept is to go through the alphabet one letter at a time, using mainly words that start with that letter before moving on to the next letter (Blackalicious's "Alphabet Aerobics" and Papoose's "Alphabetical Slaughter"). Concepts are often considered a key part of being a respected MC.

AZ

Back in the day it was more lyrical, more conceptual. Right now it's more partying and sing-along songs, but it's a different part of the game—can't be mad, I'm not mad at it at all, it is what it is—[but] back then you had to be a dart thrower to even be considered an MC. You had to have concepts.

Conceptual lyrics have made for some of the most memorable songs in hip-hop, as O.C. of Diggin' in the Crates notes: "Nas did the song backwards ['Rewind']—that's awkward, that's some awkward shit to do, so for him to do that, that was a brilliant idea."

Coming Up with Concepts

Many MCs like to have a concept before they begin writing. Evidence of Dilated Peoples believes that having a concept can give you something to aim toward: "If I'm hooking up with a group or I'm being a producer, it's good to have a direction so we're not all sitting in there twiddling our thumbs." Even just coming up with a title first can help solidify a particular concept for the track.

Chuck D, Public Enemy

With a title you can fill in the blanks and have a clear conversation about what you're talking about. . . . I mean, how can you have a clear conversation about something if you don't know what the hell you're talking about?

Sometimes inspiration can come from the production process itself. Working with producers who supply choruses for a song can give you a ready-made concept to follow—Royce Da 5'9" notes that "usually the producers got hooks and stuff already, like Pharrell [of the Neptunes]—if he come with a hook then he's pretty much giving you a concept." The music you're writing to can also give you an idea for a particular concept.

Tech N9ne

I love to have a concept before I start writing. When the beat talks to me, it'll usually give me a concept right then—I'll know exactly what the beat feels like. If you hear a beat and it's party, that's what I'ma talk about. If you hear a beat and it's sad, I'ma tell you what hurts me. If you listen to it and it's dark, I'm gonna go real sick with it. So the beats are gonna tell me whether it's dark, whether it's party, whether it's sad, whether it's sexual.

Occasionally, a concept may simply come to you, or it may come from things you experience day to day.

RBX

Sometimes concepts just hit me out of the blue.

MC Shan

Something you might see on TV might make something click, something that somebody says. You might be listening to another guy's song and like, wow, whatever he said might make something click into your brain. One word could turn into a whole song. Concepts can come from everywhere.

Writing a Concept Song

One of the main keys to writing a good concept song is sticking to the actual concept and not going off on a tangent. If you come up with ideas that don't fit the concept, don't try to make them fit—just put them to one side.

Killah Priest, Wu-Tang Clan affiliate

I stick to the topic. It all has to relate.

Big Daddy Kane

[If it's] the type of thing where I'm really trying to target a certain subject, I might sit down and just think of all the types of twists and turns and different events that can happen in the situation, and I might just jot those down and then put it into rap form.

Royce Da 5'9"

If I gotta write a concept, then I'm coming to the table telling myself I need to stick to that concept. Even if when I'm writing that song I think of something, if I think a line will sound better on a battle verse, then I'll write it down and put it to the side and not even put it in that song, just so it makes sense. That's what makes the process a little different.

Lateef of Latyrx has a concept song called "Storm Warning," in which he and Lyrics Born go back and forth trading verses and lines on the concept of the weather and storms and the destruction they can cause.

Lateef, Latyrx

[With] "Storm Warning," DJ Shadow had that beat and we were trying to come up with a concept for it. We had like three or four different concepts, and then we started talking about that concept and it really started working, and Shadow had his own things that he was adding to it. We sat there and we talked about how we were going to do it, what was going to happen, and what the story line was going to be. And [also] how we were going to intensify it as the song went on, and how we could have it not be too linear or contrived.

On the song "Trust," Wordsworth raps on the concept of how having a daughter made him reconsider the way he treated women.

Wordsworth

When I thought of that concept I was like, this is something that nobody's touched, and it's important because I got kids and it was something that I was feeling. So that was an idea I felt that nobody never spoke about from that perspective, just dudes, and how guilty we could feel when it happens, to be in that situation with having a daughter.

Since a concept song is usually all on one topic, artists need to be able to say a lot about that specific subject—and they may not have enough information just off the top of their heads. So most MCs would agree with Vinnie Paz of Jedi Mind Tricks when he says, "When I do something conceptually, I try to make sure that it's well researched."

Concept Albums

Concepts can be applied not just to songs but to whole albums as well, where an idea or theme joins all the tracks on the album together. For instance, Little Brother's concept album *The Minstrel Show* was based on satirizing stereotypes.

Big Pooh, Little Brother

When you're writing a concept album, it has moments where it's difficult, because you gotta search and find that different topic for [each track, and also] stay under the umbrella of the main concept.

A concept may also cover a series of albums. For example, Eminem's first mainstream album, *The Slim Shady LP*, was centered around his alter ego Slim Shady, while his second album, *The Marshall Mathers LP*, focused on his "real" self (Marshall Mathers is Eminem's real name). This created the concept of the two albums being linked, the first showing one side of his personality and the second the other side. A similar overarching concept linked his third and fourth albums, *The Eminem Show* and *Encore*, with *Encore* continuing the idea of a "show" that started with *The Eminem Show*.

Story Form

Storytelling has always been an important technique of the hip-hop MC. Being able to structure content in the form of a story is important to being a well-rounded hip-hop artist.

Tajai, Souls of Mischief

[As an MC you should] read stories and understand plot structure, tell stories, and expand your knowledge of storytelling.

MC Serch

A lot of my writing was focused on being a complete lyricist, like, not only going through braggadocious stuff but being able to tell eloquent stories and do story-type writing. That's what I came up with, watching Slick Rick and Dana Dane in high school and watching the Kangol Crew—"Indian Girl," "La

Di Da Di," all the stuff that Slick Rick, Dana, Lance [Brown], and Omega [the Heartbreaker] were doing during those days in the High School of Music & Art—and me watching them, it was all story rhymes. So I was heavily, heavily influenced by telling stories.

Most stories in hip-hop follow a pattern similar to traditional stories in books, movies, and TV series. They have characters, settings, and a structured plot—a beginning, a middle, and an end. Using one of Kool G Rap's epic stories, "A Thug's Love Story" from his *Roots of Evil* album, we can see how a story fits together.

Kool G Rap

[In the first verse] I met a broad, we kicked it, she gave me the numbers, we hooked up later. Shorty got a man—her man was like some big cocaine dealer dude, drug dealer cat or whatever, real jealous type. Shorty took me to her crib in the Poconos, we up in the crib, we be chilling and shit together, and we get busy and all that.

The story begins with the introduction of the main characters (Kool G Rap in the lead role, a woman, and her man), the setting where the story is taking place (at the woman's house in the Pocono Mountains), and what happens to set the story up (G Rap and the woman have a sexual encounter).

Kool G Rap

And then the next morning, her man caught up with us, bust in the crib out there and starts shooting at us. We had to jump off the balcony, jump on a snowmobile, couple of other dudes jump on snowmobiles chasing us, they popping at us, I'm popping back. I get wounded, but we get away, shorty tended my bullet wound for me.

In the middle of the story a complication arises (the woman's man sends people to kill them), which results in a difficulty (they have to escape on a snowmobile), leading to further developments (G Rap gets shot, but they make it away alive).

Kool G Rap

Then we hit the crib in the Hamptons to pick up some paper, because the dude she is fucking with is so caked out—this dude got money. So we get the money, we're trying to bounce, but then they caught up to us in the crib in the Hamptons. I'm wetting at them, they're wetting back, but they got the drop on shorty, so I had to drop my gats. Then they took both of us out on the yacht, they was probably planning on rocking me to sleep, put two in my head and throw me in the water. But I seen a flare gun when they took me to the bottom deck of the boat, so I did what I did to get away from the dude that had the drop on me, and I got the flare gun and I shot a flare in the dude, then I grabbed his gat and I started popping people. And then after a crazy shootout, I merked everybody, but after the smoke cleared, I seen the chick on the ground and she got hit with a slug—she caught one in the chest.

There is a new setting (in the Hamptons), there are further incidents (G Rap and the woman get caught and taken onto a yacht, where there's a gunfight), and the situation ends, tragically (the woman gets shot and killed).

Writing the Story

Although for a story like "A Thug's Love Story" the characters, settings, and plot could be worked out beforehand, Kool G Rap says that he prefers to write stories as he goes along, to keep himself interested in them, and that the process is largely subconscious.

Some MCs create the general outline of the story first and then write the lyrics based on that. MURS says he has a general idea of the story's plot, but then he writes the lyrics straight in rap form rather than writing it out step by step as a regular story first: "I might think of the story line and then put it into lyrics, but I never write out the story and then try to go back [and make it into a rap]."

But Kool G Rap does caution that the rhyming words shouldn't dictate what happens in the story—you should decide what will happen next and then figure out the rhymes to convey the story. "It's gotta make sense. You can't just put whatever comes next that rhymes—the story gotta be right too."

Sometimes stories can come from real-life events simply retold in the form of a rap. Schoolly D wrote the classic "Saturday Night" based on events that actually occurred.

Schoolly D

"Saturday Night" came off of just sitting there thinking about my mom, and somebody was like, "Well, why don't you write a song about what happened last week?" I came up with the story first. I'd create the beat and put the beat on—I'll start the story, and I keep going and I keep creating the story, and I keep it as true to the story or as true to the fantasy as possible. "Saturday Night" was easy to write because that was shit I had actually done. We all got high, we all got drunk, we all got in the bar fights. You're 18 or 19—you all go home trying to sneak a girl in the crib, so that was easy to write.

Abstract Form

Abstract lyrics are those that are written in a way that's not straightforward or obvious—terms and descriptions may not apply to concrete things, or the language may be figurative, so that even though a song may be about a simple subject, it is not described in a simple way. This can make the lyrics very cryptic and hard to decipher—but according to Evidence of Dilated Peoples, this can be good, as long as it sounds good: "I like that. I'm into abstract shit, [where] it makes sense to you and doesn't to everybody else. Great, as long as it's presentable."

Kool Keith, MF Doom, and Rammellzee are known for using abstract lyrics. Aesop Rock is also often commended for his intricate, abstract lyrics, though he says, "That's not really a label I'd put on myself, but people kind of consider me [abstract]."

Aesop Rock

It's kind of what comes naturally to me. The way I write is how I like to write and how I prefer to write. It comes more naturally for me to be into an abstract idea, I guess. It takes a while to sit and hatch it all out on paper, but it's what I want to write, so it's what gets me excited. I don't go out of my way to listen to only abstract hip-hop or anything like that. I like it when people do whatever comes naturally to them.

Humorous Form

Many MCs like to include humor in their lyrics, sometimes creating whole songs in a humorous style, such as the Pharcyde's "Ya Mama," which is based entirely around "ya mama" jokes, and Eminem's "Rain Man," in which the majority of the lyrics are tongue in cheek—he sounds serious but he is joking around.

Myka 9 of Freestyle Fellowship points out that humor has always been a part of hip-hop alongside more serious content: "At that same time [as Rakim, KRS-One, etc.], you had a lot of silly songs that would come out—Fat Boys, stuff like that." But the humor in today's hip-hop differs from the humor of the past.

Devin the Dude

It's a different kind of humor, I guess. It's a hard humor now. It's not really a "Just relax, chill out, everybody's tripping and laughing" type of humor, like, say, "Indian Girl" from Slick Rick or some of the other stories from back in the day.

Shock G, Digital Underground

These MCs these days are straight comedians in their wise-guy battle raps, and in their retaliations on each other, and to their perceived enemies. Yes, it's wiseguy/gangsta/Italian/cowboy funny, but it's still funny. When 50 Cent [in the song "Window Shopper"] said, "The store owner's watching you, before something gets stolen, stolen, stolen," you gotta admit that's a creative and humorous way to call somebody a broke motherfucker.

Humor can be the inspiration for the content as a whole, especially if you're naturally good with humor.

AMG

[Some of the ideas come from] just being witty. I got jokes, so I like to sit up and bag on people and tell jokes and come up with different words and terms and shit. It's just me, it's just the creative process of me, it's just who I am.

Humor can also be very useful for drawing people into your content.

Schoolly D

I think it's always important [to have a sense of humor]. I learned that from being a huge, huge, huge Richard Pryor fan. People want to laugh a little bit—some of the most historically gangsterized gangsters have always been nice guys. They always appear happy and nice in public, and they had this secret demeanor—so it's like if you really want to get something across, you bring people in with a little laughter.

3

Content Tools

I don't care what you are—a political rapper, a conscious rapper, a gangsta rapper, a backpack rapper—have some pride in the lyrics you're putting together, because it's important.
◄ Crooked I ►

While a content form is the basic structure of a song, content *tools* are the specific techniques you use from line to line in your lyrics to help better convey your content. The overall structure of a song might be conceptual or abstract, but within that structure you might use a number of different content tools, such as imagery, metaphor, or wordplay. Most of these tools are the same ones found in poetry and other forms of literature.

Fredro Starr, Onyx

That's what a rap is—a rap is a form of a poem. It's poetry on music. The first time I wrote a rap, it actually was a poem. I love poetry and I love English—that was one of my best subjects—and I guess it transcended into rapping.

Mastering the different tools is very important. It lets you express your message in a way that will move the listener, and it helps you to add substance and depth to your lyrics. It can also let you make old topics seem new and fresh again.

Q-Tip, A Tribe Called Quest

Your stuff has to have substance. It's just like seeing a hand-some man with a suit or a pretty girl with a dress—if it's appealing to the eye, but once you talk to them, if there's nothing inside, then it's kinda like, whatever.

Stressmatic, The Federation

We're basically doing the same thing all these other dudes did 15, 20 years ago. We're just saying it in a different way—we're saying it in our way.

Content tools can make your lyrics clearer and more direct by giving you a range of ways to explain what you mean—to make sure every line is powerful and makes an impact.

Cappadonna, Wu-Tang Clan affiliate

Look at many different ways to deliver that message, deliver that mail. [You] gotta be a good mailman, man, gotta be a good mailman.

Guerilla Black

I always wanted to make sure that I was real clever, and when I rhymed, everything had a purpose to it, that it would be strong—that every word was like a bullet, every sentence meant something.

Imagery

The first content tool, imagery, is the use of vivid language and description to create a picture or movie in the listener's mind. Imagery is simply describing something in an effective way in order to capture the scene or mood in the lyrics. A number of MCs compare imagery to painting a picture with words.

N.O.R.E.

I feel like it's a blank canvas, and I've got all the paint and I got all the brushes. I got all the everything and I can just paint a picture.

Kool G Rap

A lot of people say what I write is very descriptive, because I'm a writer kind of rapper. I'm not just a rapper, like, that try to get people to dance or to move and stuff like that—I'll write that shit that's gonna have you sit there and you gonna see visuals of what I'm talking about. You're gonna see a short little movie—I'm gonna give somebody a visual of G Rap doing something.

Wu-Tang Clan affiliate Killah Priest is known for the vivid imagery in his verses, as shown in these lyrics from his verse on the classic track "4th Chamber" from GZA's *Liquid Swords*:

I judge wisely, as if nothing ever surprise me,
Lounging, between two pillars of ivory,
I'm lively, my dome piece, is like building stones in Greece,
My poems are deep from ancient thrones I speak.

Killah Priest creates an image in the listener's mind by the particular way he describes things. He starts by creating an image of himself—"I judge wisely"—and then says how he is "lounging, between two pillars of ivory." So now the listener has the picture of Killah Priest, his composure, and his surroundings. He then continues to create pictures by using specific descriptions like "building stones in Greece" and "from ancient thrones I speak."

By using this kind of descriptive imagery, Killah Priest says, you're able to "take a listener, affect their emotions, take them through worlds, take them through mazes, never knowing what you're gonna say next." Like Kool G Rap, he says he can "hear a movie in any beat": "I go back and I edit the clips, make the movie fit right. . . . I do a little take in a way, replace it—it's like making a movie."

Another great example of the use of imagery is in the Geto Boys' seminal track "Mind Playing Tricks on Me" off their album *We Can't Be Stopped*. Scarface, Willie D, and Bushwick Bill all describe their paranoia in rich detail, creating haunting pictures in the mind of the listener. The Notorious B.I.G. also used a lot of strong imagery in his work, as Guerilla Black explains: "B.I.G. was a dude who made you feel his struggle and explained it so vividly that it just played out in front of your mind, almost as if you were watching a television show."

Similes, Metaphors, and Analogies

Similes, metaphors, and analogies are all very similar in that they use examples for comparison to make a point clearer (as Paris says, "Plenty of people have good things to say but difficulty conveying their thoughts"). They all use examples in different ways, however, and those differences are outlined in the sections below.

Regardless of which of the three techniques you use, a clever example can convey more to the listener in fewer words. Pigeon John says, "I'm learning the whole thing about how less is more. A person like Posdnuos [of De La Soul], you can tell every syllable means something." These tools also give the lyrics more depth, as the listener may take a while to grasp all the comparisons.

Tajai, Souls of Mischief

I grew up in the era where the best guys were like Big Daddy Kane, Kool G Rap, and Rakim—those dudes where you can't listen to their rap once and figure out what they're saying. You gotta listen to it a bunch of times, and then after that it's even deeper.

Artists are constantly on the lookout for examples to work into a simile, metaphor, or analogy.

Myka 9, Freestyle Fellowship

The average dope MC that's really tight, they'll tell you [that] in your mind you're constantly thinking of metaphors. Every time you see a street sign or a billboard, you're thinking, how can I tie that into a rhyme? So constantly think of metaphors, analogies, things of that nature.

Similes

A simile is a way of directly comparing one thing to another thing, usually using the word "as" or "like."

In the Blackalicious track "Clockwork," Gift of Gab uses several similes, including "I'm like a mathematician," "an array of pages that'll slay you like a ninja," and "cramming it in like a sandwich." All of these examples use the word "like" to compare one thing to another thing—Gift of Gab is *like* a mathematician, he has many rhymes that will kill you *like* a ninja, and he says his rhymes so quickly that he's cramming them in *like* a sandwich.

Chino XL is also known for his inventive similes. In his song "No Complex," he uses the word "like" many times to compare one thing to another, such as "flows I creates, 'Unforgettable' like Nat King Cole," and "my clique is stoned like their eyes gazed upon Medusa."

Similes can also be formed using the word "as." In Masta Ace's track "Acknowledge," he has the line "found out that he was as fake as a tooth-fairy." M.O.P.'s song "Cold as Ice" uses an "as" simile right in the title, and the song also includes the line "you'll be stiff as a log in a suit looking nice."

Metaphors

Metaphors resemble similes except they don't use "like" or "as"— instead, the thing that's being talked about is actually replaced with the example it's being compared to. With a metaphor, one thing is used to represent another thing.

In Blackalicious's "Clockwork," Gift of Gab also uses metaphors—for example, "I'm an ancient Zen master." Here, he compares himself to an ancient Zen master by saying that he *is* an ancient Zen master, instead of saying he is *like* an ancient Zen master. The song's other metaphors include "I'm a chef eating all you carnivores," "I'm a hip-hop astrologist," and "I'm a bartender all into your mental."

The lyrics of Master P's track "Hot Boys and Girls" are made up mostly of metaphors, such as "I'm a diamond on a ring, I'm your brains when you think," and "I'm the past that always seems to come back and haunt you." In each comparison in the song, the MC is saying he or she is the thing that is being used as a comparison.

Clever metaphors are a great way to make the lyrics more descriptive, and they are often used as a way to impress the listener.

AZ

[Use] more metaphors. Try to draw a better picture for whatever topic.

MURS

Metaphors are impressive—it's like a slam dunk.

Remy Ma

With real lyricists, you have to hear it a few times before you catch every metaphor.

Analogies

An analogy is basically an extended metaphor—the metaphor lasts longer and can cover a whole verse, song, or album.

Jedi Mind Tricks' song "Uncommon Valor: A Vietnam Story" can be seen as an analogy, as Vinnie Paz says, "for the war going on right now" (referring to the war in Iraq):

I don't know why I'm over here, this job is evil.

They sent me here to Vietnam to kill innocent people.

My mother wrote me, said, the president, he doesn't care,

He trying to leave the footprints of America here.

Even though the subject is the Vietnam War, there are several parallels that might make the listener think of the war in Iraq. And instead of comparing Iraq to Vietnam for just one or two lines, the metaphor runs throughout Vinnie Paz's whole verse—creating an analogy.

Another analogy can be found in 2Pac's track "Me and My Girlfriend," where at first he seems to be rapping about his girlfriend, but it soon becomes obvious that he's actually talking about his gun. 2Pac never says that he's referring to his gun, but it's made very clear through the language he uses that the entire song is an analogy. Making an entire song into an analogy like this shows a level of craft and intelligence that often gains the MC a lot of acclaim.

Guerilla Black

You gotta really be clever, because there are a lot of clever dudes out there. Cleverness is always a winner, man. If people are always hung on what you said last, and they keep repeating it or replaying it or rethinking, "Where the fuck did he think of that at?" that's what makes you a great MC—being clever and outthinking your competition.

Slang

Many if not most MCs use slang words and phrases in their lyrics. New and interesting language helps make the content more colorful. It also helps connect the song to a particular time, place, or movement, since different groups of people follow different trends in slang and the language is always changing.

Q-Tip, A Tribe Called Quest

It's never quite the same every time. You may say "I love you" a certain way one year, and five years later the parlance of the day, the culture, has moved on to give us different expressions, and you start to express your lyrics in a different way than you did before. It's just like in the '60s some people would say, "Yo, that's groovy," and people today say, "That's hot," and 10 years prior to today they say, "That's dope," but it's the same kind of emotion.

Omar Cruz

There's hood Ebonics [African American English], then you have your own slang, West Coast have their own slang, East Coast have their slang—you mix it all in together and you fit it in right. That's what separates MCs from all sounding alike: dialects and slang.

Vast Aire, Cannibal Ox

I have a decent amount of English in my brain, plus I have Ebonics in my brain, which is like my natural way of speaking from growing up, being a black kid, growing up with black slang, African American slang, in the ghetto—that's a whole 'nother dictionary in itself.

E-40 is known as a West Coast master of slang, and many of his songs use slang extensively. He has his own explanation for why slang is so popular.

E-40

Everybody wanna hear a little razzle-dazzle, they wanna hear something slick, they wanna hear new words. The world revolves around slang, whether it's corny slang or hip slang from the hood. They just wanna hear it, and that's just how it goes. Some people have different ways of doing their slang, but I spit that hood slang.

At the end of his hit single "Tell Me When to Go," produced by Lil Jon, E-40 uses several slang phrases that are associated with the Hyphy Bay Area style of music, such as "ghost-ride the whip," "put your stunna shades on," "thizz face," and "go stupid."

E-40

That was one of those situations where it's got a lot to do with the movement out here in the Bay Area, and I just kind of narrated exactly what is going on in the Bay Area. "Tell Me When to Go" was just one of them songs that had something to do with the movement, and it was one of those songs that everybody in the nation could feel because I was giving them instructions on what to do, and what we do, at the end of the song.

Sometimes slang can actually help you come up with the subject of a track. The slang that was being used in N.O.R.E.'s neighborhood helped him come up with the idea for his Neptunes-produced hit "Oh No."

N.O.R.E.

At the time I went to my hood and everybody was like, "What up, what up with the tineam, everybody good-good, everybody hood-hood? Alright, holla at your bidoy," and I was like, you know, my hood is crazy, like, my hood changed up the slang, so I took my hood's slang and [wrote the lyrics].

There are many other hip-hop tracks known particularly for their use of slang. Snoop Dogg's "Drop It Like It's Hot" uses the West Coast "izzle" slang, where the end of each word is replaced with "-izzle" (Snoop Dogg uses the same technique on a number of other songs). Wu-Tang Clan are known for their dense slang, which is very specific to their group, giving their tracks a distinct and instantly recognizable feel.

Vocabulary

An MC's vocabulary consists of all the words he or she knows and uses to write raps. Most artists recommend having a wide vocabulary, as it helps you to express your topics in the most effective way.

Akil the MC, Jurassic 5
Study vocabulary. Vocabulary is a must.

Omar Cruz
Of course [you should have a large vocabulary]. If not, every other word is "motherfucker," "motherfucker."

2Mex, The Visionaries
The bigger your vocabulary is, the more ammo you have.

RBX
[It helps to have a large vocabulary,] especially in a game where words are the weaponry. In any kind of situation, the one with the most weaponry usually wins, and so if this is a war of words then definitely to have a vast vocabulary would be to your advantage.

Knowing a lot of words can make it easier to describe your feelings. And the more words you know, the more topics you can tackle in a powerful way.

Crooked I

How can I express the anger and how can I express the pain we're going through if I don't have excellent command of the English vocabulary?

K-Os

You need new words to communicate your soul all the time.

Wise Intelligent, Poor Righteous Teachers

There's a word for every feeling that I have that I can make rhyme with something else.

Speech, Arrested Development

I love vocabulary. I think words are beautiful and I think that they can paint incredible pictures. If your vocabulary is bigger, I think the more pictures you can paint and the better.

A large vocabulary can also allow you to reach a wider audience.

Glasses Malone

[I try] to make sure I use a variety of words—I think that's definitely a plus. Any great speaker, everyone can relate to him, from a 4-year-old to somebody 94 years old. That's definitely the key to doing any type of speaking—you want people to understand and believe in what you're saying.

Expanding Your Vocabulary

The more new words you come across and find out the definitions to, the larger your vocabulary will become. Many MCs suggest reading a lot to improve your vocabulary.

K-Os

When you're an MC, you're like a vacuum cleaner. When you read stuff, you make mental notes all the time of new words. It's almost like you're a purveyor of words just for survival.

MURS

I read constantly. I read the newspaper as much as possible, I read eight different comic books a week, and then I'm always reading a novel or a biography on top of that.

Omar Cruz

I read a lot—I've always loved reading. Just reading, period, is gonna help your vocabulary. It doesn't matter what you read just as long as you're reading—your vocabulary expands.

Being interested in specific subjects can also increase the range of words you know. The Lady of Rage says that her knowledge of science helps her to impress listeners.

The Lady of Rage

[It helps to have] just a good intellectual base, because you can say things that most people may not even know about. I was good at science, so I might throw an "amoeba" in my rhyme or "paramecium"—the average person may not know about that, so it's like, damn, what the hell is she talking about! Or did you hear what she said? So I think it all helps and adds up.

Besides reading and studying, there are other ways MCs suggest to increase your vocabulary, from simply growing as a person to participating in other activities centered on the written and spoken word.

Royce Da 5'9"

I believe that as you get older and you develop as a person and start dealing with different kinds of people, you mature, and along with that maturity comes a bigger vocabulary.

Myka 9, Freestyle Fellowship

Crossword puzzles, they have like built-in punch lines, reading word games in general, Scrabble, things like that. Talking a lot, communicating with people, watching the news a lot, watching what's going on in the world, current events, things of that nature, where there's a lot of linguistics going on and language.

Getting Your Point Across

Depending on the audience you're trying to reach, you may want to use more elaborate and unusual words, or you may mainly want to use words from everyday speech.

Lord Jamar, Brand Nubian

I think it depends on the audience that you're trying to talk to. I think it's good to have a big vocabulary and then use what you need to use at the proper time.

AMG

It's a communication factor—it's still just about getting people to understand what you're talking about. You can be complex or you can be simple, as long as they get it.

You don't need to use complicated words all the time to be considered a great MC. Some artists find it more effective to use regular words.

Big Daddy Kane

You take someone like Biggie Smalls. I think that he was a great rapper, but he didn't use a large vocabulary. He just put his words together a slick way and it worked real good for him—[he] got his point across and was recognized as being a hot MC.

Del the Funky Homosapien

I may know what it means, but for others to know, I gotta

keep it somewhat conversational. I don't wanna dumb it down, and I don't feel that that's necessary, but [I] keep it in layman's terms as much as possible without getting boring. That's the challenge of good songwriting—it's a tightrope. [I think] it's best to stay somewhat conversational in tone—then you have no problem. You're using the language you actually communicate with.

Alternatively, some MCs like to fill their lyrics with more obscure words, especially if the audience they are aiming for admires that in an MC.

Vast Aire, Cannibal Ox

I have an elaborate vocabulary.

will.i.am, Black Eyed Peas

It depends on who you're writing it for. If I'm rhyming for other rappers then I want to go over their heads. It all depends on what the environment is.

Chuck D, Public Enemy

Well, you'll go over some heads and hit some others. You shouldn't always worry about other people all the time—sometimes just do what you feel.

Using a Dictionary/Thesaurus

A lot of artists use a dictionary and/or a thesaurus to help them discover new words to use in lyrics. You can look up a word in a dictionary to make sure you're using it correctly or to discover additional information about a word and its meaning, which can help you come up with more ways to express yourself.

Tech N9ne

If I say the word "bestowed," I'd be like, *bestowed*, did I use that in the right context? So I sit next to a dictionary to make sure I'm using everything in the right context, because you don't want to sound like an idiot.

Big Noyd

Sometimes a word will come to me and I don't know the definition, [so] I'll look that word up, and then from there I get into more details of where the word comes from and try and elaborate with the meaning of the word. Like I'll look up the real meaning of "death," for example, and then I'll elaborate on something like that.

Similarly, by looking up a word in a thesaurus you can find out its *synonyms* (words that have the same or almost the same meaning) and *antonyms* (words that have the opposite meaning).

Myka 9, Freestyle Fellowship

The quick-and-easy tool to just becoming a good lyricist, I think, is reading *Roget's Thesaurus*. That way you get an idea of synonyms and antonyms.

A dictionary or thesaurus can be a helpful tool—as long as it doesn't become a crutch.

K-Os

There was a time when I was listening to a lot of the Genius [GZA, of Wu-Tang Clan]. I just felt kinda dwarfed by how well [developed] his vocabulary was, and I just started reading a dictionary every day. It helped me for a bit, but then . . . There are terms in hip-hop called "dictionary rapper," but I did go through that stage just to experience it, to try it. I think if you really do it with good motives, you can pull some good stuff out of that, but if you're consulting that all the time as a way of communicating, then I think it can be sometimes pretentious.

Wordplay

Wordplay is simply playing around with words and their meanings—using language in clever ways.

Royce Da 5′9″

I'm like a word guy. I like to play with the words.

Hell Rell, Dipset

Wordplay is very important to me.

2Mex, The Visionaries

I do a lot of wordplay kind of rhyming. Sometimes I just play off of the words.

For example, in R.A. the Rugged Man's song "Black and White," he plays around with the word "white," using that same word in a lot of different contexts, while rapper Timbo King does similar wordplay with the word "black." Some of the wordplay with the word "white" includes:

"In the White House," "White Sox," "white rocks," "white cops in donut shops," "white sneakers," "white wife beaters," "white powder," "Snow White," "white snakes," "white knight," "great white hype," "Uncle Ben's rice white," "whites in your eyes," and "white lies."

A lot of wordplay plays off the double meanings of words and phrases. In this example from De La Soul's "Ghost Weed #1" skit,

Pharoahe Monch uses the words "kill" and "killing" in one way for the first two lines and then uses different meanings of those same words in the third and fourth lines:

> How many niggas who will actually kill still rhyming?
> How many niggas who are actually signed still killing?
> And when it comes to killing a mic, they ain't willing,
> And I'm supposed to be shook? That's the shit that kills me.

For many MCs, being good at clever wordplay comes from being a good English student or being good at writing poetry.

AMG

I've always been good with words, man. I've always been an A+ student with the English skills and the creative writing.

Masta Ace

English was my favorite class when I was in school, and when I went to college I excelled in English. Learn the English language, and the better your [knowledge of it], the better MC you're gonna be.

The Lady of Rage

I used to write poetry a lot, so the transition from poetry to rap is not that hard. It's just music to poetry.

Phife Dawg, A Tribe Called Quest

I had a lot of practice because my mom is a poet, so she did a lot of poetry—I was doing a lot of poetry at the time. Our poetry was just a little more street, but it still was the same thing as far as I was concerned.

Masta Ace notes that hip-hop is still moving forward as a craft, and wordplay is one of the key areas where this is happening: "To a certain extent innovations are still happening right now—the cleverness in terms of wordplay and subject matter, that's what you see being more prevalent now."

Punch Lines

A punch line is a particularly strong phrase in the lyrics that "punches," or hits, the listener. It can be something funny, an interesting metaphor or simile, clever wordplay, or anything that makes an impact.

Guerilla Black

That was one of the first things of me wanting to rhyme—making sure that my punch lines were proper.

Big Noyd

I'm not a punch-line rapper, but at the end of the day you do have those [scenarios where] by the time you get to the end of the bar, you want to say something fly—you want to say something catchy.

The track "Uni-4-Orm" by Heltah Skeltah, Canibus, and Ras Kass from the *Rhyme & Reason* soundtrack has a lot of punch lines. For example, Canibus raps the following two lines; the first is a kind of setup for the second, which contains the punch line:

If you try to battle me face to face,
I'll bring your career to a stop quicker than anti-lock brakes.

Sometimes MCs create the punch line first, and the rest of the song comes later.

Big Daddy Kane

There's sometimes where I'm just trying to write a rhyme, and I'm just jotting down little hot, little slick lines that I thought of, and then I just put it in the rap until a whole verse forms.

Yukmouth

Sometimes I'm just walking around and a punch line will hit me, and I just keep it in my data bank. I just keep it locked in my head until I come up with a song that I'm feeling, and I'll put the punch line in this song.

Punch lines are often used in battle rapping to diss opponents. Many of the lines will end in a punch line to get a response from the people listening.

Flow

4

How Flow Works

*Study the art form and once you know the art form, you can
improve on it, because you got cats that already did all them
things that you're trying to do in hip-hop.*
◄ R.A. the Rugged Man ►

The flow of a hip-hop song is simply the rhythms and rhymes it
contains. For some MCs, this defines rapping as the next stage in
poetry. But rap is not just poetry spoken aloud, because unlike
the rhythm of a poem, a song's flow has to be in time with the
music—the rhythm of the lyrics must fit with the basic rhythm
of the music. This basic rhythm is referred to as the *beat*, and the
same term is often used as another name for the music itself.

MURS

Not only do you have to make everything rhyme, but you
have to add a rhythm to it. Poetry doesn't have to rhyme, it
just has to sound beautiful, but in rap it has to sound beautiful and it has to be on time and it has to rhyme, so to me it's
the next level of poetry evolution.

Myka 9, Freestyle Fellowship

Sometimes I might write a poem, a spoken-word poem, but
then morph that into a rap rhythmically.

Sean Price, Heltah Skeltah

It's down to attaching flow to the beat. . . . Like Bruce Lee said, if the water is in the jug, it becomes that jug. If water is in that bowl, it becomes that bowl. That's how I approach it.

The rhythm and rhyme of the flow are as important to rapping as melody and rhythm are to playing musical instruments.

Mighty Casey

Rap is music, so there has to be some musical value to it, and if you're not adhering to certain musical values . . . Like if you're a trumpet player and you're off [the] beat, you're not a good trumpet player. If your melodies and your rhythms don't sound good and you're a musician, you're not a good musician.

MCs agree that a strong flow is extremely valuable, either as a way of conveying the content clearly and effectively or as an element that takes center stage to impress the listener. Even artists who focus more on the content of the lyrics still stress how important flow is. Creating a song's flow is often the main priority for MCs, as it has an immediate impact and largely determines what the song sounds like.

Wordsworth

The flow can grab somebody before the [meaning of the] words.

Zumbi, Zion I

I think the flow comes first, because I don't wanna be a boring MC where it's all about what I'm saying but it doesn't really sound that good. I'm a fan of cats who flow dope and then are saying fresh stuff within it. So I think the flow is what I'm trying to lock in first. The meaning is a close second, but the flow has got to fit first.

A lot of artists believe that most listeners pay attention to the flow first, and if the flow is not entertaining, they never even get into the content of the lyrics. If you don't know how to flow well, then it can even sound like you don't know how to rap.

Big Pooh, Little Brother

You have some people who don't care about what you're rapping about. They just want the flow to be crazy.

Havoc, Mobb Deep

I'm a flow person, and without the right flow, subject matter probably won't even matter. It's all about styles, just the way you're getting your subject across. If people can't feel how you're saying it, it doesn't even matter what you're saying.

Vinnie Paz, Jedi Mind Tricks

I think there's a lot of people that I listen to, even people that make records, where I'm like, yo, this dude can't rhyme. I'm not even talking about, like, from a lyrical perspective, just like, yo, this dude sounds like shit. He could be saying the most amazing shit, but I grew up in an era where that doesn't matter if you sound wack. I put a lot of energy into the mechanical aspect of it and the flow, like Kool G Rap, and [Big] Pun.

A strong flow is often responsible for making a song popular—Rah Digga suggests that "you actually [can] say 'Mary had a little lamb,' but if the flow is proper, it'll be a hit."

Royce Da 5'9"

[Jay-Z's track] "Money, Cash, Hoes"—the song ain't really about nothing, really he's just rhyming. But the thing that catches your ear is that flow—it's the way he rides the beat that makes me like the song.

A lot of MCs have distinct styles of flow. Eminem often has a reasonably fast and dense flow, using many words and complicated rhyme schemes, while Snoop Dogg often has a sparser flow with more pauses, which suits his unique delivery and his melodic voice. Some artists suggest using many different types of flow to help yourself stand out as an MC.

Fredro Starr, Onyx

I think to be one of the best MCs, you gotta have the crazy flow. You have some rappers who rap the same on every record, flow-wise. Then you got some rappers who change up their flow on every record. OutKast, them dudes, you can't never know where they're going with their flow. Lil Wayne is on his thing—his flow changes up on every record.

Kool G Rap

I never just did one flow. I mean, you hear a flow I did on "Men at Work," and you heard a different flow on "Road to the Riches," so it's like I never just did only one flow.

As hip-hop has progressed, flows have become more and more complicated. The flows of earlier hip-hop records sometimes sound more simplistic compared with the advanced techniques used by today's artists. This means that to have a basic, ordinary flow today requires a reasonably high level of technique.

Esoteric

I think people's expectations of what makes an MC dope has changed over the years. Before, some people were using real simple lines, whereas some of the verses that Eminem is releasing are mind-blowingly intricate, and people kinda expect that now.

The Flow Diagram

The easiest way to see how flow works is by looking at the lyrics in a diagram that shows how they line up against the music. The flow diagram used in this book was created based on the systems many artists use to write down the flow of their raps.

Spider Loc

Sometimes the way you actually write the words onto paper will remind you where to pause, where to break, or where to breathe. Sometimes the way it's written on the paper expresses the flow—they go hand in hand.

Nelly

[When I write on paper,] if I want to stretch something out a little bit, I might put a little line by it or I'll write it real short if it should be short.

Vinnie Paz, Jedi Mind Tricks

I've created my own sort of writing technique, like little marks and asterisks and shit like that to show like a pause or emphasis on words in certain places.

Aesop Rock

I have a little system of symbols and shit—I think a lot of people do, that I've seen. I thought I was crazy, and then when I started seeing other rappers, everyone has their own little symbols. I have a system of maybe 10 little symbols that I use on paper that tell me to do something when I'm recording.

Several artists note that these systems are similar to regular musical notation.

Del the Funky Homosapien

Music theory has helped tremendously. [I use] basic music transcribing, some staff paper, and [I'm] just writing out the rhythm of the flow, basically. Even if it's just slashes to represent the beats, that's enough to give me a visual path.

The flow diagram uses a similar system of notation to show how flow works. Here are the opening lines from the Pharcyde's track "Drop," from the album *Labcabincalifornia*, written normally:

Let me freak the funk, obsolete is the punk that talks
More junk than Sanford sells. I jet propel at a
Rate that complicate their mental state as I invade their
Masquerade. They couldn't fade with a clipper . . .

Now here are the same lyrics, this time shown in the flow diagram:

1	2	3	4
Let me freak the	**funk**, obso-	**lete** is the	**punk** that talks
more junk than	**San**ford sells.	I jet pro-	**pel** at a
rate that compli-	**cate** their mental	**state** as I	**in**vade their
masquerade.		They couldn't **fade** with a	**clip**per . . .

Beats and Bars

The numbers along the top of the diagram represent the beats in the music, and each new line represents a new *bar* of music. A bar is simply a way of measuring a unit of time in music—in almost all hip-hop tracks, one bar is four beats.

To see clearly how the lyrics match up to the beats and bars, simply listen to the song in the example. In the first line, you can say "let . . . funk . . . lete . . . punk . . ." along to the lyrics and it is the same as counting "one . . . two . . . three . . . four . . ." in the music. That means those are the places where each beat falls:

1	2	3	4
Let me freak the	**funk**, obso-	**lete** is the	**punk** that talks . . .

Each line of the diagram is four beats, or one bar of music. The example below shows the first two bars:

1	2	3	4
Let me freak the	**funk**, obso-	**lete** is the	**punk** that talks
more junk than	**San**ford sells.	I jet pro-	**pel** at a . . .

The first bar has the lyrics "Let me freak the funk, obsolete is the punk that talks," and the second bar has the lyrics "more junk than Sanford sells. I jet propel at a . . ."

Many rappers write down their flows by counting bars (Rock of Heltah Skeltah says, "When I'm writing it on paper, I do count my bars—I mark them down"), and using one line to represent one bar is a common way of doing so. As Crooked I says, "I used to get the legal pad, man, the yellow one, and I used to write each bar as one line, so at the end, 16 lines, 16 bars."

But regardless of whether they note it in some written form, all MCs recognize the importance of the beat and being able to count bars. It's central to being able to rap.

Tech N9ne

The beats are the pulse. . . . Without no beat there's no life, without the pulse there is no life—gotta have the beat.

Brother J, X Clan

I've always loved rhythm, so I'd say as long as I've known how to clap my hands on time is as long as I've been conditioning to learn how to rhyme.

Thes One, People Under the Stairs

[It's bad if an MC] can't get the count right and they don't know when to come in. I've worked with dudes like that where I'm like, yo, come in on the 1, and they're just sitting in the booth and they miss [it].

Twista

The advice I'd give to people who want to be better at MCing is know how to count bars. When you know how to count bars, you can plan where your most potent punch lines [can go]. When you don't know how to count bars, you're just all over the place.

Fortunately, counting bars is a skill that can be learned.

Cage

I don't think anyone just comes out and understands timing, and not everybody even knows how to count bars—or measures, for that matter. It's all a learning process. And some people just never learn what timing or rhythm is and make horrible music—they didn't realize they didn't possess those things.

Syllables and Stressed Syllables

Lyrics are broken up into syllables, which are single units of sound. Breaking lyrics down into syllables, rather than just words and sentences, helps us look at flow in a lot more detail.

In the same Pharcyde example from the track "Drop," some of the shorter words are made up of only one sound—for instance, "let," "me," and "freak"—so each one is considered a single syllable. Longer words may consist of more than one sound, in which case they are split up into separate syllables. For example, the word "obsolete" consists of three sounds: "ob-," "-so-," and "-lete."

Ob-so-lete

Each separate sound is its own syllable: "ob-" is a syllable, "-so-" is a syllable, and "-lete" is a syllable.

So if we look at the second line of the song, we can see that it is made up of twelve syllables:

1	2	3	4
more junk than	**San**ford sells.	I jet pro-	**pel** at a . . .

The syllables are "more," "junk," "than," "San-," "-ford," "sells," "I," "jet," "pro-," "-pel," "at," and "a."

Stress is the emphasis put on particular syllables. Syllables are stressed by saying them slightly louder and/or longer, making them more distinct. In normal speech we stress certain syllables naturally, depending on our accents and personal preferences. For example, when speaking, we would probably stress part of the Pharcyde lyric in the following way:

obso**lete** is the **punk** that **talks** more **junk** than **San**ford **sells**

The syllables "-lete," "punk," "talks," "junk," "San-," and "sells" would be stressed.

In a hip-hop song, however, different syllables than normal may need to be stressed in order to keep the lyrics in time with the beat.

Fitting the Lyrics to the Beat

This is a very important point to note: a stressed syllable must be said *at the same time* as each of the four beats in a bar (unless there is a *rest* on a particular beat, something we will look at shortly). Stressing a syllable on each of the four beats gives the lyrics the same underlying rhythmic pulse as the music and keeps them in rhythm.

In the flow diagram, the important stressed syllables are shown in **bold** type. Because they have to come in time with each of the four beats in a bar, they are always under one of the beat numbers at the top of the diagram:

1	2	3	4
Let me freak the	**funk**, obso-	**lete** is the	**punk** that talks
more junk than	**San**ford sells.	I jet pro-	**pel** at a . . .

You'll notice that these stressed syllables do not always match up with the syllables that would be emphasized in ordinary speech:

Normal-Speech Stress:
obso**lete** is the **punk** that **talks** more **junk** than **San**ford **sells**
On-the-Beat Stress:
obso**lete** is the **punk** that talks **more** junk than **San**ford sells

Other syllables in the song may still be stressed, but the ones that fall in time with the four beats of a bar are the only ones that need to be emphasized in order to keep the lyrics in time with the music. Stressing these syllables may not make them seem louder or longer in comparison with any of the surrounding syllables, but they will be more distinct when compared with how those particular syllables are said normally.

Keeping lyrics perfectly in time with the beat is sometimes called being "in the pocket." It's one of the most important skills for any MC.

2Mex, The Visionaries

I wanted to be that "in the pocket" rapper, like the flow is effervescent, sort of like a Nas or the way Large Professor [of] Main Source [did it]—he was completely in the pocket.

Mr. Lif

I always have a strict gauge as to whether something is on beat.

B-Real, Cypress Hill

[I learned to rap by] listening to the rap that was on the radio, emulating that—eventually figured out how to put the words together in the right places to make them on beat and everything.

Rests

A rest is basically a pause, during which no syllable is said on the 1, 2, 3, or 4 beat of a bar. In the flow diagram, rests are shown by a space under one of the four beats in a bar on which no syllable is said. In the following example, a rest is highlighted:

1	2	3	4
Let me freak the	**funk**, obso-	**lete** is the	**punk** that talks
more junk than	**San**ford sells.	I jet pro-	**pel** at a

The highlighted space is under the 3 beat of the second bar, where there is no syllable. At this point on the track, a beat is heard in the music but no syllable is heard—there is a pause instead.

Lots of MCs have a way of notating when they will rest or pause in the lyrics.

Rock, Heltah Skeltah

Sometimes I put a lot of dots in front of a word if I take a long pause.

Thes One, People Under the Stairs

I use slashes, kind of like the old way they used to when they were putting verses in *The Source* way, way, way back. I'll put a slash kind of when there's a pause.

Vast Aire, Cannibal Ox

I put two back slashes—that means to chill, let the beat drop, and then come right back in on time.

Big Daddy Kane

The method I always used was commas—that means there is a pause.

Kool G Rap

Sometimes I might write "pause" in parentheses so I don't forget, because when you're writing, you get so trapped up into your wordplay sometimes, you might forget, oh, I gotta pause before I say this. And if you forget that little pause, that could throw your whole flow off and then you start falling off beat.

MURS

I have different pauses. I might write two words per line and then five words the next line if that's how I'm pausing, or I put an asterisk or I'll draw a line to know when to pause and break it up at.

MCs like Method Man of Wu-Tang Clan and Pharoahe Monch use a lot of rests to give their flows rhythmic variety, while other MCs such as Nas and Big Daddy Kane have fewer rests, since their flows are densely packed, with a lot of syllables in each bar. Rests can be used in several different ways, as we will see when we look at rhythm in more detail (see chapter 7, p. 127).

Overlapping Bars

Hip-hop lyrics often overlap bars. A verse doesn't have to start at the beginning of a bar or end at the end of one. It can begin or end anywhere within a bar.

Here are the opening lyrics of N.O.R.E.'s hit single "Superthug" from the album *N.O.R.E.*, as shown in the flow diagram.

1	2	3	4
			Ayo, we
light a candle,	run	**laps** around the	**Eng**lish channel.
Nep-	**tunes,** I got a	**cock**er spaniel.	We on the . . .

The verse doesn't start at the beginning of a bar on the 1 beat; it starts at the end of the previous bar. He says, "Ayo, we," and then "light" falls on the 1 beat.

The following lyrics are from the end of the first verse in Blackalicious's song "One of a Kind," from the album *Quannum Spectrum*:

1	2	3	4
Time and	**days** of the	**last** breaths of	**life** leave your
spine a-	**blaze** when my	**ass** bless the	**mic**, come
on.			

The end of the verse finishes with the word "on" being said on the 1 beat of a new bar, rather than finishing within the previous bar.

Esoteric

I'll know if I wanna start before the 1, or if I wanna hit it after the 1, or come in on the 1, I'll have that already predetermined before I step in front of the mic.

How Is the Flow Diagram Useful?

The flow diagram lets you see the techniques used in the flow very clearly. By diagramming different complex flows, it is easy to see exactly how they work and how they're put together, and it will allow us to break down rhythm and rhyme techniques in more detail in subsequent chapters.

Esoteric

I think [the flow diagram is] a pioneering move, because anybody can spit with [a simple] flow but not everyone can rhyme like [the best MCs]. I think that it's a very valuable contribution, and that would be a tremendous help to MCs that have been stuck in the same old rhyme flow, and they can look right there and see how [it can be broken down like that]. I never really thought it could be explained, and [it's] kinda put it into a mathematical context, which is crazy!

The majority of MCs learned how to flow by listening to other artists' records, picking up techniques, and combining them to create their own style. The flow diagram is a tool that helps with this method of learning, by providing a visual guide to the techniques.

R.A. the Rugged Man

I learned from listening to other rappers that were great, because you don't start off good—you start off pretty wack and you just get better and better, and you kinda teach yourself by listening to others.

Steele, Smif N Wessun

When I first started rapping, I would write like every artist that I liked. I had a Treacherous [Three] rhyme, I had a Kool G Rap rhyme, I had a [Big Daddy] Kane rhyme, I had a Chuck D rhyme—I would try to rhyme like everybody who I liked.

Havoc, Mobb Deep

I learned how to rap just copying from the styles of the artists that was out back then—Big Daddy Kane, Kool G Rap, Rakim, stuff like that. I used to memorize their stuff and try to get a style—like, form a technique—see how their technique was.

Rock, Heltah Skeltah

I think every rapper, I think every artist in general, is a combination of themselves and all their favorite artists, because everything you see, you learn from, you take in, it changes you. So Kool G Rap, Big Daddy Kane, Rakim, KRS-One, N.W.A was basically what shaped my shit when I was young.

Big Daddy Kane

The flow that I use, I really developed my rap style in the mid-'80s based on Grandmaster Caz from the Cold Crush Brothers, from listening to him. That's like really who I pretty much patterned my style from, and I just took it to another level once I had the opportunity to get out amongst the world myself.

Sean Price, Heltah Skeltah

I'm one of those dudes who listens to everybody, and I take a little bit of everybody's style and then put it in my bowl, mix it up, and come up with that gumbo flow. I can adapt to all kinds of situations however you want to kick your rhyme. You wanna rhyme like this, you wanna rhyme like that? No problem, I got that. So you gotta work on your craft, get that gumbo flow, man. Be able to adjust to anything that's going on right now.

Gift of Gab, Blackalicious

I'm a style junkie, so I was always into new styles. I always liked hearing albums like [De La Soul's] *3 Feet High and Rising* or Freestyle Fellowship's *Innercity Griots*, or Public Enemy's *It Takes a Nation of Millions*. . . . It helped me to grow as an artist to hear artists like KRS-One and Kool Keith who were really flipping styles, because I was really into styles—I was really into, "Wow, I've never heard anybody rap like that before." So as I grew, I would listen and I would take pieces from each of these artists until I developed my own sense of who I was as an MC.

The flow diagram is also a useful way to remember the flow of your own songs.

Thes One, People Under the Stairs

I have written rhymes before where I'd go back and I can't get the rhyme to fit correctly over the beat, because I've forgotten [the flow], and it just kind of unravels.

Tajai, Souls of Mischief

[I've forgotten flows]—that sucks. I think that's why I started being rigorous with [writing it down], because that'll make or break a rap. You can have the same lyrics and if you kick it wrong, it's wack. Forgetting the flow sucks—it's like a wasted rap.

More Examples

Below are a couple more examples to help you get used to how the flow diagram works so you can better understand the techniques covered in upcoming chapters. It will help a lot if you can listen to the tracks while reading the lyrics in the diagram, as that will make it clearer how the flow is notated and how the lyrics fit to the beat.

Here are some lyrics from "Keys Open Doors" by Clipse, from the album *Hell Hath No Fury*. These are the first four lines of Pusha T's first verse, right after the opening chorus:

1	2	3	4
	Eeyuck,	make ya	**skin** crawl
press one	**but**ton let the	**wind** fall.	**Who** gon'
stop us? Fuck	**the** coppers! The	**mind** of a	**ki**lo
shopper, seeing my	**life** through the	**wind**shields of	**chop**pers.

Note that the verse doesn't start at the beginning of the bar—it starts after the 2 beat, rests on the 3 beat, and then doesn't use any rests for the next three lines.

The second example is from "Time's Up," the classic single from O.C. (of Diggin' in the Crates), from the album *Word . . . Life*:

1	2	3	4
			You lack the
minerals and	**vi**tamins,	**i**rons and the	**ni**acin, fuck
who that I of-	**fend**, rappers sit	**back** I'm 'bout to	**be**gin, 'bout
foul talk you	**squawk**, never	**e**ven walked the	**walk**, more less
destined to get	**test**ed,	**nev**er been ar-	**rest**ed. My . . .

He starts his verse on the 4 beat, saying "You lack the" before the first full bar begins. O.C. is known for his dense, complex lyrics—we can see that he packs more syllables into these opening four bars by not including any rests.

5

Rhyme

I'm not one of those dudes that settles for the basic, simple, easy
line all the time. I really try hard, and when you listen to the
rhymes, you can hear the effort in a writer's song.

◄ **Masta Ace** ►

Rhyme is often thought to be the most important factor in rap writing—MCs often refer to rap lyrics as "rhymes." Along with rhythm, rhyme is what gives rap lyrics their musicality, because similar sounds being repeated are interesting to listen to.

Making words rhyme in an effective way is one of the central challenges of writing hip-hop lyrics. If an artist takes his or her time to craft phrases that rhyme in intricate ways but still get across the message of the song, that is usually seen as the mark of a highly skilled MC.

Rah Digga

People like Nas, people like Eminem, I don't think they're just flying through their verses in 10, 15 minutes. That type of rhyming and intricacy, that's not done with the snap of a finger—that's writing on a daily basis, constantly jotting down lines and phrases.

Evidence, Dilated Peoples

Definitely, [it's difficult to rhyme and get your point across].
. . . That's why people get props! That's why it's an art form,
that's the challenge of it, because we can sit here and say
witty stuff all day long if we don't have to [make it rhyme. If
I didn't] have to worry about it rhyming or sounding good,
then it wouldn't be as much of a challenge.

Being able to make words rhyme in different ways allows you to
grow as an artist. You are able to express yourself more effectively,
develop your own signature style, and make sure your style continues to evolve.

MURS

There's so many words in the English language, I've never
come to a point where I can't express how I feel and make it
rhyme at the same time.

Devin the Dude

Everybody has their signature ways of doing things, just the
combination of different styles.

Gift of Gab, Blackalicious

I continue to change my flow. That's part of my goal as an artist—to remain unpredictable. I don't want anybody to ever
be able to pinpoint what I'm gonna do next or say, "Oh, this
is the way Gab raps, he raps like that." I want to always keep
it unpredictable.

Perfect Rhyme

A perfect rhyme is the simplest and most obvious form of rhyme.
It's when one word has exactly the same ending as another word.

For example:

cat / hat
mug / plug
hit / grit

Here is an example of perfect rhyme from Melle Mel's lyrics in Grandmaster Flash and the Furious Five's track "The Message":

A child is born with no state of mind,
blind to the ways of mankind.

Here, all the rhyming words end with the same sound: "-ind."

Perfect rhymes are still used a lot today, but earlier hip-hop songs used them more frequently, since other forms of rhyming had not been fully developed.

Speech, Arrested Development

The rhyme styles is more simple from back in the day to some extent, but it was because it was so fresh—the whole thing was just fresh, the whole idea. MCs today [are] adding on to what's already there, whereas cats back in the day, they really was creating something from scratch—the foundation hadn't been laid as much.

Today, perfect rhyme includes rhyming by repeating the same word or phrase. This technique was not always considered valid, but it has become more widely accepted.

Yukmouth

Back in the day it used to be wack for you to say the same shit, but now you can say the same phrase over. Like you can say, "Yo, I went to the store and I copped that *coke*, / And I came back on the block, now I got that *coke*"—saying the same word. It used to be corny to say the same shit over and over again, but now it's hot, so hip-hop has definitely changed.

Assonance (Vowel Sound Rhyme)

Assonance occurs when two words don't have exactly the same ending but instead use a shared *vowel sound* (sounds made by the letters *a, e, i, o,* and *u*) to create a rhyme. As long as the vowel sounds are the same, the other sounds that surround them (the *consonant sounds,* or sounds made by letters other than *a, e, i, o,* and *u*) can be different. Examples of assonance include:

fit / hip
cat / back
hot / dog

Here is an example from the Madvillain song "America's Most Blunted":

The most blunted on the map.
. . . alley with a hood rat.

Here, "map" rhymes with "rat" using assonance: both words have the same vowel sound in the middle, the "a" sound. The surrounding sounds are not the same—one word ends with a *p* and the other ends with a *t*—but the vowel sounds are, and this creates assonance.

Assonance is the most widely used type of rhyme in hip-hop lyrics today, since it is so versatile. With assonance, you don't have to find words that rhyme perfectly, so a lot more words can be rhymed together. As R.A. the Rugged Man says, "I'll always have some shit rhyming with some shit. I'll always figure it out."

Bending Words

Assonance can be stretched even further by using words with similar vowel sounds instead of the exact same sounds. MCs sometimes "bend" words, pronouncing them in a way that makes two different vowel sounds sound alike:

arms / Mom's
three / Dre

This technique can be seen in Eminem's "Lose Yourself," when he rhymes

arms are heavy

with

Mom's spaghetti

The words "arms" and "Mom's" do not have exactly the same vowel sound, but they are close enough for them to work together as a type of rhyme. Stat Quo says, "With Eminem, he makes words rhyme that typically don't rhyme together—he's good at that. It's about how he pronounces it."

Steele, Smif N Wessun
It's always difficult to come up with words—there's nothing new under the sun—but you can twist words. Like, you got individuals like Redman who will bend the shit out of some words—he can make them fit into a [rhyme].

Planet Asia
[When you bend words,] things rhyme without the words actually having the same vowels and letters--you can rhyme without rhyming.

K-Os

I think Guru from Gang Starr is probably my favorite example of somebody who rhymed words that shouldn't sound like they rhyme. I think that comes from freestyling a lot, because when you freestyle, you're in survival mode, so you're looking for the next word that's gonna fit, and it just ends up fitting.

Alliteration and Consonance

Alliteration occurs when words *begin* with the same letter or sound. It's more subtle than the other types of rhyme, and it does not produce the same effect. It is mostly used to improve the overall sound of the lyrics, rather than to link particular rhyming words (2Mex of the Visionaries says, "I used to write a lot of alliteration type of rhymes—I was just really into the way words sounded"). Examples of alliteration include:

Jimmy / joke
mama / might
light / ladder

Here's an example of alliteration by Snoop Dogg from Dr. Dre's song "Dre Day":

Here's a jimmy joke about your mama that you might not like.

Here, "jimmy" and "joke" both start with a *j*, and "mama" and "might" both start with an *m*. Alliteration is being used in two ways in this line—with words that are next to each other ("jimmy" and "joke") and with words that aren't directly next to each other, just relatively close ("mama" and "might"). Either way, as long as the words that start with the same letter are heard soon after each other, the flow sounds more musical and interesting.

Consonance is created when the consonant sounds in a word are the same but the vowel sound is different:

sock / sack
cut / cot
bell / bill

Consonance has a similar effect to alliteration—some of the same sounds are repeated, adding another level of interest to the overall flow of the lyrics.

Here is an example of consonance from Kool G Rap's "A Thug's Love Story":

The other six started to pop, felt something hot,
I think I got hit, my jacket is ripped.

The words "hot" and "hit" use the same consonant sounds, but different vowel sounds in the middle. The term *hip-hop* is itself an example of consonance, where the vowel sounds in the middle of *hip* and *hop* are different but the surrounding consonants are the same.

Compound Rhymes (Multisyllable Rhymes)

Rhymes can be one syllable long, such as "cat," "bat," and "hat." However, this is rare in today's hip-hop, as most lyrics use compound rhymes, also known as *multisyllable rhymes*, *polysyllable rhymes*, or *multies*. Compound rhymes are created when a rhyme is more than one syllable long. In Wu-Tang Clan's song "Triumph," Inspectah Deck uses the following compound rhyme:

dropping these
mockeries

Here, "dropping these" rhymes with "mockeries," and they are both three syllables long.

Compound rhymes can incorporate a mixture of any of the types of rhyme previously mentioned. In the previous example, the syllables "these" and "-ies" use perfect rhyme, while "drop-" and "mock-" use assonance.

A number of MCs are known for their complex compound rhymes. Big Daddy Kane and Kool G Rap are known as pioneers in the field who have taken the technique to its limits, influencing other MCs such as Eminem and the late Big Pun.

Kool G Rap

[With] multisyllable rhyming, it's not like you're just rhyming "*fight*" and then "*light*" and then "with all my *might*." You're rapping "*random luck*" with "*handsome fuck*," "we cop *vans and trucks*"—it be shit like that. It ain't just doing the basics, because that's not ear catching—[more basic rhymes] don't catch the ear like that.

You often need to use compound rhymes in order to come up with new rhymes that haven't been used before. The more you can create interesting combinations of words, the more you set your-self apart from less sophisticated rappers.

Speech, Arrested Development

Most of the time I try to find rhyming words that haven't been rhymed yet, and in order to do that, I combine two words to rhyme with another word that has a number of syllables.

Masta Ace

You got guys that just rhyme "cat" with "bat" and "hat," and that's it, but there's so much more to it if you want to put some time in. If you don't know many words, then you can't write many words—you hear those kinda rappers all the time. To hear a whole album of "cat," "bat," "hat," it just sounds boring. That's why as an artist, when I listen to other rappers, there's guys that I really appreciate because they'll come up with combinations of words that rhyme [where] I would have never thought of that.

Linking Compound Rhymes Together

Because compound rhymes can be of different lengths and can use different sounds, there are different ways to join them together. Knowing how to do this can make your rhymes more interesting.

Killah Priest, Wu-Tang Clan affiliate

The words have to fit together—they have to be put together right, like sewing.

Pharoahe Monch

Make the flow interesting enough to be entertaining to people as well as the subject matter—that's what I'm constantly trying to do.

Linking with Rhyme

When compound rhymes are linked with rhyme, the rhyming syllables themselves create the link between them, even though they may have an entirely different rhythm. The compound rhymes may not have the same number of syllables or be stressed in the same places, but strong rhymes can create a clear link.

Here is an example from the Lady of Rage's "Unfucwitable":

1	2	3	4
			. . . the mic
brawler, the	**night** crawler,	I smoke them	**like** I'm off that
water.			

The compound rhymes "mic brawler," "night crawler," and "like I'm off that water" are each stressed in completely different places, and the last one has more syllables than the others, but they are all linked through rhyme. The first syllable in each phrase rhymes ("mic," "night," "like") and they all end with two syllables that rhyme ("brawler," "crawler," "water").

Linking with Rhythm

When compound rhymes are linked with rhythm, the rhythm of the words creates the link between them, even if the rhymes themselves are only slightly similar. Although the rhyming syllables may create some level of connection, the rhythm can help to establish a stronger link.

Here is an example from Snoop Dogg's first verse of Dr. Dre's "Nuthin' but a G Thang":

1	2	3	4
One,	**two,**	**three** and to	**the** four,
Snoop Doggy	**Dogg** and Dr.	**Dre** is at	**the** door.

The compound rhymes end with a perfect rhyme—"the four" and "the door"—but the beginnings are only joined by bending the words "three" and "Dre." The link is made far stronger by the rhythm: both compound rhymes are exactly the same number of syllables long—five each—and the stress falls in exactly the same places within each phrase, on the first syllable and on the fourth syllable. Even though the phrases don't match up exactly with rhyme, there are enough links in both rhythm and rhyme to make the phrases work together.

Rhythmic linking can help when you are trying to make a particular point but you can't find a way to phrase it in the form of an exact rhyme. As Nelly says, when you're trying to "get your message across, you get it across—you're not worried about if it rhymes," but by making the rhythm the same, you can create a stronger link.

Partial Linking

With partial linking, other rhyming sounds work with compound rhymes but do not form complete compound rhymes themselves.

You may have two fully formed compound rhymes, and then a couple of separate words here and there that are linked with those main compound rhymes. The partial links may be one-syllable-long rhymes, or incomplete compound rhymes that connect in some way to the main compound rhymes.

Consider this example from Jay-Z's "22 Twos":

1	2	3	4
too. To all my	**broth**ers it ain't	**too** late to	**come** together,
'cause too much	**black** and too much	**love** e-	**qual** forever.

There are two main compound rhymes that end each line—"too late to come together" and "too much love equal forever." They are joined by perfect rhymes at the beginning of each phrase ("too" with "too") with assonance at the end of each phrase ("together" with "forever") and with the assonance of "come" and "love" in the middle.

The partial link is the phrase "too much." This connects to the "too" and the "too much" in the main compound rhymes, but it is not a complete compound rhyme, since it doesn't have all the other elements found in the main compound rhymes.

Partial linking helps you add more rhymes to a verse, because you can connect extra words and phrases to the main rhyming phrases without having to create any more complete compound rhymes.

Coming Up with Rhymes

A common method of coming up with rhyming words and phrases is to make a list of things that rhyme before you start writing the lyrics.

Tash, Tha Alkaholiks

I think of the [rhyming] words before I think of the line.

Termanology

Sometimes I think of a word and then I'll think of all the words that rhyme with that, and I'll piece it together.

Rah Digga

I write the alphabet, A to Z, across the top of every single page that I write on—it just kind of helps me come up with a lot of my rhyming words. So I'll go in my head, "at," "bat," "cat," "dat . . ." as I'm writing—it just helps formulate my lyrics.

If you're stuck on a particular rhyme, try looking for assonance instead of perfect rhymes.

El Da Sensei

When you get stuck doing a line and you're trying to rhyme the next one, you try to find every word you can think of that has the same vowel sound.

Fredro Starr, Onyx

If I wanted a word that rhymes with "black," I'll write on the paper all the words that rhyme—"black," "tack," "rap," "cat," [etc.]—and then build my sentences around those words.

Some MCs use a dictionary or a *rhyming dictionary*, which has lists of words that rhyme with other words.

Wildchild, Lootpack

It can be difficult. Depending on the flow or certain words, you gotta go to your dictionary or rhyming dictionary.

El Da Sensei

Hell yeah [it's hard to come up with rhyming words and phrases sometimes], because you never want to say the same thing twice—you barely wanna hear the same words all the time. If you're kinda good at English in school, it kinda helps a little bit when you're doing these rhymes too—either that or you find yourself looking in the dictionary and you're just trying to fish for certain things that you probably never said before, which is not bad either.

Part of the challenge of rhyming is to avoid using cliched rhymes that have been used many times before by other artists. This may make it more difficult or time consuming to write a verse.

Akil the MC, Jurassic 5

I think there is a word or a way to phrase everything—it's just harder trying not to do what someone else already did.

Termanology

Sometimes it'll take me like six hours, 'cause I'm sitting there trying to think of a word that rhymes with a word that nobody really rhymed before, and it might take me like six hours to write one verse.

Keep in mind that it's not necessary to make everything rhyme all the time. Sometimes it's better to have a line that doesn't rhyme than to force a rhyme.

David Banner

It doesn't necessarily have to rhyme, if the feeling is there.

Big Noyd

I have stuff that I want to say and it might not actually rhyme with the last sentence or the last word that I said, and sometimes I'll still do it even though it might not rhyme. I still say it anyway, because I'm really trying to make a point.

Bootie Brown, The Pharcyde

I don't think you [always] have to make words rhyme. I think there are MCs that don't make words rhyme [constantly]. Prodigy from Mobb Deep doesn't make words rhyme all the time—he'll say something and it sounds charismatic—and Nas the same way. The way that they say it, you'll just feel it so much—you'll be like, that really didn't rhyme, but you don't care, because the way that they're saying it, you're like, damn, that shit sounds dope.

6

Rhyme Schemes

A good MC should hold his rhyme patterns in the same regards that a graffiti artist holds his illustrations—with his own style, flair, and originality.

◄ Shock G, Digital Underground ►

MCs often use rhyme to give structure to their lyrics, by arranging rhyming words and phrases in specific sequences throughout a verse or song. These patterns are referred to as the verse or song's *rhyme scheme*. Using a rhyme scheme can be compared to putting together a jigsaw puzzle: the individual rhyming words and phrases are like pieces of the puzzle, and the rhyme scheme is the picture that tells you where all the pieces should go.

MURS

It's a puzzle. I pace a lot when I write, I might go back and forth for two hours trying to find it, but to me that's the best part, because when you find it, it's like, aw, it's like figuring out a Rubik's Cube. It's like, aah, I knew I could make it work.

David Banner

I think [creating rhyme schemes is] an evolution. I think over time it becomes something—it becomes like a new monster.

It's like every day you piece something new to your style and that morphs it into something else.

Using different rhyme schemes to structure the rhymes makes each song sound unique and attention grabbing.

Papoose

It's never the same. I always use different formats and different strategies and shit.

AZ

I try to never be one dimensional, and when I write, I try to use different formats on every song to make it different. Every rap to me has its own personality and every rap has its own emotions, so every time I write it's for a certain emotion depending on what zone I'm in, and that's how I come up with different formats.

Havoc, Mobb Deep

Be versatile. Don't limit yourself to no one style, and concentrate on your lyrics. Be lyric-conscious.

Stat Quo

If you notice some MCs that don't really have a large vocabulary, their rhymes, the basic patterns, are the same. They never use anything different.

The Lady of Rage

You might put a pigeonhole on someone and feel that that's all they can do, that they're gonna stick to this one style, [but] when you change it up all the time, they never know how you gonna come. It's impressive to hear different types of flows. It shows your growth, it shows your ability to not just being one limited thing—you have style.

B-Real, Cypress Hill

You just get whatever beats and [start] writing to them and constantly practice what you've written and constantly come up with new, different types of [rhyme schemes].

Rhyme scheme is one of the elements of hip-hop that has developed the most since rap's early days. Schemes are constantly evolving, and new combinations are created as hip-hop moves forward. Earlier MCs often had great vocal deliveries and strong content, but complex rhyme schemes hadn't been developed at that point. (R.A. the Rugged Man says, "Melle Mel, 'The Message'—very basic flow, but his voice was so ill and he was so lyrical.")

Many MCs credit Rakim with the big shift toward more complex rhyme schemes and flows.

Planet Asia

When you're talking about Rakim, you're talking about the next level, the shift, the literal shift . . . like, bam—no more simple rap. It upped the ante for lyrics.

Masta Ace

I remember when Rakim came out—that was like a big moment. . . . Only guys that's really around my age that was rapping would remember how important that was. When he said, "I came in the door, I said it before, I never let the mic magnetize me no more" [on "Eric B. Is President"], everybody's mind was blown, because nobody had ever put three words that rhyme together in a sentence, and that just opened up so many doors. That just like really got the ball rolling in terms of creativity, as a lyricist. There was no limit to what you could do and figure out how to do it with words, and that's what got me really excited about being an MC— the endless possibilities in terms of the cadences, the flows, and how to make words rhyme.

Around the same time as Rakim, other pioneering MCs were crafting complex rhyme schemes.

MC Serch

I think everyone as a writer who came up in the '80s was influenced in some way, shape, or form by Rakim—[and] I definitely appreciated Big Daddy Kane, Kool G Rap. . . . Those were a lot of my early influences.

Brother Ali

In the late '80s, when people like KRS-One, Chuck D, and Rakim came out, I started writing. I was really inspired by the jump that the art of writing rhymes took in the late '80s and early '90s, and that's when I started writing myself.

Today, the patterns of rhyme an MC uses can be as important as the content.

Shock G, Digital Underground

I believe there are rappers who walk around with patterns in their heads that are just as intense and sacred to them as another rapper's words and topics may be, and who also are waiting for the right opportunity to bust the pattern out. Sometimes a person's creative new flow pattern does as much for the art form, and can change the game as much, as a person's lyrical content can.

Some MCs have their own way of notating the rhyme patterns they use.

Tajai, Souls of Mischief

I got a key, a flow key that I use. The best way for me to describe it is colors and directional lines, so if you look at two lines, the words that I say that sound the same will be the same color. [Though] it's in my head: if you look at the paper, the only way you can tell is instead of a color I'll maybe just draw a double line under something or draw a line with three dots—the same pattern for each matching portion of it.

Types of Rhyme Scheme

There are several different types of rhyme scheme that can be used. Each type is based on the number of bars that the rhymes join together.

Couplets

A couplet is a rhyme scheme in which two bars of lyrics are joined together through rhyme. Below is an example from the Beastie Boys' "Shadrach":

1	2	3	4
Riddle me	**this**, my brother,	**can** you	**han**dle it?
Your style to	**my** style, you	**can't** hold a	**can**dle to it.

The couplet is made up of the compound rhymes "handle it" and "candle to it," which join the two bars together.

In fact, the whole first verse of "Shadrach" is made up entirely of couplets: the first two bars are joined by "handle it" and "candle to it," the next two lines are joined by "right" and "night," the two bars after that are joined by "win it" and "cynic," and so on. A lot of lyrics are written in this way, entirely in couplets, where the first two bars are joined through rhyme and the next two bars are joined through a different rhyme—continuing throughout the verse or song.

Couplets are easily the most commonly used of all rhyme schemes and are the simplest to come up with. R.A. the Rugged

Man notes that it is still fine to use simpler rhyme schemes like couplets: "There's nothing wrong with that. If you're as lyrical as Melle Mel, you don't need a different flow every goddamn paragraph. It all depends who the person is." A couplet can often be the starting point of a whole song.

Esoteric

Each song is different, but I will usually come up with a couplet or a couple of rhyming words like "Maybe I'm a dreamer / because I think I can pull Adriana Lima" or something like a little rhyme like that, which I've never said, but just for an example. Then I'll be like, OK, I wanna use this rhyme, so I gotta come up with some kind of song—about a girl or about a relationship, or setting my sights too high or whatever—that might spawn a concept.

Single-Liners

A single-liner is a rhyme scheme in which a bar of lyrics has no rhyming connection to any other bar, and instead syllables within that one bar rhyme with each other—as Planet Asia says, "Some people rhyme on just one bar."

Below is an example from the Game's "Put You on the Game":

1	2	3	4
first, Af-	**ter**math, the	**Chron**ic is	**back**,
this is	**in**do,	**pro**duced by	**Tim**bo.

Here, there is no obvious rhyming link between the first bar and the second. But the compound rhyme "indo" and "Timbo" works just within the space of the second bar.

The Notorious B.I.G. also often used the single-line rhyme scheme to add variety and interest to his flow, as Lateef of Latyrx points out: "Biggie obviously has some pretty intense and complex flows."

Multi-liners

A multi-liner is a rhyme scheme that joins together three or more bars of lyrics. Below is an example from Public Enemy's "Bring the Noise":

1	2	3	4
D, Public	**En**emy	**num**ber one.	Five-
O said	**freeze**	and I	**got** numb.
Can I	**tell** them that I	**real**ly never	**had** a gun?
But it's the	**wax** that the	**Term**inator	**X** spun.

In the example, all four bars are joined together by the same rhyme scheme, through the rhymes "one," "numb," "gun," and "spun."

Making a rhyme scheme work across multiple bars can take more time and effort than using a couplet or a single-liner, but it increases the number of things you can do with the flow. Rah Digga offers this advice: "Don't rush. If you can make four lines rhyme instead of two, it's only going to make you a better MC."

Combinations of Schemes

Combinations of single-liners, couplets, and multi-liners can be used within the same verse, creating varied rhyme patterns that keep the listener entertained.

Some MCs like to change the rhyme scheme around frequently, and some like to keep it consistent—it depends on the artist. KRS-One often uses different combinations of rhyme schemes in his songs, such as in "MCs Act Like They Don't Know." Pharoahe Monch also uses combinations, as in "Simon Says."

R.A. the Rugged Man

A lot of people rhyme with a similar flow throughout their verses a lot of times, and then you got guys like the Pharoahe Monches or Busta [Rhymes] who flow all different kinds of flows. I got several different flows throughout my whole shit.

Wordsworth

Don't be afraid to try new flows. A lot of people stay stagnant with what they're in. I'm on just having fun with it.

Mighty Casey

There's so much variation you can put in the flow. You can have a four-bar flow pattern, two-bar flow patterns, [etc.].

For example, multi-liners and single-liners are often used together in a verse to good effect: an odd number of bars are joined together by a multi-liner, and they're followed by one final bar containing a single-liner, to create a verse with an even number of bars. Or the combinations may be more complex: a verse may start with a couplet, then have an eight-bar multi-liner scheme, then a different five-bar multi-liner scheme, and finish with a single-liner—creating a 16-bar verse in total.

Different rhyme schemes can also partially link to each other, so that some of the same syllables are part of more than one rhyme scheme.

Whole Verse

A whole-verse rhyme scheme links all the bars of a verse together with the same rhyme. It can be challenging to write so many consistent rhymes without losing track of the song's message.

Mighty Casey

If I'm doing a whole 16 bars rhyming the last few syllables, that might be tough.

Planet Asia

Flows can come in like two-bar and four-bar rhymes, and some people can rhyme their whole shit and make sense, like every line, in between and front and back all rhymes and still makes sense.

Below is an example from Busta Rhymes's "Put Your Hands Where My Eyes Could See," which shows two bars of a whole-verse rhyme scheme:

1	2	3	4
it's a must that	you heard of us,	yo, we murder-	ous. A
lot of niggas	is wondering	and they curi-	ous how . . .

The compound rhymes "heard of us," "murderous," and "curious" join these bars together, and the rest of the verse follows in the same way, using the same rhyme scheme for 16 bars.

Another example is in Kool G Rap's verse on "The Anthem," from Sway & King Tech's album *This or That.*

Kool G Rap

That's the challenge of rapping like that—you have to be very articulate to do a whole 16-bar verse where you're rhyming with the same rhyme and you are making it make sense, you're not just saying anything.

Extra Rhymes

In addition to creating the main rhyme schemes that link bars together and provide a structure for the verse, you can add extra rhymes that add to the overall sound of the lyrics. Here is an example from B-Real's verse on OutKast's song "Xplosion":

1	2	3	4
Dre,	pass	**me** the glass	**of** wine so
I can pour it	**o**ver my	**hom**ies' graves and	**mine** for . . .

The words "wine" and "mine" link the two bars to create a couplet. Here are the same two bars, this time with the extra rhymes highlighted:

1	2	3	4
Dre,	pass	**me** the glass	**of** wine so
I can pour it	**o**ver my	**hom**ies' graves and	**mine** for . . .

The words "pass" and "glass" rhyme with each other but not with the main rhymes that link the two bars together. If the two bars were not already linked, "pass" and "glass" might be considered a single-liner, but since the couplet provides the main rhyming structure, they simply add an extra rhyme on top of it.

Number of Rhymes in a Bar

Any of the rhyme schemes described previously can incorporate multiple rhyming elements per bar. For example, a couplet does not have to be limited to only one rhyming element in the first bar and one in the second—each bar can contain several elements that rhyme with one another, and as long as the same rhyme joins together the two bars, all the elements are considered part of the couplet.

But the number of rhyming elements in a bar does affect the way the lyrics sound. A lot of earlier hip-hop lyrics used relatively few rhymes per bar. Here is an example from Run-DMC's classic track "Sucker MCs":

1	2	3	4
			Two
years a-	**go** a	**friend** of	**mine**
asked me to	**say** some	MC	**rhymes**, so I . . .

The only rhyming syllables are the two halves of the couplet that link the bars together: "mine" in the first bar and "rhymes" in the second.

As hip-hop evolved, some MCs started to pack more and more rhymes into each bar.

Masta Ace

Up until [Rakim], everybody who you heard rhyme, the last word in the sentence was the rhyming [word], the connection word. Then Rakim showed us that you could put rhymes within a rhyme, so you could put more than one word in a line that rhymed together, so it didn't have to be just the last word. Now here comes Big Daddy Kane—instead of going three words, he's going multiple, seven and eight words in a sentence.

For an example of lyrics with a lot of rhymes, look at this couplet from Kool G Rap's verse on the track "Know Da Game" with Mobb Deep and M.O.P., on Frankie Cutlass's album *Politics & Bullshit*:

1	2	3	4
concrete. Get	**blown** at home or what-	ever **zone** you	**roam**, get two
flown to your	**dome**, blow chromo-	**somes** out your	**flesh** and **bones**

In the first bar, there are four rhyming syllables ("blown," "home," "zone," and "roam"), and in the second bar there are seven rhyming syllables ("flown," "dome," "blow," "chrom-," "-o-," "-somes," and "bones"). This adds up to a total of 11 syllables that rhyme in just these two bars.

Termanology

What I try to do is I try to rhyme two words every bar, versus a rapper that rhymes one time per bar. It's a lot harder—you're actually writing double the rhymes. There's only a few rappers that really can rap like that, like Kool G Rap, Eminem. . . . There's not really too many MCs that can do that.

Rah Digga

I like all the phrases, the whole line, to rhyme if I can help it. Instead of just the last two syllables in the line and two lines that rhyme, I like to rhyme four, five, six, seven syllables, like the whole line if I could, for as long as I can. I think when you spend time on your rhymes, you have outcomes like that instead of the simple [flows].

Some MCs vary the number of rhymes per bar within a single song, using only a few rhymes in certain parts but adding more rhymes in other parts.

Dray, Das EFX

I always try to start off calm with the flow, [then] by the sixth, seventh, eighth line . . . by the middle of the song I'm really trying to do something complicated flow-wise.

The music you're rapping over may make you want to add more rhymes in places as well.

El Da Sensei

The music should make you wanna change it up anyway, depending on what the producer's doing with the track. If he do a drum roll here or he do an extra snare here and there, you should actually want to try to double the rhyme up in certain places. For me, that's the thing that keeps the listener interested: it's not just the same flow all the way through the song—that's like a main ingredient.

Rhyme Placement

Rhymes can be placed anywhere in a bar, though the most common place they occur is on the 4 beat of the bar. Below is an example of this from LL Cool J's "I Can't Live Without My Radio":

1	2	3	4
			My
radio, be-	**lieve** me, I	**like** it	**loud**. I'm the
man with a	**box** that can	**rock** the	**crowd**. Walking...

Even in the case of a single-liner, one of the rhyming syllables frequently falls on the 4 beat. Extra rhymes, however, are usually spread throughout the bar for variety.

Some MCs prefer to put even the rhymes from their main rhyme schemes all over the bar rather than mostly on the 4 beat—Planet Asia says, "You can rhyme at a place where you normally don't rhyme at." Here is an example from Eminem's "Yellow Brick Road" in which the main rhymes fall on other beats:

1	2	3	4
so much they	**called** me a	**drift**er. Some-	**times** I'd
stick up a	**thumb** just to	**hitch**hike,	**just** to get...

Rhymes can fall not only on any of the four beats in a bar but also on the *offbeat*, one of the syllables that isn't on a beat. Here is an example from Method Man's verse on Wu-Tang Clan's "Shame on a Nigga":

1	2	3	4
head from the	**shoulde**rs. I'm	**bet**ter than	**my** competor,
you mean com-	**peti**tor, what-	**ev**er. Let's	**get** together.

As the rhyming syllables are not on any of the four beats that are prominent in the musical backdrop, they are not as obvious as rhymes that fall on the beats. This creates a subtler, more conversational type of rhyme.

Rhymes can also run over from one beat into the next or even into another bar—they don't have to be confined to any particular area. Below is a couplet from Nas's "N.Y. State of Mind":

1	2	3	4
Rappers, I	**mon**key flip em	**with** the funky	**rhy**thm I be
kicking. Mu-	**si**cian, in-	**flict**ing compo-	**si**tion . . .

The compound rhyme "funky rhythm," for example, starts before the 4 beat and ends in the following offbeat, and the compound rhyme "I be kicking" starts in the first bar and runs over into the second bar.

Rhymes often spill into other bars when they are longer compound rhymes, as there is only so much space in each bar. When a rhyme runs over into another bar, we determine the rhyme scheme by looking at the rest of the bar that the rhyming pattern has spilled into. If the same rhyming pattern continues for the rest of that bar, then it is joined to the previous bar (as in the previous example from Nas—the same rhyme scheme continues in the second bar with "musician," "inflicting," and "composition," and so the two bars are joined as a couplet). But if a new rhyme scheme is introduced in that bar, then the pattern that runs over is only considered part of the previous bar, as in this example from the Notorious B.I.G.'s "Ready to Die":

1	2	3	4
Tef-	**lon** is the ma-	**ter**ial for	**the** im-
perial.	**Mic** ripper,	**girl** stripper, the	**Henny** sipper.

The rhyme between "material" and "imperial" spills over into the second bar but is considered part of only the first bar's rhyme scheme, because there is a new rhyme scheme that dominates the second bar (the single-liner made from the compound rhymes "ripper," "stripper," and "sipper").

An easy way to make rhymes fall in unexpected places is to write lyrics with standard rhyme placement and then shift the whole verse so it starts at a different point in the bar.

Tajai, Souls of Mischief

Sometimes I'll write a rap, and then I'll just scoot it over and it'll sound like the craziest rap ever, but all I did was scoot it over and add a couple of words in the beginning and take off a couple from the end.

But simpler rhyme placement—and simpler rhyme schemes in general—may actually be a better strategy in certain situations. If the content of a song is especially strong, then more straightforward, consistent rhyming techniques, such as putting most of the rhymes on the 4 beat, might be a better way to highlight that content. On the other hand, if you want a song to showcase your flow, use more varied rhyme placement and more complex rhyme schemes.

R.A. the Rugged Man

As an MC, I think you should try to do both versions: do a song where you keep [changing the rhyme] schemes—do a few songs like that—and then on the flipside of that, show us what you got lyrically. I think a rapper that does that very well is a guy like Redman. He'll be very lyrical on a joint and kind of keep the same flow, [and] when he keeps to the same flow, his lyricism is crazy—certain songs like "Rated R" he was straight lyrical, didn't change up his flows. Then you got songs like "Green Island" and "Redman Meets Reggie Noble," and the "Tonight's Da Night Remix" where he just annihilated every flow possible known to man. Red was the master at it, so I think Redman is an ideal MC when it comes to doing both.

7

Rhythm

A lot of those little patterns and rhythms are what people find
attractive about all this stuff—it's such a rhythmic form of vocals.
◄ Aesop Rock ►

Rhythm (sometimes called *cadence*) refers to the way syllables
are placed on the beat and the different patterns that are created
by different numbers of syllables. Rhythm makes the lyrics sound
musical and interesting. It's also what makes the lyrics a rap, rather
than just words spoken in a random way over a beat.

Tech N9ne

[Me learning] rapping came from rhythm. My aunties and
my uncles were really musically inclined, so they taught me
rhythm beating on the breakfast table, taking the forks and
spoons to glasses—my mom too.

Since hip-hop lyrics place a lot of emphasis on new and interesting flows and intricate rhythms, and all those different rhythms
require a lot of syllables to play with, you usually have to write
more lyrics for a hip-hop song than you would for a song in
another genre.

Evidence, Dilated Peoples

That's why rapping is also, I think, respected by other genres of music and people who sing—because they can hold one note for so long and have to say so few words to get the message across. "I love you," "You're in my heart," "You'll be here forever," and "It's hard to sleep without you" . . . that's a whole verse right there if you held the notes right. With a rapper, we can't do that—that's not even half a bar.

Many people are drawn to hip-hop music initially because of the interesting rhythms, and their favorite artists are often those with a keen rhythmic sense. A listener can appreciate interesting rhythms even if he or she doesn't know what the lyrics mean.

Chuck D, Public Enemy

I was turned on by the fact that these guys out of the Bronx were making these tapes, and I was intrigued by the rhythm, how they delivered their raps.

Evidence, Dilated Peoples

It doesn't have to make sense to me. That's the example of me liking rap music in other languages, or some dancehall reggae that's real deep—I can't understand it, but I can appreciate the rhythms and the way they sound, and that's what makes me like them.

Being versatile with rhythm is also seen as a valuable skill for MCs.

Fredro Starr, Onyx

You got rappers like Jay-Z, who's a master of the flow—he can flow fast, he can flow slow. Biggie was a master of the flow, 2Pac was a master of the flow—they can come in different ways.

Coming Up with Rhythms

Artists have different ways of coming up with the rhythm of a song, but many MCs share some of the same basic techniques.

One Be Lo, Binary Star
That's all about feel, man. I gotta feel the rhythm or the cadence.

Twista
[I] change it up each song. I just try to do something different than I did the last time, and that helps me create flow patterns.

Bootie Brown, The Pharcyde
Dancing has a lot to do with our rhythms. Sometimes the way I rap is almost like the way I used to dance. You have to feel that rhythm inside of you, and it comes out of you in a certain way. That whole body movement and everything has to do with the way I feel I rhyme.

A lot of MCs come up with the rhythm of the lyrics first, before coming up with the content or any rhyming words.

N.O.R.E.
A lot of times I have the flow and then won't have the words yet.

will.i.am, Black Eyed Peas
I just improv[ise] over the beat—I lay down the rhythm first, and then I fill it in [with words].

Other artists wait until they're actually recording the song to finalize the rhythmic patterns.

Pigeon John

When I go to record, it's working out the patterns sonically, so you know that it works. If it's too many syllables, if it's too wordy, or if it's not wordy enough . . . all of those things kinda work themselves out when I start recording—when I put it into the sonic realm.

Scatting

Artists who create their rhythms first usually use a technique called *scatting*, based on jazz scat singing. With scatting, you improvise random noises or syllables over a beat, just to work out the rhythmic structure.

Tajai, Souls of Mischief

[Sometimes my rhythms come] from scatting. I usually make a scat kind of skeleton and then fill in the words. I make a skeleton of the flow first, and then I put words into it. That's where vocabulary comes in—you can make anything fit anywhere.

Vursatyl, Lifesavas

A lot of times when I'm listening to a beat, I hear different patterns—it's almost like math in my mind. And what I try to do is, I'm just kinda scatting or mumbling those patterns or those rhythms that are in my mind—then I find words to fit in those patterns. We call that *styling*, when I really come up with a dope style. I try to plug [in] the words that make sense, and that paint the picture, into those patterns.

Following the Music

Picking out particular instruments or other sounds in the beat you're rapping over and following their lead is another popular way to come up with rhythms.

Big Pooh, Little Brother

I end up picking out certain things in the beat. Whether it's the bass line or it's drums or a piano, I always end up picking out something that I use as my guide.

Akir

More so than anything else, I'd say that my flow usually tends to follow the percussion. I'm also a producer, so I realize the importance of the percussion section as the backbone of the music, and I usually try to adhere to that.

Devin the Dude

When the music changes, it lets you know what to do and how to change as far as the flow patterns.

Being Another Instrument on the Track

Instead of following the rhythm of sounds within the music, some MCs like to picture themselves as a separate instrument on the track. They create new rhythms that complement the existing patterns.

Gift of Gab, Blackalicious

I'm basically trying to be like another instrument on the track. I want to ride it like the bass line is riding it, only with words. I wanna ride it just like the guitar or the violin or whatever instrument, just riding it.

Omar Cruz

I come from the school of Nas, Big, 2Pac, Big Pun, Jay-Z, those type of cats—they're very big on cadence, almost like instruments on a track.

Crooked I

I just think of different ways that I can ride beats, and I think of different rhythmic patterns that I can use that will complement [the music that] the producer made.

Similarly, some artists mimic rhythms from other records that complement the beat they're rapping over.

Akil the MC, Jurassic 5

Maybe I already have a rhythm. Maybe I may have taken it from a jazz record—I might take a horn riff, follow that horn riff from some other record, and then put that on a hip-hop record, a beat. The vocal is an instrument in itself, so I like to listen to other instruments in other songs for other cadences. It might be a singer—I like old 1920s music—or African rhythms, just cadences, [or] the Arabic language, the cadence of that.

The Pattern Diagram

The easiest way to see how rhythm works is by using a diagram that shows how many syllables are in each bar. (Rah Digga puts it this way: "For me, writing rhymes is almost a little mathematical—I like to look at it like a blueprint.") The pattern diagram is similar to the flow diagram, but it replaces the song's lyrics with numbers that represent the syllables in each bar—it shows the "patterns" created by the different numbers.

Here again is the flow diagram for the opening lyrics from the Pharcyde's track "Drop":

1	2	3	4
Let me freak the	**funk**, obso-	**lete** is the	**punk** that talks
more junk than	**San**ford sells.	I jet pro-	**pel** at a
rate that compli-	**cate** their mental	**state** as I	**in**vade their
masquerade.	They couldn't	**fade** with a	**clip**per . . .

To put the same lyrics into the pattern diagram is very simple—
just add up how many syllables are in each quarter of the bar and
write the number in place of the words. This is how the same lyrics
look as a pattern diagram:

1st	2nd	3rd	4th
4	3	3	3
3	3	3	3
4	4	3	3
3	3	3	2

In the pattern diagram, just like in the flow diagram, each line represents one bar of music—the first line is the first bar, the second
line is the second bar, and so on. Look at the first bar/row. As you
can see, in the first quarter of the bar (labeled "1st" at the top of
the diagram) is the number 4. This represents the four syllables
that are in that quarter of the bar—"let me freak the." There's a 3
in the second quarter of the bar (labeled "2nd" at the top), which
refers to the three syllables "funk, obso-" in the second quarter,
and so on.

When there is a rest on one of the beats, the number is simply
shifted to the middle of the quarter to indicate that there is a rest
before those syllables are heard. Recall how a rest is shown in the
flow diagram:

1	2	3	4
more junk than	**San**ford sells.	I jet pro-	**pel** at a

Here's how the same rest is shown in the pattern diagram:

1st	2nd	3rd	4th
3	3	3	3

The pattern diagram is useful because it helps to break down the patterns of rhythms very clearly. Many MCs have mastered rhythm by listening to how other MCs use it, and the diagram helps you to go through this same process with a visual aid, to clearly see how other artists' rhythms work.

One Be Lo, Binary Star

[When I was learning how to rap,] I would take like a Rakim verse, or like Treach from Naughty by Nature—I would take certain people's verses and I would like spit the same verse with my own words, so I would just basically take the patterns.

Ill Bill

That's the first part—that's where it comes from: first memorizing not just the rhymes but the rhythm of the rhymes, the cadence. That's how I started—it was patterned after LL [Cool J]'s cadences at first.

By breaking down the rhythmic patterns of existing songs, the diagram helps to show the scope of what you can do with rhythm and how you can incorporate more complex rhythms into your flow.

Patterns of Rhythms

A flow's rhythm is largely decided by the number of syllables that are used in each quarter of each bar—the more syllables, the faster the rap. Some artists like to rap fast, some like to rap slow, and some prefer to mix it up. Some like to create random rhythms throughout a song, while others prefer to try to stay in one set pattern.

Pay close attention to the rhythms you're using, Mighty Casey says—"It's not just your ideas you're putting down, it's patterns and repetition and variation"—and experiment with different rhythmic patterns. As Wordsworth suggests, "Practice different flows, and don't be afraid to try different things on record and find yourself." Some MCs believe that the rhythms you settle on simply reflect who you are.

Fredro Starr, Onyx

I think there's something instilled in your personality. If you're a laid-back person, the lyrics come out laid-back. If you're a person with a lot of energy, your lyrics are gonna have a lot of energy. My flavor is a fast-paced, energetic way of being—that's my personal way of living and it shows in my [flow], I think.

Matching Patterns and Random Arrangements

Matching Patterns

Some MCs like to pick one pattern of rhythm and use it for several bars or even for whole verses or songs. This technique connects the lyrics together in a strong, clear way, and listeners are often impressed if the artist can successfully fit all the lyrics into a single set pattern.

Gift of Gab's solo track "Rat Race" is a great example of a song where each bar's pattern of rhythm closely matches the next bar's, throughout almost the entire song. Here are a couple of lines from the first verse in a flow diagram:

1	2	3	4
	. . . just an-	**oth**er clip	**add**ed in my
catalog.		Get your	**mon**ey, young	**play**er, I ain't
mad at y'all . . .			

Now here are the same lines in a pattern diagram:

1st	2nd	3rd	4th
	2	3	4
3	2	3	4
3			

As we can see, each bar includes the same number of syllables in the same places. Gift of Gab stays with this pattern for the majority of the song, adding or removing a few syllables here and there to create slight variations.

Other tracks that use a lot of matching rhythm patterns include Busta Rhyme's "Put Your Hands Where My Eyes Could See," Eminem's verse on D12's "Git Up," and Tech N9ne's "Killer."

Of course, writing in this style means that you mostly have to use a precise number of syllables in the correct places, so it can mean playing around with the lyrics until they fit.

Planet Asia

You might come up with a pattern in your head and be like, I'm digging that, and you try to keep that flow going and never stray away from it. And that's what makes the whole song a certain type of song—because you kept a certain type of flow.

Mr. Lif

There's always ways to go back and fill in the gaps in terms of balancing out your syllables and making sure that the flow is just tightened up.

Random Arrangements

Alternatively, a lot of MCs use a random arrangement in which each bar has a new rhythm instead of matching the rhythm of the previous bar. The constantly changing rhythm makes the flow unpredictable and surprising.

Below are four bars from Big Daddy Kane's classic track "Set It Off" in a flow diagram:

1	2	3	4
Go with the	**flow**, my rhymes	**grow** like an	**af**ro, I
entertain a-	**gain**, and	**Kane**'ll never	**have** no
problem.	I can sneeze	**snif**fle or	**cough**. E-E-
Even if I	**stut**ter I will	**still** come	**off**, 'cause . . .

And here are the same lines in a pattern diagram:

1st	2nd	3rd	4th
3	3	3	3
4	2	4	2
2	3	3	3
4	4	2	2

The syllables are arranged differently in each bar and don't follow any set rhythm. This keeps the listener guessing as new patterns are created in each new line.

MCs like Pharoahe Monch, KRS-One, and E-40 also use varied rhythms within single verses, which many listeners find very appealing.

Vast Aire, Cannibal Ox

Just when you think I like a slow, murky vibe, I pop out of nowhere with a quick momentum. Just when you think I was gonna go left, I go right.

Combining Patterns and Randomness

Most MCs like to use a combination of matching patterns and random arrangements, so that the syllables match in some bars but not in others.

One way to combine the two techniques is to create a verse that has a random arrangement of syllables but to copy that exact arrangement in a later verse.

Myka 9, Freestyle Fellowship

There aren't many MCs that I know of that are writing an entire verse, then matching that verse with the next verse and the third verse, and it's all cohesive. Those are things that I'm doing now as far as arrangement and composition goes.

Many and Few Syllables in a Bar (Rapping Fast and Slow)

Many Syllables in a Bar (Rapping Fast)

Having a lot of syllables in a bar means you have to say them faster to stay on the beat. This creates a rap that sounds fast.

Das EFX debuted with a unique style in which they would add "-iggedy" to the end of a lot of words—this increased the number of syllables per bar and meant that those bars had to be said faster. Here is an example from the first verse of Das EFX's "Mic Checka":

1	2	3	4
biggedy burn	**rig**gedy rubber	**when** I blabber	great. I
miggedy make the	**Won**der Twins	**de**acti-	vate. It's
crazy, I'm	**big**gedy breaking	**backs** and busting	lips. I
friggedy freaked	**Glad**ys Knight	**and** those freaking	Pips.

And here are the same lines in a pattern diagram:

1st	2nd	3rd	4th
4	5	4	2
5	3	3	2
3	5	4	2
4	3	4	1

As you can see, the pattern uses a lot of 3s, 4s, and even 5s—especially at the points where the "-iggedy" words add more syllables.

Dray, Das EFX

We came out in '92 and we started doing that style in '90, let's say, so it was a good two years before the public and the world heard our style. It just kind of grew. At the time that was just a natural way for us to rhyme—we didn't sit down and say, hey, let's make up a style.

Similarly, in a lot of rapping styles that were influenced by dancehall/ragga, artists incorporate more syllables and faster rhythms. KRS-One does this in a number of his songs, as does Wise Intelligent of Poor Righteous Teachers.

Wise Intelligent, Poor Righteous Teachers

[Using the Jamaican style of rhyming and faster rhythms came from] a lot of reggae, a lot of reggae music in the community we grew up in, a lot of yard parties. There'd be dub sessions at everybody's house—a lot of Jamaican kids in the community, so we were at the dub sessions all the time, so it became a part of us. You are what you eat and that's what we were taking in, [so] that's what we became.

Many rappers from the Midwest are also known for using very fast-paced rhythms—for example, Tech N9ne, in tracks such as "Welcome to the Midwest" and "Be Warned."

Tech N9ne

When you think about Twista, when you think about Bone Thugs-N-Harmony, Eminem, Ludacris, all those people from Chicago, when you think about Midwest artists, a lot of us got that choppy flow, that gunny flow. . . . I think there is just so much information [from being in the middle of the United States, surrounded by different styles] that we just gotta spray.

A number of MCs add more syllables when a beat is slow, contrasting the slow beat with rapid-fire rhythms. Sheek Louch of D-Block/The LOX says, "If the track is slow, you might want to speed up, just because it's slow."

Twista is known for being one of the fastest rappers ever. He explains how he developed his style:

Twista

[I created my fast style] by just trying to expand with the rap style. It started with just tripling up the words with one sentence and then a whole four bars, and then it's like a whole verse. Probably around the time I wrote one complete verse like that was when I realized that this is a hot style for me. I think when I really had it down pat was when I made the song "Mista Tung Twista" back in like '91—that was my first song where I wrote the whole song in that rap style.

To develop your own fast-paced style, you may want to practice freestyling (see chapter 9, p. 181). Coming up with lyrics spontaneously as the music plays is a good way to learn how to put together faster rhythms.

Zumbi, Zion I

I probably rap fast more freestyling than writing. You kinda learn how words fit together and how the phrasing goes and that certain words [are] harder to fit in the quick flow like that, or certain syllables, the way they knock together is more difficult to put them together. So I think freestyle has taught me certain flows that I can use in that quick pattern.

Making a lot of syllables fit into a fast rap often requires some editing. It's also important to know which words fit together smoothly with other words.

2Mex, The Visionaries

I wanted to do a style that was fast and exciting yet completely coherent. I started realizing that it all depends on what words you put together and how you put them together—like a run-on sentence that sounded very smooth. Sometimes I rap so fast that there'll be one syllable too many, and then I have to figure out where the fuck do I edit the syllable from. . . . And then you take a syllable off, maybe you took one or two out, and now you're one short and then you gotta add one—it's just a word game.

Few Syllables in a Bar (Rapping Slow)

Having only a few syllables in a bar means that there is less to say. This creates a rap that sounds slower—and often is clearer and easier to understand.

A lot of old-school hip-hop had very sparse patterns with very few syllables per bar. Here's an example from Melle Mel's lyrics in Grandmaster Flash and the Furious Five's "The Message":

1	2	3	4
			A
child is	**born** with no	**state** of	**mind,**
blind to the	**ways** of	**man-**	**kind.** God is . . .

And the same bars in a pattern diagram:

1st	2nd	3rd	4th
			1
2	3	2	1
3	2	1	3

The highest number of syllables in a quarter of a bar is three, and there are some quarters with only one syllable in them.

Even now, a lot of MCs prefer rhythms with fewer syllables.

O.C., Diggin' in the Crates

I try not to cram so many words, so people can easily gravitate towards what I'm saying, whereas 10 years, 12 years ago, I was trying to cram every word, and not everybody can do that and get across.

Twista

Today's MCs, they do it with a little more ease—it's not as complicated as it was when we did it. When I think of, like, Rakim, KRS-One, LL Cool J, Ice Cube . . . you threw a lot more into the rhythm. Today people rap a little more looser, a little more easy, [but that's] not to say that it's wack or anything.

Sometimes a certain song will benefit from not including so many syllables.

Gift of Gab, Blackalicious

If the music takes me to a place where I feel it's appropriate to go on some superlyrical, ill-cadence-type stuff, that's where I'll go. Sometimes the music calls for a real simple flow, like a song like "Swan Lake"—that didn't call for being extra, extra lyrical, it called for a really straightforward flow.

Combining Fast and Slow Rhythms

A lot of MCs like to change up the speed of their rhythms frequently. They may rhyme fast for part of a bar before rapping slow again, or they may rap fast on one song and slow on another.

E-40

Sometimes I rap fast, sometimes I rap slow, but the majority of the time, I'm not rapping too fast—a lot of cats is just listening too slow. I had to slow it down on my most recent album, just so that everybody else could catch up—I had to let them make like Heinz and catch up, that's why I did it. But I still turn it up a notch when I spit my fast rap—I do that every once in a while. I mix it up, I do it all, I still do my thing with the fast rap, but I also had to [slow] it down because everybody ain't got a lot of patience to figure out what I'm saying.

Rests

As we discussed in chapter 4 (p. 73), a rest occurs when an MC pauses on the 1, 2, 3, or 4 beat of a bar instead of rapping the next syllable right away. Rests are a key element of rhythm—there are several different things they can do in a verse.

Creating Breathing Spaces

One of the main uses of rests is to create breathing spaces within the song so the artist can perform smoothly without running out of breath.

E-40

You know you have to take breaths in between your lyrics. You gotta know how to map that out.

Joell Ortiz

I usually have cues on the paper for breaths.

Gift of Gab, Blackalicious

It's all about making the breath part of the flow. You gotta take little short breaths where there are pauses, that way you get to breathe. When you're rhyming you're exhaling, and when you find a pause you have to take a quick inhale and then keep flowing.

More rests can be added once you've had a chance to try to perform the vocals. If you find them difficult to deliver without running out of air, you may want to adjust the flow to create more breathing spaces.

Masta Ace

Sometimes I'll write stuff down and it'll be in this difficult cadence that in my mind, it sounds great, but I'm not actually trying to say it as I'm writing, so I don't realize how tough it's gonna be in the booth spitting it. [Then] I figure out all that—that line there has too many words, let me pull a couple of words out and make it easier to say without having to struggle with the breath.

See chapter 13 (p. 271) for more on deciding where to breathe.

Structuring or Dividing a Verse

Like patterns of syllables, rests can be used to create more of a structure for the flow. For example, in the first verse of Jay-Z's "22 Twos," he puts a rest on almost every other 1 beat so that each set of two lines begins with a rest. Slick Rick uses a similar technique in every verse on his track "I Own America."

Rests can also be used to divide a verse into different parts. In the second verse of Eminem's "Yellow Brick Road," he raps for 8 bars with no rests, and at the end of the 8th bar he includes a rest on the 4 beat. He then uses a different rhyme scheme and flow for the next 12 bars. So the rest signals a change in the flow and acts as the dividing line between the two different sections of the verse.

Adding Rhythmic Variety

Rests can also be used to add variety to the rhythm, by creating pauses in unexpected places.

Vinnie Paz, Jedi Mind Tricks

At certain times I purposely create pockets. The use of spaces is as important as words are sometimes.

Ill Bill

It's super-random, where I put a pause or anything that you see in the rhymes. It could be as random as how I set it up when I initially wrote it and just sticking to that, or it could be where I'm not exactly sure how I want to deliver it when I'm in the vocal booth and pauses and different rhythms are actually created right on the spot.

The Lady of Rage's track "Get with Da Wickedness (Flow Like That)" has a number of rests in surprising places to break up the lyrics and to create an interesting flow. So do Mystikal's tracks "Danger" and "Shake Ya Ass."

On the other hand, some verses have very few or sometimes no rests in them at all, creating a denser rhythmic feel. Having fewer or no rests is a good way to add more syllables to each line, which can then be used to create more complex rhythmic patterns.

Emphasizing Content

Rests can also be used to emphasize the content of the lyrics. This is usually done by putting a rest after an important line so that there is a brief silence after it. This lets the line sink in with the listener.

An example is in GZA's lyrics on the track "Clan in Da Front," from Wu-Tang Clan's album *Enter the Wu-Tang (36 Chambers)*:

1	2	3	4
'Cause I don't	**know** you, there-	**fore** show me	**what** you know.
I come	**sharp** as a	**blade** and I	**cut** you slow.

The lyrics in the first bar are followed by a rest on the 1 beat of the next bar. This gives the preceding line more of an impact.

A different way to add emphasis is to put a rest on the 4 beat, which draws attention to the syllables in the offbeat *after* the pause. In the song "Dear Mama," 2Pac uses this technique several times, as in the example below:

1	2	3	4
you al-	**ways** was a	**black** queen,	Mama.

The rest on the 4 beat makes the following word, "Mama," more prominent.

◀ III ▶
Writing

8

The Writing Process

The process of writing makes it easier to write—
the more you write, the easier it is.

◄ Lateef, Latyrx ►

The writing process is the way you come up with the content and
the flow and join them together to create the finished lyrics. Some
of the most memorable and classic hip-hop tracks are created not
just by great flow or great content but by the skillful combination
of the two.

K-Os

I think that's what makes Mos Def great, I think that's what
makes André 3000 [of OutKast] great, and I think the originator that I think in my mind of that is Q-Tip [of A Tribe Called
Quest], and Black Thought [of the Roots] also—they all have
wicked flows but they say so much.

Cormega

If you got subject matter and flow, that makes you a well-
rounded artist.

Shock G, Digital Underground

Many of the classics we enjoy today are a result of this rare combination. I say "rare" because of the millions of rappers out there today, the majority of us usually have one strength or the other—[flow] or content. The true greats always possess, and are aware of, both.

There is no one "correct" way of putting together content and flow. Different rappers rely on a wide range of different techniques, and looking through all these methods will help you to experiment and find the process that works best for you. Developing and practicing your own writing techniques are key to becoming a better MC.

B-Real, Cypress Hill

It's like someone who trains in the gym, or an athlete—you have to practice and work all your skills and tools constantly to become really good at what you do. So you have to constantly be writing.

Research

If you don't already know enough about the subject you're creating a song about, you may need to do extra research before you start writing.

Immortal Technique

It depends on what the song is about. If it's about your personal life experience, then really the research you have to do is within yourself, and that's something that's probably already going on internally. If it's about a specific subject matter, I've usually done the footwork beforehand.

Del the Funky Homosapien

For Deltron 3030 [the supergroup produced by Dan the Automator], I had to do a lot of research, so much that it was hard to remember the lyrics for performances!

Shock G, Digital Underground

To a self-critical perfectionist like myself, accuracy is crucial. [For Digital Underground's classic *Sex Packets* album,] we researched MDMA [Ecstasy], as well as psilocybin mushrooms, LSD [acid], and DMT [dimethyltryptamine]—the three major hallucinogens—before we settled on the "official" lingo for the *Sex Packets* lyrics and album literature.

A lot of MCs do research because they feel they have a duty to the listener to get the information in their songs correct. And if they make sure everything they say is accurate, that also helps make the arguments in their lyrics more convincing. If their information is wrong, listeners will question what they're rapping about and call them out on it.

Omar Cruz

As an MC you're also a teacher to a certain extent, and if you're a teacher and you don't have your info right, you're just the blind leading the blind. So for me it's important if I am spitting something [that] it's at least accurate in terms of what is facts and not what's my opinion.

Akir

I always wanna be able to come with an intelligent grasp. As you can tell from my music, it's very important for me to maintain a message.

Devin the Dude

You really, really have to know what you're talking about

when you're writing, because once it's out, there [could be] people like, hey, that's not right!

There is also an art to how you use the information you dis-cover through your research. Instead of inserting these facts into a song in an obvious way, talented MCs use their own words to subtly weave the research into their lyrics.

Tajai, Souls of Mischief

I definitely do a lot of research, but I try to really disguise it so it doesn't seem like I do. I would rather drop a key word or something so somcone who does know what I'm talking about is like, "Oh, he really knows what he's talking about," but so it's not like I'm reading verbatim from an encyclopedia when I rap. I think you listen to certain guys and they do that and it's like, this isn't a report, it's a fucking song, what's up?

Where to Do Research

There are many places to get information on the subject you're rapping about. The Internet is a very popular research tool.

Ill Bill

That's what's dope about the Internet—the fact that you're one touch away from a billion encyclopedias' worth of infor-mation. . . . That's a huge asset when researching a song. Take for example a song I have called "The Anatomy of a School Shooting"—I definitely researched that before I wrote it.

MURS

I just did a song about NASCAR, [and] recently I've really been on a Wikipedia kick, so I went on Wikipedia, found everything about NASCAR, rented like five movies on it. I started watch-ing races, I went to a race, and then I wrote the song.

It's good to supplement information from the Internet with other sources, to get different viewpoints from diverse places.

Imani, The Pharcyde

It's good that you can Google shit, but Google ain't everything. You [can] do research in books, and we travel a lot, so sometimes the shit you see on TV and the shit that you read in the paper here ain't always the same when you go other places. They have a different perspective, so then I'm writing from a worldview sometimes versus just a regional California or L.A. type of view.

A lot of MCs research by getting information from their friends and family.

40 Cal, Dipset

I might ask a friend about a line.

Dray, Das EFX

I remember having to call a couple of friends—"Yo, how does that show go?" or "What does that guy really say?" I don't want to misquote—I wanna get the line right. I had a crew, so we would feed off each other.

R.A. the Rugged Man

I wrote [a verse for the Jedi Mind Tricks' song "Uncommon Valor"] about my father [and his experiences as a soldier in Vietnam], and me and him were back and forth on the phone—"What happened then, Dad, what was this?"— because it was a factual-based thing. When you're dealing with somebody's true-life story like I was doing with my father, you wanna go, "Did this happen, what's this, what's that, what did they do?" He told me shit like, "They were killing the village elephant—[they'd] murder the village elephant to piss off the head," stuff like that, which I would have never thought of, so I said, "Kill a village elephant" [in the song]. Little wild shit like that, just little factual shit like that, made the shit a lot tighter, because it was all shit that I wouldn't have known.

Gift of Gab, Blackalicious

[With] "Chemical Calisthenics," I *had* to research that, because I never knew about none of that stuff. I actually had to get a book from Cut Chemist [who produced the track] with the definitions of each word to make sure that what I was saying made sense in the context of the rhyme.

Research from Life in General

Many MCs avoid having to call on outside sources of research by focusing on topics they're already very familiar with—particularly real-life experiences.

AZ

Anything I ever wrote, I've had direct contact with it, so I never had to research on anything, because I live the life I speak about. I was a product of that environment.

But calling on your own experiences and the things you've learned in your life can be considered just another form of research.

Gift of Gab, Blackalicious

Research is just observation. You could watch the news and get that information and that's research, or you could see a certain situation happen or be in a certain situation and observe that and that's research.

The Lady of Rage

I said something in a rhyme about "botulinum toxin" [from] watching the Discovery Channel. At the time I didn't know that was botox—it's a poison, and they use it to decrease the wrinkles in your face. So I was watching that, and instead of saying "botox," I just used the whole "botulinum toxin," which sounded better. So I watch a lot of things on Discovery, *Forensic Files*, and I just use all of that. I learn stuff every day, so it's how you use what you know.

One Be Lo, Binary Star

I only rap about stuff that I know. If I'm talking about the ghetto or I'm talking about hip-hop, I'm just talking about hip-hop from my perspective, or the ghetto from my experience—I'm not trying to give you the history of hip-hop and who was the first DJ. In general I just read what I read and I learn what I learn, and if it turns into a verse, that's cool, but I don't read books so I can rap about it.

Ways of Writing Lyrics

Once any necessary research is done, there are different ways of actually "writing" the lyrics of a song. They range from physically writing them down on paper, a phone, or a computer to composing them in your head, rapping them into a tape recorder, or simply freestyling them off the top of your head in the recording booth. Some MCs change their writing method over time, while others stick to the method that works best for them.

Writing Lyrics Down

Reasons to Write Lyrics Down

One of the main reasons for writing lyrics down in some way is so you can see everything in front of you. Because you don't have to keep everything in your head, you can make the flows and wordplay more complex, and you can edit things more easily.

Rock, Heltah Skeltah

I'm able to see and put down more intricate flows [writing it down].

Joell Ortiz

I'm a perfectionist, and sometimes I feel like I might lose something special if I just rhyme into a mic.

Akil the MC, Jurassic 5

[On paper] I think your thought process might be a little more thought out, more complex—you have to really think about it. I think if you sat down and wrote something, you can write something a lot more complex.

Writing the lyrics down also means that you won't forget them and lose some of the great lines you thought up.

Cormega

Some of the best rhymes I ever thought of, some of the most unique rhymes I ever thought of, you'll never, ever hear them, because I [didn't] get up and write them down with a pen. I went to sleep and I tricked myself into saying, "Oh, I'll write it down in the morning," and then when the morning came, it was gone.

Writing on Paper

The most obvious way to write lyrics down is to handwrite them on paper. To some artists this method is almost a tradition.

Mr. Lif

I like the pen and paper. It's an unparalleled experience for me.

Big Noyd

I write everything down on paper. Now with the technology, a lot of people use their BlackBerries and [T-Mobile] Sidekicks and stuff to write, but I'm old school—I'm straight pen and pad.

Spider Loc

I really enjoy writing, even doodling. If I sit around and there's pen and paper somewhere handy, I'll just do something on the paper. I enjoy writing for the purpose of just the physical act of writing—it's just something I like to do.

Part of the appeal of writing on paper is having copies of your original lyrics on paper, as you wrote them.

Steele, Smif N Wessun

I love to have a pad. I'm one of the last artists that still has doodles and draws shit on the side of your pad. I think that's like memorabilia.

Many MCs have special books in which they write down all their rhymes to keep them organized and all in one place.

Vursatyl, Lifesavas

I've got literally thousands of rhyme books. All of my stuff is in books and notepads.

Fredro Starr, Onyx

I like to write in a black-and-white composition book—for some reason that book is the perfect rap book. You got spiral notebooks and you got pads and shit like that, but [with] the black-and-white composition book, the way the lines [are] on the pages is perfect for writing a rhyme. I see kids writing rhymes on two-ways, and I see kids writing rhymes on computers nowadays, but I always think writing rhymes in a composition book is the best way to preserve your raps.

Writing on paper doesn't have to be limited to actual sheets of paper, a notepad, or a composition book. As 2Mex of the Visionaries comments, "I just write on anything, man. I write on pizza boxes and other people's papers."

Writing Electronically

Technology has become such an important part of our daily lives that many artists like to write their lyrics on their phones or computers.

E-40

These new devices nowadays is good—that's how I do my lyrics. I write either on paper, [or] if I don't have paper, I'll use my Sidekick. [I'll] use that to write down notes and every-thing, like on the airplane—you can do your own editing and everything.

Rah Digga

I do all of my writing on a laptop—I type all my lyrics out.

Many MCs like the fact that if you write electronically, you can easily save your work in a portable form and send the lyrics some-where else immediately—though with phones and laptops, you do have to be careful to not run out of power while you're writing.

Akir

Since I started working with a Sidekick, I've been writing a lot of music on my Sidekick, because I'm able to e-mail that to myself and so I don't have to transcribe my lyrics.

Glasses Malone

I write everything down on my Sidekick—I always got it with me. And when I'm done, I can e-mail it to myself to copyright the lyrics. The only disadvantage is when the battery goes dead and you in there laying a verse—that ain't really cool.

Even if an artist writes lyrics some other way to begin with, he or she may then convert them into electronic form to make the editing process easier.

Chuck D, Public Enemy

[I write on paper], but also the computer has helped out a great deal over the last 10 years for me, because I write it out on paper but I kind of arrange through the computer.

Techniques for Writing Lyrics Down

Different artists have different techniques for writing down their lyrics. They may use a variety of symbols, as we have seen in previous chapters, or they may write in their own form of shorthand.

Cappadonna, Wu-Tang Clan affiliate

Sometimes I'll have no respect for the loose-leaf paper at all. I'll write upside down, write graffiti all over the place, I'll do some of it in script, some of it small, some of it big.

Big Pooh, Little Brother

I write everything like one big run-on sentence, no slashes, no nothing, like one big block of words.

E-40

I write real quick, because I've gotta remember what I'm gonna say—when the ideas come in my head, I've gotta hurry up and put it down. So when I do that, I write a word down the way I say it. I don't write down the correct spelling, I just hurry up and write in a way at least I can understand.

Writing in Your Head

Instead of using a computer, phone, or pen and paper, some artists prefer to "write" lyrics in their heads, working out the words and flow ahead of time but never actually writing them down. This method was popularized by MCs such as Jay-Z and the Notorious B.I.G.

Pusha-T, Clipse

Anything that you've ever heard of anybody saying about seeing Jay-Z in the studio, what does he do? He mumbles to himself, he walks around, he mumbles to himself, he walks around, he mumbles to himself, then he's like, OK, I got it. It's not like, stroll in the booth and [record immediately]—he plays with the idea. Paper and pen is nothing but comfort, to me, it's nothing but being comfortable and being able to look at it, digest it, and say, OK, this is how it's supposed to [go]. But if you can train your mind to do it without that, that's dope.

Styles P, D-Block/The LOX

A lot of people brag about not writing, but I think I stopped writing at like 12 because I just couldn't say the rhyme that was on the paper—I just couldn't get it out, like I never could flow exactly what was on the paper. So I got accustomed to just keeping it in my head and being able to say it.

Ill Bill

I'm in shock every time I'm in the studio with Everlast [of House of Pain] and I see how he does it. He constructs the rhyme in his head, on the spot, sits there and like 20 minutes, half an hour later, he's like, OK, I'm ready to go . . . [and he] goes in the vocal booth with no paper and spits it.

Reasons to Write in Your Head

The main reasons to write in your head are if it makes the writing process easier for you and if you can come up with better lyrics by doing it. It can also be an advantage when you don't have access to paper, a phone, or a computer. Bobby Creekwater says, "Sometimes I might be riding and I might not be able to get to paper, so I just memorize the lines in my head."

Some MCs find that writing in their heads allows them to come up with the flow and delivery more spontaneously.

Hell Rell, Dipset

I feel [writing it in your head] is better, because when you're doing it off the paper, it's like you're reciting. When you're saying it off your head, it's like it's coming from the heart.

Bishop Lamont

[Artists who write in their heads are] basically synchronizing themselves with the beat [as they come up with lyrics]. It's not some words and lyrics they put down and tried to structure it to follow the beat.

Guerilla Black

One of the key things in writing without paper—you have the expression memorizing in your head. [It's] how it sounds after you actually say it, because everything is spoken, like how does that sound, or how will that sound, how will this sound, or where will this go, or where am I going with that. Everything is sounded out so that I know what rhythm I'm gonna go with.

This can be especially helpful if you prefer to memorize a song before you record it (see chapter 13, p. 264), because writing in your head means you'll be memorizing the lyrics automatically as you come up with them.

But MCs caution that you shouldn't write in your head just so that you can brag about it, because your lyrics may suffer as a result.

Evidence, Dilated Peoples

I know a couple of rappers who can [write in their heads], and it's really dope in the studio session itself. Like when you and the engineer and the producer and the rapper is in there and does it, it's really impressive to everyone that's in the room. But the people [who listen to your records] don't care—the people just want to like your music, they just want to enjoy it. So I'd say [writing in your head is] dope if it doesn't really affect the wordplay and the continuity of your lyrics—[but] if you're doing it for shock value or something, the three people in the studio, that's cool for them, but I don't know if the rest of the world is gonna get it.

How to Write in Your Head

Most MCs who write in their heads describe the process as building up a verse, line by line, until it's complete. Esoteric says, "Basically, as I'm coming up with bar 1 to bar 16, the lyrics are getting memorized in my head as I try to fine-tune them. I'm memorizing it as I'm doing it." Akil the MC of Jurassic 5 breaks down this process further, explaining that he comes up with the first part of a verse, goes over it in his head until he has memorized it, then adds something to it and goes over the entire thing again before adding something else—essentially going over the whole verse every time he adds a section, so that it gets firmly memorized.

Akil the MC, Jurassic 5

In the very beginning I was writing on paper, but then I started working at this restaurant and every time I would be sitting down writing a rhyme, a customer would come in, so I would have to get up and go cook their food or whatever. Every time I would go back to my paper, I would forget how I said it—I would have the words but I would forget how I said it. So I started developing this process of just memorizing it in my head, sort of how you learn your ABCs:

A, B, C . . .
A, B, C, D, E . . .
A, B, C, D, E, F, G . . .

And then by the time I'm up to Z, I know [the rest of it] already—it's already memorized. So I developed that process of writing like that—I'll always know how I said it if I keep repeating it.

Recording the Lyrics or Flow

In addition to using the techniques discussed above, a number of MCs "write" their lyrics by rapping them into a tape recorder, a cell phone with a voice recorder, or a similar device.

Crooked I

I got a tape recorder that sometimes I record rhymes on for two purposes—one is when I'm just having certain ideas and I don't want to forget about them and I'm nowhere near the studio, and the other one is when I'm sleeping—I dream raps, I dream verses, I dream hooks, choruses, so I wake up in the middle of the night and I put them on this tape recorder.

MC Shan

I also use my telephone when I come up with an idea or melody for a style. I use the voice comment thing, [record] it in there, and then go back and put words into the melodic structure that I made—sometimes you gotta record the style in actual real time, opposed to just writing it down.

Recording the lyrics can help you remember how the flow goes, which is important because as Royce Da 5'9" comments, he's forgotten the flow "plenty of times, and that's when songs get scrapped right there." If your flows are very intricate and complex, recording them as you think of them may be a particularly good idea.

R.A. the Rugged Man

Sometimes when you write like a crazy amount of flows and you come back and try to spit it two weeks after you wrote it, you're looking at your notebook [and] you don't remember. One syllable could throw that whole flow off—it's not perfect no more. I have my little tape recorder and now the second I write the flow, I record it into my tape recorder so it's forever, so I know what the flow is. I can go back to that flow in like four months and go, "Oh, shit, that flow was ill."

The recorder can be used to help you remember not just complicated flows but your delivery as well (see chapter 12, p. 239).

Tech N9ne

After I write it down I put it in a little Dictaphone recorder and I listen to it constantly, so when I get in the studio I damn near have it. If you listen to my music, [the flow is] real intricate—I've got to be on it. My Dictaphone recorder really helps me with pitch, like how I'm gonna say things, because I don't want to lose it—if I don't do it, [then] back in the studio it'll be different. You can be riding in the car and get an idea and you don't wanna lose an idea—stuff you want to remember you might put on the recorder and it might go on the album, so those Dictaphone recorders, man—that's a good idea.

Freestyling in the Vocal Booth

MCs who are good at freestyling (rapping off the top of their heads) sometimes record songs simply by going into the studio and coming up with lyrics on the spot.

The Lady of Rage

[Snoop Dogg, when I worked with him earlier in his career,] that's how he created his stuff. He would freestyle—he wasn't a writer then, he was a freestyler.

Myka 9, Freestyle Fellowship

I freestyle whole songs. I love it—those are my favorite. I'm talking about one freestyle all the way through, as soon as they turn the mic on, all the way through the whole song. I have a song on every album I've ever done, I've either had freestyle verses or complete freestyle songs, where I'm not only freestyling verses, I'm freestyling choruses, then I'm freestyling the arrangement and composition of the entire song, and I'm keeping it cohesive to what the song is about. Those are my finest moments, those are my brightest moments and my finest hours, that's Myka 9 at his best, when I [haven't] heard the [beat] before, turn on the mic, I react—verse, song, arrangement, everything.

Cashis

[I sometimes freestyle whole verses or songs.] I've got a bunch of records like that—some of the records that I did on *Eminem Presents: The Re-Up* was like that, some of the records on *The County Hound EP* was like that, the majority of the records on my mixtapes are like that, and a couple of the records on the *Loose Cannon* album are like that.

One of the main benefits of freestyling is the spontaneity that comes from creating lyrics in the moment.

DJ Quik

At that point you're just open—you're open to creativity—and keeping it in rhythm is just like thinking fast, thinking on your toes. Sometimes the magic comes out of that. Some of those lyrics we'll keep, some of them we'll structure more, or whatever.

T3, Slum Village

I think that part of the thing that has been lost in hip-hop is the spontaneous feel and fun and doing things effortlessly—I think that the spontaneous part has been lost in the music game. Certain rappers have a few premeditated rhymes and they freestyle [too]—to me that's the best rapper, so I keep it spontaneous and try to be the best I can be on both ends of the spectrum.

Evidence, Dilated Peoples

When you're freestyling, the dopest thing happens—you'll just get in a zone and then you'll be rhyming one way, and then out of nowhere you'll just hit a word that shouldn't be there and you'll take a left and start rhyming something on that word. That's something that doesn't happen all the time when you're writing, because you're looking at the words, you're trying to line them up—it's more organized, it's more premeditated.

An MC does not always have to freestyle an entire verse all the way through. He or she might freestyle in sections, restarting at a particular bar if something goes wrong or piecing together the verse from the best parts of different attempts. Or the MC might use the freestyle take as a jumping-off point but then go back and rewrite it.

Myka 9

Sometimes I'll do what's called a *punch-in* style, where you're in the studio, you might [freestyle] four or five bars or eight bars, then you might mess up or you lose your train of thought—then the engineer would just punch you back in right where you messed up. [See chapter 13, p. 274, for more on punch-ins.]

Mr. Lif

I take the best parts of a freestyle and put them into the verse.

Zumbi, Zion I

[Sometimes I'll] freestyle, record, and get an idea, and [then] go back and rework the idea. Maybe I said a couple of things, a hook was nice, maybe the general idea of the rhyme was cool—I'll go back and edit the rhyme a little bit, tighten it up.

However, sometimes it may be better to run with the original freestyle take. As will.i.am of Black Eyed Peas notes, "Sometimes you could do a freestyle and you want to go redo it perfect and you fuck up the song."

Incorporating the Different Methods

Instead of using only one of the methods described above, a lot of MCs incorporate several different techniques into their writing process. For instance, a rapper might freestyle some lyrics and write some other parts down.

Nelly

I probably haven't wrote anything down [completely] since

Country Grammar. Not saying that I wouldn't jot down a line or two, just so I could remember it, but as far as just writing the whole rap down, nah. It's basically, you get in there and you kinda do it as you go. A lot of it is freestyling, but you kind of go over it a little bit—you get a vibe and you try to put it down as much as possible, and then you come back after you've listened to it, and you might change a few things or make it a little tighter or sweeten up the flow a little bit.

Schoolly D

I remember James Brown gave this interview and he said he would never write his lyrics down, he would only write one word down that reminded him of what he was going to say in the verse, what he was going to say in the chorus. So I kind of took that. I wanted to keep it fresh—that's why I don't like to write everything down, because I always leave some room so when I get in front of the mic, [there's] room for me to come up with something else on the fly.

Places to Write

Another aspect of the writing process is where you choose to do your work. Some MCs like to write in specific locations, while others don't have a preference.

Lateef, Latyrx

I have a couple of different places that I write—I have some places that are like my go-to spots. I have my nice, pretty hillside view with a picnic table.

will.i.am, Black Eyed Peas

I write anywhere and everywhere—airplanes, buses, trains . . .

Cappadonna, Wu-Tang Clan affiliate

Anywhere is fine with me. As long as there's some paper and some pens, I start writing.

In the Studio

A lot of MCs prefer the professional atmosphere of the studio for writing their lyrics.

Nelly

I always write in the studio, unless I get an idea just from being out and seeing something.

Big Noyd

I rarely write at home—I don't get that vibe. I need that studio vibe—the beat really loud and a couple of homies around.

DJ Quik

In some cases, when you're on the spot, when you don't have a lot of time to experiment, I'll write in the studio—not forcefully, but I'll catch a vibe and write in the studio. And that's actually my safe haven, like those are the records that more aptly become hits because they were done structurally.

Sean Price, Heltah Skeltah

I don't have a rap book, man. I write on the spot [in the studio]. If I don't go to the studio for two months, that means I ain't writing for two months.

At Home

Many other MCs prefer to write at home, where the atmosphere is more relaxed.

Vast Aire, Cannibal Ox

Most of the stuff is done at home with beats on and video games and cracking jokes with your friends—I like a good atmosphere when I'm creating.

RBX

I would prefer writing at home in front of the TV, watching Martha Stewart, some beats banging, in my own little zone—no pressure, no hip-hop atmosphere, no gang of guys gambling in the background.

Schoolly D

A lot of those earlier songs were written at the breakfast table, four o'clock in the morning, sitting there with some headphones, sitting up all night. So I like to do most of my work at home first.

A number of MCs have studios in their homes so that they can combine the studio setting with the home setting.

Yukmouth

My first album, *Thugged Out,* was written all in my little game room in my house. I got a three-story house, [and] I got a game room that I just chill and write all my raps at. So mainly in my game room—then I got my own studio, and I write them in my studio.

In the Car

Coming up with lyrics while driving or riding in a car is another popular way to write hip-hop songs. Some artists are inspired by what they see while in a car.

DJ Quik

I remember an interview I saw a long time ago with OutKast, and it was saying that Big Boi would drive around and write his lyrics—just, like, driving around the city getting inspiration from just what he sees. I used to do that too—I'd drive around in my Lexus just writing lyrics down, whatever I felt, whatever I heard.

Fredro Starr, Onyx

I like to ride through Manhattan or ride through the city, writing while somebody is driving me around—that's my inspiration. I like to write in my car, right while I'm seeing things. Like if I'm just passing down a street in Southside Jamaica, I might see some people outside on the corner with some type of clothing on or doing something, and it'll give me inspiration to write something. So a lot of my rhymes have been written inside of a vehicle.

In a Quiet Place

Some MCs like to write in a quiet place, where they have room to think and be alone with their rhymes.

Devin the Dude

Sometimes you have to have a little quietness. I prefer it, just being locked up with the music.

Termanology

I like to be by myself, man. I hate writing when there's a lot of people around. I go to the studio and there's like 20 motherfuckers in there, trying to talk to you, or party, or be like, "Hey, listen to this shit." The pressure of it is kinda wack, because you can't really be yourself and just zone out. I'm the type of MC that likes to zone out, because I'm a thinker. When I write rhymes it takes me quite a while, because every time I write a rhyme it's not just to rap—I'm trying to write one of the best rhymes ever, because that's the way I wanna go down in history.

Whether your surroundings are quiet or noisy can also influence the kind of song you'll write.

O.C., Diggin' in the Crates

If it's a deep-thinking joint that I'm trying to put down, then I usually need peace and quiet, whereas if I'm doing something that's totally opposite to that, I can be around noise.

Times to Write

Lyrics can be written at any time (Akil the MC of Jurassic 5 notes, "Lyrics come at all times of the day—throughout the day you'll think of different subjects"), but some MCs do prefer to do their writing at specific times of day. Akil the MC adds that "for the most part, for me, when I wake up in the morning, that's when my thoughts are freshest," and many other MCs like to write at night.

Mr. Lif

I'd say if there's a bias, it'd be in the middle of the night, when everyone else is sleeping.

Vinnie Paz, Jedi Mind Tricks

I usually drink a lot, and it's always late at night—they're the only two things that are like a constant.

Omar Cruz

I kinda write better at night, when most people are going to sleep. My antennae is out—I guess I'm clearest at that moment to be able to create.

Some artists wake up with rhymes in their head, which they then write down before going back to sleep.

Wise Intelligent, Poor Righteous Teachers

Sometimes I'm resting or I'm asleep, one o'clock, two o'clock in the morning, [and] I'll get up with rhymes in my head and just put them down and go back into a coma.

Tash, Tha Alkaholiks

I'll go to sleep and I'll think of a whole rap in my head and wake up in the morning and say, "Hand me a pen—I just wrote this rap in my head." Some nights I had a whole rap written out—it's almost like I'm a machine and I'm built to rap.

Some MCs write simply whenever the inspiration hits them.

One Be Lo, Binary Star

[I write] whenever I get the urge to write something down—I could wake up in the middle of the night, or I could be driving, or I could be at a show. It could be a word [and] I wanna write down that word, because I wanna think of something to go with it later. I got stuff laying all around my house, just stuff that I scribbled on paper all the time because I get the urge at any given moment and I just gotta write it down.

How Long Does It Take?

The length of time it takes an MC to write a verse or whole song varies, depending on both the artist and the song.

R.A. the Rugged Man

People got different strategies, so every rhyme is different. It's like anything—filmmaking: Stanley Kubrick will take three years to make a movie, while Roger Corman will take two days—so it's all everybody's style and the way they do it.

Immortal Technique

"Bin Laden" took me a night, an evening of writing that, and then a song like "You Never Know" took me over the course of like three years, because it was a progression in my life. "Dance with the Devil" took a couple of months, "Caught in the Hustle" took an afternoon—it just really varies.

Stat Quo

I've had good ones that took a couple of days, and I've had good ones that took five minutes. [Eminem and Dr. Dre] just prefer you to make a hot song, no matter how long it takes— if you make a hit record every six months, nobody's gonna be mad at that. If it takes you three months to write one "In Da Club," that's fine—records like that stay around forever.

Writing Quickly

Many MCs like to write their songs quickly, or they simply find that some of their best songs were written that way. For instance, B-Real says that some of Cypress Hill's biggest songs were written relatively fast.

B-Real, Cypress Hill

I think if you're on a roll and you're feeling the vibe, songs sort of just write themselves. Definitely "Insane in the Brain" came like that, "Rock Superstar," "Dr Greenthumb"—a lot of the songs. I think sometimes those faster ones turn out to be the really good ones. With "Dr Greenthumb" I think I wrote that song in like 40 minutes and recorded it in another 40 minutes, maybe an hour tops. That's like an anthem for us—that beat just took me somewhere really fast. I couldn't explain it—how fast I wrote it, how fast we laid it down.

The lyrics may come out more easily when you write about certain subjects, and particular situations can sometimes inspire you to write more quickly. Even the beat of a song may sometimes inspire fast writing.

Tech N9ne

It depends on what the song is talking about—[that determines] how long it takes me to write a song. If I'm pouring my heart out—like a song I got called "The Rain," I'm talking about being away from my children—I can just pour those out.

Schoolly D

The *Aqua Teen Hunger Force*, that theme song, it took me like a half hour. I couldn't come up with anything for like two months, then these guys show up in town and say let's go to the studio—we go to the studio and it just comes to me.

Chuck D, Public Enemy

The song "Harder Than You Think" was totally inspired by the music to write the words rather fast, so "Harder Than You Think" is probably the fastest song I wrote and probably the quickest executed song.

An artist might also write a song quickly simply as a test of his or her ability to do so.

2Mex, The Visionaries

Our friends will walk in the house and say "Ready?" We got 10 minutes to write—just do the dopest verse you can write in 10 minutes—and we'll be like, "Go," and we'll write under pressure and write the most we can. It's like a mental exercise.

Writing Slowly

On the other hand, some MCs like to take their time while writing their lyrics.

The Lady of Rage

It can take from an hour to a week. It's not a fast process for me—it definitely takes time, depending on the beat. Working with Snoop and Dre, they're so fast and they write just like that, so when I go in with them, I usually have something already. If they call me and say, "Rage, I want you to do this song," I start right away on it so they won't have to be waiting on me like, damn, you're slow. But I saw an interview—I think Eminem said sometimes it may take him a week or some days to write a rhyme and I felt much better, because I thought it was just me.

O.C., Diggin' in the Crates

[The classic track "Time's Up"] actually took like a year. At the time I got the song, it was actually Pharoahe [Monch]'s record, and I asked him for it for about six months. I think at that time they was working on *Stress: The Extinction Agenda*, and he had my man Buckwild's "Thirteen" track that he did— he came up with something for "Thirteen," so that's why he gave up the "Time's Up" joint. And that right there, it really bust my ass, man—it's an awkward beat to write to.

Some topics may require that you spend a longer time on a song than you usually would. For instance, if you're writing a song about something that's especially important to you, you may feel you need to spend more time perfecting it.

Shock G, Digital Underground

[One type of rhyme] is the "thought about it my whole life" gripe you gotta get off your chest, which is a rhyme you've been loosely creating and upgrading in your daydreams all day, all week, all year, several years even, waiting for the right music or the right situation to record it. An example could be when 2Pac would take one of his older works from his poetry or rhyme book and "adjust" it to fit the current beat. Rhymes like these are usually things a person feels they "have to say" and remain urgent to the writer year after year, regardless of style changes or trends in the industry.

Quality over Quantity

The majority of MCs stress that you should look for quality over quantity in your lyrics—that it's better to not rush. Writing a really memorable verse is more valuable than quickly writing a number of forgettable ones.

Royce Da 5'9"

I take my time—I don't never feel it's a rush. I can take two hours and write a verse, [and then] somebody else can write [a verse], not even write it down, memorize it off the top of the head, and go spit it in 30 minutes, and if my verse is better, then who'd you rather be? So I pride myself on quality over quantity, even though I can knock out a lot of shit pretty fast, but that's just icing on the cake—that's not something I strive for. If I can get it done fast, then cool, but I just go for the quality.

If you're tempted to rush the creative process, keep in mind that you may have to live for a long time with a song you wrote quickly. Make sure it's something you're completely comfortable with.

Shock G, Digital Underground

Everyone around me usually writes faster, [but] I never understood what the big rush is. If it becomes popular, you're gonna have to say that shit a thousand more times in your life anyway, and it may get listened to around the world for years and years, or even forever; so you might as well make sure it's what you really wanted to say. From touring I learned to constantly review my material first, test it for long-term meaning, moral position, breathing space—can you jump around on a 90-degree outdoor stage saying it? Because you might just wind up having to perform it for the next 20 years!

Writing in One Go or in Pieces

A song or verse can be written all in one go, or you can write it in several different pieces at different times. As Bishop Lamont says, "You can write a whole song, or you can take your time and write it in bits and pieces—it just depends on the inspiration level and what level of discipline and quality you're trying to get out of it."

Writing in One Go

Some MCs like to write a song or a verse all at once.

Zumbi, Zion I

[I write] mostly in one go. I'll write the first verse, proof it, the second verse, proof it, the third, whatever, and then I'll proof the whole thing and make sure it all works together—it's usually in one sitting.

Mr. Lif

I try to sit down and write a verse beginning to end.

MC Serch

It's funny—the records that came the most naturally are the ones that people remember the most. Like "Pop Goes the

Weasel" I wrote in one shot, "Daily Commute," "Steppin' to the AM," "Wordz of Wisdom," "Back to the Grill"—I wrote [them] in one shot. There's a couple of records where people say, well that was one of your best performances, and those are the records that usually everything kinda just flowed out of me and I went to the studio and I was able to just knock it out.

Writing in Pieces

Alternatively, you can write a song or verse in different pieces at different times. Vast Aire of Cannibal Ox says that "sometimes I've got to leave a song alone and come back to it—I'll have the first two verses, but the third verse I waited on a bit and plotted on a bit."

Some MCs have a writing technique in which they make various notes and write sections of lyrics, which they then piece together.

Aesop Rock

I always just take notes and stuff during the day, and then when it comes time to make a song, I look at all the little notes and fragments that I've taken throughout the day, couple of days, or a week.

Other MCs like to go back to old lyrics that they've written but never used and pick out different lines to piece together a new rap.

Vursatyl, Lifesavas

There's always little things that I've written in the past that jump out at me, so sometimes I'll thumb through an old notepad and see stuff that, wow, what was I thinking at that time? So I find little dope rhymes, pieces of rhymes, [or] maybe it's just words.

Akil the MC, Jurassic 5

Sometimes I write raps and then I don't find a place for them until years later, [like,] oh, OK, that goes with this, now I have a chorus that may go with that. Maybe I haven't finished the whole thought or maybe it's just that one verse—you might have some other verses like, oh, these go together.

O.C., Diggin' in the Crates

I learned [about creating new lyrics from old lines] from Pharoahe [Monch]. Pharoahe is the king of one-liners. He'll write down a line five years ago, and it'll end up on a song five years later. I asked him one time why he do that, and he was just like, sometimes you can't sit there and write a whole record or write a whole rhyme—it might fall off after the 6th bar, the 10th bar, the 2nd bar, whatever the case is, but you don't force it—it's got to flow.

Working on Several Tracks at Once

A number of artists work on several tracks at the same time, so that they're effectively writing them in pieces rather than concentrating on one song at a time.

Paris

I rarely work on one song until it's finished. I usually have multiple projects going at once.

MC Serch

Me doing an album, [I'll often go from track to track]. Sometimes you have five or six different thoughts because you're holding on to five or six different beats, and there are definitely times when I'm like, you know what, I don't really feel like writing this record right now, let me listen to this track [instead] and write to this beat.

Some artists believe that switching their attention among different songs helps keep the inspiration alive.

Esoteric

Most of the songs we've done, I would start something and go real hard, go real heavy with it, and then drop it and work on a new track and then come back to that track—to put the finishing touches on it. For me that works better, because I can become inspired and then get really uninspired and I start rhyming "cat" with "hat," where I'd like to be able to continue with a real visual every time.

Keeping or Changing the Process

All the elements discussed in this chapter combine to form your overall writing process. If you've found a particular process that works for you, it may be a good idea to stick with it.

Shock G, Digital Underground

[I use the] same process . . . but the processes themselves have changed out there, so my era's style of writing has become old school in itself, therefore making it seem like I have changed, but in fact it's the world that has changed.

MC Serch

It's been the same [process]—I write the same way that I've been writing since I was 11 years old.

Rock, Heltah Skeltah

It depends on the MC—it depends on what the people have grown to expect from you. . . . If you've sold millions talking about nothing, then don't try to get smart now!

On the other hand, many MCs change their writing process over time, for various reasons. For instance, growing and changing as an artist or a person can influence the way you write your lyrics.

Q-Tip, A Tribe Called Quest

As time moves on, so does your approach to things. I welcome change—I definitely move along with things.

Buckshot, Black Moon

I change with the evolution of time—I've definitely changed the way I write stuff. Hip-hop's changed, so of course I've changed the way I write. Everything changes—times change, people change, hip-hop's changed—so of course I'm gonna change my pattern of doing things. I still have that same Buckshot Shorty, but it's just evolved now.

Dray, Das EFX

My process and things I think about are different now—I wouldn't say half the stuff I said back in the day. Right now, I'm a damn grown man. I'm trying to say grown shit but not sound like I'm preaching.

9

Beats and Freestyling

There's so many different reasons that people make records—
different records are for different purposes.
◄ Pusha-T, Clipse ►

One aspect of the writing process deserves special attention: how
to tailor your content and flow to the beats you'll be rapping over.
These musical backing tracks are created by a hip-hop producer,
but the MC is responsible both for deciding whether to write the
lyrics while listening to a beat and for actually picking a good beat
to rap to. Some MCs even produce their own beats, which can
influence the way they create their songs.

In this chapter we will also examine the basics of freestyle rap,
which allows you to create lyrics spontaneously and is a great way
to improve your rapping skills.

Writing With or Without the Beat

You may want to write your lyrics as you're listening to the beat
you'll be using for the finished track, or you may prefer to write
without listening to a beat at all. And sometimes you may write

the song to one beat and then change to a different beat either before or after the vocals are recorded.

With the Beat

Many MCs prefer to write to the beat they will be using for the finished song. That way the music can serve as the main source of inspiration and direction.

Dray, Das EFX

I'm just following what the beat is leading me to, like a dance, and the beat is the lead on the dance floor. I'm just following what the beat is doing, just trying to keep up—not trying to step on the beat's toes. I like to write the rhymes right to the track—if the track pauses, I pause . . . if the track called for me to do something, I did it, lyrically.

Phife Dawg, A Tribe Called Quest

I write to the beat, because the beat pretty much leads you to where you wanna go with it.

Q-Tip, A Tribe Called Quest

It's based on the music for me. I always connect to [the music] so I can become like an instrument—that's the way I do it. [With the song "Excursions,"] the key that [the beat] was in, the notes that were being played, the mood of it, all played a part in what I did.

Brother J, X Clan

I may hear several tracks that talk to me and tell me, *I'm the one, let's do this, I know your theme, this is what you need to focus on, this kind of sound.* It talks to you.

For many artists, some of their most popular tracks were written to the beat.

Shock G, Digital Underground

On "Same Song," as I was finishing the beat at home, 2Pac and Money-B would call occasionally to hear it over the phone as they wrote and perfected their verses from their homes, [and] I wrote mine immediately after I saved the pattern. "Kiss You Back" and "I Get Around" were both written while listening to the actual tracks they became—at the "Get Around" session, Pac came into the studio with his verses ready after having the beat for a few weeks.

Writing to the beat can help you match the feel of the music more closely. Some artists believe that every beat calls for a unique way of rhyming over it.

Nelly

I like to listen to the beat, get a nice groove for it, and see where the beat takes you. It's impossible to do the same style on every beat, I feel. . . . Some people do it, but I can't really do it.

Wordsworth

Visualizing what the song could present—does this song sound like somebody's hurt? does this song sound like something to get people amped?—you first gotta generalize, what does the beat sound like? That's the first thing. Once you find out what the beat sounds like to you, then you figure out what do you want to give the people on that track so that they feel where you coming from. The beat is gonna have a specific way of asking you to rhyme a certain way sometimes.

Using the music to write to also allows you to come up with a flow that works well with the particular rhythms that are already part of the beat.

Bishop Lamont

You gotta write with the beat, or the rhythms won't be in sync. I mean, you can make it work, but it's always better if it's customized specifically for that. That's where the energy is—that's the template for whatever you're going to utter over it.

Sometimes a beat may even contain a vocal sample that directs the content of the song.

Lord Jamar, Brand Nubian

If I get a beat and the beat already has something in it, like some sort of vocal sample or something that is saying something, [then] that can lead you down a certain road a lot of times.

MURS

When I do my albums with [producer] 9th Wonder, I go to North Carolina and it's two weeks of him giving me beats and me staying up all night in a hotel room by myself just playing the beats over and over again and writing songs, and when I leave it's done. A lot of times with the soul samples, they'll say one phrase and you try to think of what that means to you.

Artists often describe writing to a beat as creating a "marriage" between the beat and the lyrics. Pusha-T of Clipse says, "I like writing to the beat. That's when you marry the beat, man. That's when a marriage comes in." MCs also suggest that writing to the beat makes the track sound more complete.

Big Daddy Kane

In all honesty, I think [writing to the beat] is something very important to do—that is something, like, that the generation after me started doing. Those cats that was coming out in the '90s, they're the ones who really started making it where they sat and wrote to the beat and their style matched that beat perfectly. I think it makes a song more whole.

Without the Beat

On the other hand, some MCs prefer to write their rhymes without listening to the beat they'll be using.

Wildchild, Lootpack

If I've got a concept I've already got in mind before the beat, then usually I won't need the beat.

MC Serch

I write a rhythm and a flow, and then I wait for the right beat that matches that rhythm and flow. Very rarely [do I write to the beat].

Many classic hip-hop tracks have been written without a beat. On some of the most revered tracks, the lyrics actually inspired the beats.

Schoolly D

[With] "Gangster Boogie" in '83 [later sampled in the Game's track "Compton"], that was just a rap that I used to rap on the corner, and then I went in and created the music.

Shock G, Digital Underground

[With] "Humpty Dance," the beat wasn't made yet. It was just to the music in my head at the time, which wasn't any specific beat, more like a vague montage/fusion of all the stuff I liked at the time—my "dream beat,"' you could call it. We all have one and it can never be made or fully translated—it's the total mental collection of your personal highlights, the lifetime summary of your music listening experiences. It's the beat that's in your head when you're not even thinking about it. "Freaks of the Industry" was also written before a beat was made, and so was "Doowutchyalike"—with all three of these, the lyrical content set the mood and guided the beat making.

Some artists believe you can concentrate more on the lyrics if there isn't a beat to distract you.

Guerilla Black

Sometimes my purest thought comes away from the beat, because sometimes the beat can be a distraction. I think your purest flow comes from when you're not writing to the beat, because you just hear everything in your head and you pick your first thought.

Fredro Starr, Onyx

Sometimes the beat can alter what you really want to say, because you have to keep rewinding the beat or you have to keep playing it over and over, so I think sometimes if you have a free mind then nothing stops you, and your rhyme comes out where you can say it over almost any beat.

One way to write without the beat is to choose a particular beat and keep it in mind while writing the lyrics but not actually listen to it as you're writing. As 2Mex of the Visionaries says, "I just hear the beat for like a minute and hear the tempo, and then I can turn the beat off and then write the whole verse—but I gotta hear it for a second."

Another way is to write the song to a beat that you make up in your head.

Wise Intelligent, Poor Righteous Teachers

Sometimes I'll have a melody in my head and I'll just write the rhyme to that particular melody and then the track will come later.

Killah Priest, Wu-Tang Clan affiliate

I used to write without the beat all the time. That's the reason why "Heavy Mental" sounds the way that it does—I did it over a didgeridoo. I used to just do it over sounds and make the beat up in my head, and I could never get a producer to give me that same beat! I like up-tempo, crazy, noisy shit.

Writing without a particular beat in mind often means that you'll need to adjust the lyrics to make them fit properly once you do choose a beat.

DJ Quik

Sometimes I'll just write what I feel at the moment and then I'll try to find a track that it fits, and if I have to do a little alteration, I will.

Hell Rell, Dipset

If I don't have the track, I'll write the rhyme [and] then when I get the track, if it doesn't fit it, I'll fix it up and try to make it fit the beat.

Writing to a Different Beat

Sometimes you may write to one beat and then record those lyrics over a different beat, or you may change the beat after recording the vocals over it. A different beat can help bring a different style or flow to the lyrics.

Big Noyd

[Writing to a different beat] helps change up the flow. I'll even write to a beat that's a hit already, like somebody else's song, an instrumental of a song that's out already and that beat is hot, and I know I can't use it but I love the beat. I'll write a rhyme to that beat because I enjoy the beat so much and the beat brings out a lot of a style or it makes you wanna rhyme more, and then I go and try and get another beat that's an original track that I like and I see if it fits to that beat, to that tempo.

Cage

There was a song where I recorded the [vocals] and then the beat was changed, and it ended up giving it a different feel, because the emphasis and the words are accentuating in the way that you were to the other music. When you switch the beat around, it could end up being better or worse.

T3, Slum Village

We remix stuff all the time. We might use a beat at a particular time and then remix it later, or add live instruments to it.

In fact, some artists keep working on and changing the beat right up until the song is released.

will.i.am, Black Eyed Peas

The beat is always half-finished until it comes out. It's not finished until you have it—when you've got it, I'm done. Up until you getting it, I'm still working on it.

Picking Beats

Being able to pick a good beat is an important part of the writing process. As Del the Funky Homosapien says, "The marriage between lyrics and music is paramount."

Sorting Through Beats

The majority of MCs like to sort through beats until they find one they like, rather than taking the first beat that comes their way.

Evidence, Dilated Peoples

We were in New York City [and "Worst Comes to Worst" producer] Alchemist was out there—we went to his house and listened to like a thousand beats. We weren't settling—we were real picky, giving Alchemist a hard time that day. I remember because there were so many beats to pick from. How many tracks did we go through before we found "Worst Comes to Worst" that day? Many tracks, a plethora, and we found this beat.

Some artists will get beats from a number of different producers and listen to a huge range of options before they find something they want to use.

Tech N9ne

What we do is we send out for a gang of producers that I think is hard-core—we even find new producers if they got heat that I'm looking for at that time. They'll send like 15 beats on a CD and I'll listen, and the ones that make me feel the most, those are the ones I choose.

Most MCs pick beats that simply seize their attention as soon as they hear them. By picking beats that grab them right away, they're often inspired to write lyrics immediately.

Yukmouth

When you feel a beat as soon as that beat come on, the [chorus] usually hits you or the first five lines of your verse hits you as soon as that beat come on, like, whoo—you feeling it that bad.

Picking a beat that you feel comfortable rapping on can be very important to the final outcome of a song.

B-Real, Cypress Hill

I pick beats by the way they hit me when I hear it. If it calls out to me in some sort of way, in any way, then I'll most likely pick it to try to write something to it. If it doesn't hit me at all, like not even interest me at all, then I'll bypass it, it doesn't matter whose beat it is. I have to feel comfortable on it—I have to be inspired by it and excited by it, otherwise it might not be a good song.

Having Input into the Beats

Instead of choosing from finished beats from producers, other artists like to have input into the beat-making process.

Cage

Now I don't pick out beats so much anymore. Now I sit down with live musicians and I co-produce them.

The Lady of Rage

[On the track "Unfucwitable":] I like to help create the beat, and I can do that more with [producer DJ] Premier, because we have a real close relationship and he lets me do that. So he was going through the beginning stages of picking out some-thing and I forget what the sample was, but he was playing something and I was like, I like that. And so he kept playing it, and then he looped it, and *he* didn't like it, but I liked it and I was like, that's what I want, that's what I want! So he went on and did it.

Working with Certain Producers

Some MCs have specific producers they enjoy working with because those producers' beats suit their songs the best.

Buckshot, Black Moon

I do have a certain type of chemistry with 9th Wonder, and I have chemistry with the beats. I like different producers, but my best chemistry besides DJ Evil Dee is 9th.

Aesop Rock

[Producer Blockhead, a frequent collaborator,] will usually send me 10 beats at a time or a group of beats, 7 or 10 or 15. Whenever he's got a new batch of beats, then he'll just send them over to me and I go through them all and see if anything has a vibe that I like.

In addition, certain producers are also known for their great beat selection—for knowing which beats will suit which MC. Finding a producer with this skill can be a great asset.

Thes One, People Under the Stairs

Dudes who are just MCs, especially solo MCs, if they don't have someone helping them pick beats or a producer working directly with them, they can oftentimes make a lot of really, really bad choices beatwise. And that's why you have the great producers who are able to say, OK, this will sound dope with this—helping MCs pick out things and not go astray.

Rapping and Producing

Then there are artists who like to produce their own tracks as well as deliver the lyrics—they make their own music to go along with their vocals. Some find this process harder, some find it easier, and for others it makes no difference (Akil the MC of Jurassic 5 says, "It don't matter, as long as it's a tight beat," and Shock G of Digital Underground agrees that "it's fun to rhyme over anything hot and interesting, no matter who made it").

Finding It Easier to Rap on Your Own Beats

For certain artists, writing to their own beats gives them an advantage. If they make the beat, they can ensure that it's something they'll be inspired to rap over, and they'll have special insight into how to write to it.

K-Os

I think this is a big thing from Kanye West, and I also would cite people like Q-Tip or Diamond D, people who make their own beats. For you to create and finish the beat, you have to be able to like it—you're nodding your head in a certain way, you're like, oh, this is dope, and you're getting into your own rhythm.

Havoc, Mobb Deep

It's easier for me because I'm the one who made it, so I know how I want to rhyme to it.

Tajai, Souls of Mischief

If you listen to Kanye, it's almost subliminal how every one of his rhymes goes so well with his beats—but he made the beat too.

Some artists benefit from the similarities between programming a beat and writing a flow—Evidence of Dilated Peoples says that he finds it easier to write over his own beats "because the same way I flow is the same way I program my drums"—while others, like DJ Quik, succeed by keeping the two processes separate.

DJ Quik

It's two different hats. When I'm writing the music, I have a certain pattern of thinking. When the music is sufficient, I'll stop, take five, and put on another hat for writing. I won't even think about it—I'll subconsciously just switch over to the other pole and start writing to the track.

Finding It Harder to Rap on Your Own Beats

However, other MCs find it harder to write over their own beats. They like to have another person's input on a song, rather than doing everything themselves.

MC Shan

I don't like to produce the songs I [rap] on, because that's too much of me influencing me and no other negative voices, a devil's advocate to say, "Nah, don't do it that way—do it this way." So I basically like to have other people make the beat, and if I feel what's going on with the music, then I'll [write] a song to it.

Artists may be inspired by writing to their own music, or they may feel that they lose inspiration if they're forced to listen to the same beat so many times during the beat-creation process. They may prefer the fresh perspective that can come from hearing someone else's beat for the first time as they write.

Evidence, Dilated Peoples

It's nice to not write to your beats sometimes, because knowing how the beat was created sometimes erases the mystique of it and now you're not listening to the track as a whole, you're listening to how the kick drum was EQed, because you made it—you're focusing on the individual elements. That's why I'm so blessed I have [producers] Alchemist and Joey Chavez and all these people around me who I look up to anyway, so I'd be a fool to not take their tracks and write to those, because I can get those as full compositions and not have to really sit there and ponder all the elements of it.

Akir

Through the course of a production session, you might listen to a particular track maybe 10,000 times by the time you're about to write something to it. And when you're writing, you might have a track on repeat. So not only are you listening to it 10,000 times when you're producing it, but now you have to listen to it 10,000 times again to write to it. And the thing that first got me into being an MC [was] the improvisational art of it, so it's always better for me to hear a track, be inspired, and try to do something based on that first feeling.

When to Finish the Beat

Producing MCs may prefer to have the beat fully completed before adding vocals, or they may like to change parts of the beat once the vocals are added—or even create the track around an existing vocal take.

Schoolly D

I never have the beat finished completely—the beat is only finished after we mix it. I always leave a little bit [of room] for magic, because [when] you're working with the engineer [you might say], "Why don't I put a different snare in?" So the beat is never done until it's over.

Thes One, People Under the Stairs

In terms of making the actual song, it's always the beat, and then the rhyme is just another instrument on top of the beat to me. The beat has all these different elements to it, it has the drums and the samples and this and that. And I look at the rhyme as just one more element—it's gotta fit with the beat, it's gotta come together. Sometimes I'll write a verse knowing what I'm capable of doing later, as an engineer, and I'll know I want to put a delay on something or do this or that and then I can write my rhyme around that.

To record vocals and then create a beat based on them, an MC might rap over a *click track*. This is a backing track in which there is no music, just a clicking noise made at a certain speed so that the artist can keep in time.

Evidence, Dilated Peoples

I've heard of rappers rapping to click tracks. I've heard J Dilla rumors where he didn't have the track, and he'll just come over and just [put on a click track]—"click . . . click . . . click . . . click . . ." and you'd rap all day to that. I don't know if that's true or not, but if that is, I'd respect that—that's just treating vocals like an instrument and building around it like a remix or something. If I do something with my voice, now I can play an instrument to mock that, whereas if I had done the track first, unless I had written specifically to that instrument, it wouldn't have happened.

Freestyling

Freestyling, to most MCs, means coming up with lyrics off the top of your head. In early hip-hop, however, the term had a different meaning.

Big Daddy Kane

That term, *freestyle*, is like a new term, because in the '80s when we said we wrote a freestyle rap, that meant that it was a rhyme that you wrote that was free of style, meaning that it's not [on] a [particular] subject matter—it's not a story about a woman, it's not a story about poverty, it's basically a rhyme just bragging about yourself, so it's basically free of style. . . . That's really what a freestyle is. Off-the-top-of-the-head [rapping], we just called that "off the dome"—when you don't write it and [you] say whatever comes to mind.

This earlier definition of freestyling has evolved into the meaning that most MCs associate it with today.

Myka 9, Freestyle Fellowship

That's what they say I helped do—I helped get the world to freestyle, me and the Freestyle Fellowship, by inventing the Freestyle Fellowship and by redefining what freestyle is. Back in the day freestyle was bust[ing] a rhyme about any random thing, and it was a written rhyme or something memorized. We have redefined what freestyle is by saying that it's improvisational rap like a jazz solo, so as a result we actually helped create another trend and culture, another pastime. So now kids can do something else other than just play basketball or whatever—they can sit on the staircase and exchange rhymes instead of going around getting into crimes. It's a good thing to not only MC but freestyle, because it kinda helps promote free thinking.

A number of artists first learned how to rap by improvising lyrics on a regular basis. Some of them made freestyling into a type of game that improved their rapping and served as a fun activity at the same time.

David Banner

First four years of my record I just freestyled. I learned how to be the best freestyler—looking at stuff that was in my environment and rapping about the stuff that was in my environment.

MC Shan

We used to have a thing called the rhyming game. Somebody would start the sentence, and you gotta finish it. If you didn't make the rhyme rhyme, you're out, so it kept us on our toes all the time as far as rhyming off the top of the head and things like that. Just out of the blue, [someone] would say, "Rhyme"—boom, you better spit something!

One Be Lo, Binary Star

It was a day-to-day thing. All we used to do was sit around all day and freestyle—that's all we did. We were just trying to be the best we could be, and we were bouncing it off each other. We woke up freestyling, we went to sleep freestyling. We would just be sitting in the basement trying to come up with songs, and we'd just start freestyling. We was just having fun—we wasn't trying to make records or make history.

Reasons to Freestyle

Freestyling can be beneficial for a number of reasons. First, it can be a fun activity to do for your own entertainment.

Bobby Creekwater

[I freestyle] all the time—it's therapeutic, even, so I definitely do that as much as I can. We're in it to have fun, so I definitely try to have fun with it when- and wherever I can.

Coming up with lyrics off the top of your head can help you to formulate new ideas and discover different ways of rhyming.

K-Os

Freestyling helped me, because when you freestyle in rap, that energy, it sounds very live. A lot of times I would be like, how come when I freestyle it sounds a certain way, but when I write a rap it sounds different? So freestyling helped me learn how to make my more calculated raps sound sweeter.

Performing freestyle verses for an audience is also a great way to promote yourself as an artist.

Cappadonna, Wu-Tang Clan affiliate

In the long run, freestyling is like an investment. You have to stack as many freestyles up as you can, especially when you're first coming in the game—you gotta give everybody a little freestyle for like thousands of people. You hit up mad spots, doing a lot of advertising over the years, and people know who you are.

Finally, for some MCs, mastering different levels of freestyling is a goal in itself. It's another direction in which you can take your music and another aspect of hip-hop in which you can learn to excel.

El Da Sensei

I think it's a good practice to do both [freestyling and writing], because you wanna be able to be kinda versatile.

Myka 9, Freestyle Fellowship

The pinnacle level of MCing, I believe, is when you can actually freestyle with a rap partner and you guys can both say a series of rhymes at the same time and say the same thing— you get psychic, it gets really deep, it's spiritual.

10

Structuring, Editing, and Selecting Lyrics

You're always trying to mature and gain ability and learn new tricks—not only just writing raps but in songwriting and song structure.
◄ Andy Cat, Ugly Duckling ►

We've explored the basics of the writing process, but there's more to writing lyrics than composing the words and flow and marrying them to the beat. MCs must also familiarize themselves with different song structures and how they affect the listener, so they can vary their songs and select the best format for each one. They must learn how to edit their lyrics, improving on their song's strengths and eliminating its weaknesses. And they must decide which of the lyrics they write to actually use—and, in particular, which to release as singles—to make sure they're putting only their best work forward.

Song Structure

To turn a collection of lyrics into a rap song, you have to create a structure for them, dividing them into a chorus and verses so that they have as great an impact as possible.

E-40

Some people can have some of the greatest lyrics in the world but don't know how to make a real song.

Myka 9, Freestyle Fellowship

That's what rappers mainly do—[they] expand on an issue. They have a title, you expand on the title with the chorus, [and] you expand on that theme with the verses.

Yukmouth

When I was locked up in jail, all I was listening to was the radio and all I could hear was how they structured their songs—so learn how to structure a song. The 16[-bar verse], the 8-bar hook—learn how to make [songs], because rapping is more than just freestyling and battling, man. It's about making songs.

Thes One, People Under the Stairs

We want to try to present it in a way that people even outside of hip-hop can appreciate. We don't want a lack of structure to impede people from appreciating what's happening in there.

Different song structures are sometimes associated with partic- ular types of tracks—though an artist may choose to use structure in more unexpected ways.

Evidence, Dilated Peoples

I came up around Cypress Hill and House of Pain and QD3 and a lot of producers, so that's what I learned—song format and structure—and that's good to know. It's good to break it, but it's good to know. If there's six rappers on it and the song's six minutes and there's no chorus, it's pretty much under- stood that it's an album cut [rather than a single]. But funnier things have happened [for example, Wu-Tang Clan used that type of format on their single "Triumph"]—that's them doing what they do best, and that's why people liked it.

Choruses (Hooks)

Choruses are short sets of lyrics that are repeated more than once in a song. They're also known as *hooks*, because they're designed to "hook" the listeners and to stay in their heads. Most MCs agree that the chorus can be a very big factor in how well a song is received.

Guerilla Black

The hotter your hook is, the harder they can feel the record. If your hook is hot, they'll take time to remember exactly what you said. Can [a listener] actually remember your whole first verse after he heard your song [maybe] five times? No, I don't think so—but I think he can remember your chorus very fast. And if he can't remember it within the first five times of hearing it, I bet you he at least knows a couple of words, especially the key words that make the song what it is to him in his mind.

Brother Ali

The chorus is a really important thing, and if the chorus isn't right, [my producer] Ant won't let a song happen.

Rampage, Flipmode Squad

I think if you have a big hook, then you got a record.

As hip-hop has evolved, choruses have become more important and elaborate, for better or worse.

Tajai, Souls of Mischief

That's changed a lot—when I first started rapping, the last words you said in your rap was the chorus, like [the verses ended with] "da-da daa, da-da da daa daaa . . . and I'm in controooool!" and the song was called "In Control," and the chorus was like (mimics scratching) "I-I-I-In control." Now it's like you gotta have singers and all kinds of shit—the hook has definitely become more and more important in rap. Like, listen to Eric B. & Rakim, first album—how many hooks does he have? And that's a classic album.

For some artists, writing a chorus is enjoyable (Akil the MC of Jurassic 5 says, "I love writing hooks—my specialty is writing hooks"), though many MCs find the chorus the hardest part to come up with.

Pharoahe Monch

A lot of times you write the verse as an MC and you get stuck on choruses.

Spider Loc

I force myself to try to think of the hook first because naturally the verses come first.

Structure of the Chorus

Choruses can theoretically be of any length, but they are usually four or eight bars long. Since they are meant to be repetitive and stick in the listener's head, they work best when kept fairly short. Royce Da 5'9" says, "I don't normally write my hooks down, since they're only eight bars. Normally I just come up with the hook and then I just go in and say it." Songs with choruses that are four bars long include Dead Prez's "D.O.W.N." and Jay-Z's "Hard Knock Life (Ghetto Anthem)." Songs with eight-bar-long choruses include Ludacris's "Get Back" and Nas's "One Love."

Some hip-hop tracks have no chorus. This usually happens when an MC wants to focus purely on showcasing his or her lyrical skills or when the song is in the form of a story and a repeated chorus may interrupt the progression of the plot. Classic examples are Eric B. & Rakim's "No Omega" and Slick Rick's "Children's Story."

A lot of MCs like to write a chorus that is simpler and not as densely packed with words as the rest of the lyrics. This makes the chorus more direct and easier for the listener to remember.

Devin the Dude

Sometimes the hook lyrics are a little slower and longer . . . less words within the hook than there is in the verse—I kind of stretch some of the words.

Aesop Rock

[For the track "None Shall Pass,"] I came up with the idea of it being a really simple chorus with mostly music, and I wanted it to be a phrase. It took a while to come up with the phrase "none shall pass," but once I did it, it was such a short phrase and it's very minimal but it sounded right on the beat.

Choruses that are *harmonized*—sung or partly sung—are often very effective.

Guerilla Black

Right now in the age of hip-hop, rapped choruses aren't as popular as harmonized choruses are—50 [Cent, for example,] has a voice to make harmonizing hooks.

Ways of Writing Choruses

Writing choruses is a special skill in itself, and there are a lot of ways to do it well. Often, MCs like to use the music of the track they're rapping over to inspire the chorus.

Devin the Dude

I let the music let me know what to say, and it tells me what to do on it—certain instruments give me an idea on how the hook should be.

Brother J, X Clan

[Sometimes] a beat hits me and tells me, "This is the hook"— this is something you can play with, here are some notes, or this is a line you can play with.

Many MCs like to write the chorus of a song first. A number of popular singles have been written with the chorus in mind from the start.

Stressmatic, The Federation

When you have the hook first, you have the idea of the song or what to follow—you already have a diagram to follow.

will.i.am, Black Eyed Peas

I come up with the chorus first.

Nelly

I like to try to come up with the hook first, because then that's what makes you focus on the verses.

Pharoahe Monch

[With "Simon Says"] I definitely took the advice of a producer's standpoint more than an MC's standpoint, and producers would have you write choruses before they would have you write verses.

On the other hand, we'll see later (p. 196) that many other MCs prefer to write the verses first. They often come up with the chorus while they're writing the rest of the lyrics to the song.

Devin the Dude

Sometimes I just start writing and I'll get the hook right out of the verse. Somewhere in the middle of the verse, there might be a hook hidden in there.

Remy Ma

[Sometimes] you'll think of something while you're doing a verse, like four bars that sound so crazy, so you're like, that, *that's* the hook.

Deciding on a title will sometimes inspire the chorus, since the words of the chorus often include the title of the song.

N.O.R.E.

I used to get a title to a record—I used to sit back and say I'ma write a record [called] "Stars on my Nikes," and then two or three weeks later I'll write a [chorus] like "Stars on my Nikes, stars on my Nikes." When I have the title, usually I'll write the hook first.

If you're having trouble coming up with an attention-grabbing chorus, you may just need to get more familiar with the track. Sheek Louch of D-Block/The LOX suggests, "If you laid all your verses but you're still working on the hook, take it home, ride around with it, feel it out, then drop the hook."

Guerilla Black suggests writing several choruses and picking the best one.

Guerilla Black

Having hooks that just really stand out—you're not just gonna make a hook in one session like that. I don't advise anyone to. I'd advise them to make seven different choruses to the same song, that way they'll have a lot to pick from. That way you'll have something that actually feels good. That's how I write choruses to any record.

Choruses from Producers or Other Artists

Producers or other artists may sometimes have a chorus already on the track, so you don't have to come up with your own.

E-40

Some producers, they might already have a hook customized for your particular style, which is always good to me.

Pusha-T, Clipse

If you've got hooks in place, when it comes hook-ready, it's easy to lay it down, it's easy to run with the direction. [With] the Neptunes, sometimes you come into a studio and they've got hooks, all types of shit already together, and you're walking into a song. You walk into a song, only thing you have to do is fucking write the verse, and that's a good thing.

Some MCs ask other artists to lay down a chorus for them.

Big Noyd

[With the track "Things Done Changed,"] the hook came later. The female singer [Kira] and her writer, they sat together, listened to my song, and they came up with the hook.

Thes One, People Under the Stairs

For a song like "Acid Raindrops," we didn't even write that chorus, the homeboy Camel wrote it, who raps on the song. He was like, "Yo, I got this chorus," and we heard it and we were like, "Oh, that sounds great over the chorus part of the beat." So now that we have the written chorus and the chorus part of the beat, now all we gotta do is write a rhyme that's semi-related to that and we're good, we got a song.

Even when an MC asks another artist to do the chorus, he or she may still want input into what the other artist does. C-Murder says that on the song "One False Move" with Akon, "I definitely got an input on the chorus if it's my album, if it's for my record, so we definitely collaborate on that." Similarly, if you are writing in a group, there can be input from other artists in the group even if you're the one writing the chorus.

Sean Price, Heltah Skeltah

I'll call Rock or Dru Ha, I'll be like, "Yo, I need a hook—what we gonna do?" When it's time for me to do choruses for my album, the whole crew comes in the studio. Here at Boot Camp [Clik] we help each other tremendously—we don't write each others' rhymes, but each album is like our album. So if they got some input on the hooks, I'm all ears. Let's just get it right, because one bad album could fuck up the whole crew.

Verses

A series of verses make up the main body of a song and the majority of its lyrics. A verse is usually longer than a chorus, and it normally doesn't repeat—verses are generally more varied than choruses, to keep the song interesting. MCs often refer to the verses as the rap, the rhyme, the lyrics, or "a 16."

Structure of the Verses

There are often three verses in a song, separated by a repeated chorus. AMG breaks down the format: "You got the intro verse, [and then] you got the middle one, which should be real hot, so you can kinda like land it easy on the third one." A song may have more or fewer verses, however—Imani of the Pharcyde says, "I like two verses. I'm impatient and I don't like to write three verses."

The reason that a verse is often called a 16 is because each verse is usually 16 bars long.

Crooked I

The length of the typical verse in music today is 16 bars. Sometimes you do 24 bars, but the typical formula for writing a song is three 16-bar verses.

MURS

If it's a standard rap song, you try to keep that to 16 bars [for the verses]. I was never really a stickler for length until I listened to DJ Quik—he's so precise he almost never does anything over 16 [bars]. That's who I really learned my math from—Atmosphere and DJ Quik. . . . That let me know that you never really need to go over 16.

The 16-bar structure is particularly popular when an artist wants to reach a wide audience.

Lateef, Latyrx

I'm a fan of a good chorus and short verses. For songs that are gonna have a wider acceptance range to them, shorter verses are usually more effective, because people generally that are not music aficionados are more concerned with the hook than they are with the verse.

Some artists even prefer verses of fewer than 16 bars. For instance, Rampage of Flipmode Squad writes 12-bar verses: "I do all my songs in 12s because if you do 16s and 24s, the song is too long."

Often, different verse lengths are used for different types of songs. Lateef says, "It depends on what the song is about and who it's for, because music is for so many different things—people listen to music so differently." For instance, a story rap may be longer—MURS explains, "When I'm telling a story, I usually don't put a limit on it, [though] when I work with 9th Wonder on a song, he'll split it and say, OK, stop there. . . . I kind of cap it at 32 bars." Sixteen bars is the preferred length of most guest verses—Lateef notes that "sometimes somebody will tell me, hey, I need you to do 16 bars."

If the objective of a song is to show off the MC's rapping skills, he or she may structure it as just one long verse or a series of long verses.

Del the Funky Homosapien

Dudes used to have songs with nothing but one verse the whole song, to where you would be like, "Daaaaamn! Dude is *still* rapping!" It was amazing.

Lateef, Latyrx

If it's going to be a spitter verse, a to-rap verse, then there really are no boundaries on how long it can be. You can keep on writing and writing—it don't really matter—because most rap cats are gonna listen to you at least once to see what you were talking about, and if it's dope, then it's dope.

Other MCs never worry about the length of the verses. They just keep writing until it feels "right," and then they stop.

Big Daddy Kane

I never really paid attention to the length of verses until probably the late '90s. I'd just write until it felt good. When I feel like I wanna end the verse there, sometimes it might be a 16, sometimes it might be a 32—it just felt good. [There are] some songs I've done through my career where it's probably just one long 108-bar verse.

Del the Funky Homosapien

Sixteen bars *is* the standard song structure, so don't ignore it. Just be able to do more, then you'll always be special. That doesn't mean blow people's wigs back all the time, because that ain't good neither. Balance is key, really, in life or MCing.

Ways of Writing Verses

Although some MCs write the chorus first, as mentioned earlier in the chapter (see p. 190), many others like to start with the verses, because verses are considered the main body of the writing, where the MC can really convey a message and show off his or her skills.

Planet Asia

It's funny, because a lot of people, they come up with their hooks first. Me, a lot of times I come up with the rhyme first.

AMG

I usually start off with verses. Sometimes I don't have a hook until all the raps is done.

AZ

I start with the verses first—that's the body of the song. Once I've built the body of the song, [then I'll do the hook]—the verses lead into the hook.

Remy Ma

Ninety-five percent of the time, I'll write the verses first. I pretty much write the song first and then fill in the hook later.

Gorilla Zoe

If I feel like just expressing myself, then I'd do the verses [first].

Hell Rell, Dipset

I do the verses definitely first. Some people say that they like
to do the hook first, but I'd rather do the rhymes first, because
if you don't have a substance, if you don't know what you're
rapping about, then how do you fit a chorus around it?

Different MCs find different parts of the verses more difficult to
write and write certain verses first.

Big Pooh, Little Brother

The first two bars, the 9th and 10th bars, and the 15th and
16th bars are the hardest bars in the world—the beginning,
the middle, and the closing of the verse if it's a 16-bar verse.

MURS

I usually write the second verse first. I don't know why, but
it always comes out like that, and the first verse will be the
second one [I write].

Editing Lyrics

The editing process involves changing, adding, and removing certain sections of a song that have already been written. Effectively
editing your lyrics can turn a good song into a great one.

Pigeon John

A lot of times with the first draft, it's just like [for] an author—
you gotta edit that stuff. It's a lot of times wordy or you repeat
yourself and [have] too many syllables. I definitely cruise
each line and try to make each line deafening. I think in general the more that I learn about [MCs I admire], they really
do the down work—it sounds effortless, but I think there is
a lot of trying, a lot of editing and pounding and getting the
right tone.

Some artists edit as they go along. Others come back to a verse to edit it once the whole thing is written.

Termanology

If I'm writing it, I usually just edit it right then and there—that's why it might take me five or six hours to write one verse.

Killah Priest, Wu-Tang Clan affiliate

Sometimes I'm a bit of a perfectionist, so I do a lot of erasing, drawings, imagery—so I gotta go back on it. Sometimes it gets me mad when the first idea that I had was the best. I go back and I edit the clips, make the movie fit right. I do a little "take" in a way, replace it—it's like making a movie.

Rewrites

A rewrite is a form of editing in which you go through a completed version of a verse or song and write it over again to create a new and better version. For example, Pusha-T of Clipse had to rewrite the song "Grindin" multiple times because the beat was difficult to write to.

Pusha-T, Clipse

I wrote "Grindin" three times, and the last time I was satisfied. It took me three times to nail it—like, took it, scrapped it, took it, scrapped it, took it. [The beat] was just too unorthodox for me—I loved it, but I mean, me coming in on the beat like that, where does the shit start, where does the shit end?

Pharoahe Monch

[Writing a song is like writing a screenplay in that] you can definitely go back as a screenwriter and rewrite scenes and leave more to the imagination, leave more hidden clues for people to find, [and] double up metaphors when you're writing and you're going back and you're doing rewrites and you're touching things up.

Quality Control

Another way of editing the lyrics is to take out the parts that aren't as strong. By exercising quality control, you can weed out all the mediocre lines and phrases and make sure that every section of a song is as powerful as it can be.

R.A. the Rugged Man

There's a couple of times when I'm spitting and I go, you know what, take those two bars out and the whole verse will maybe flow a little better. Some little shit like that slowed the shit up, where I didn't like the way it sounded no more—that shit ain't flowing right. [So] take those two bars out. You thought they was ill, but they're not ill, and now your whole verse is ill because those two mediocre bars are missing.

Knowing what to keep and what to edit out is something you learn over time.

Andy Cat, Ugly Duckling

That's a maturity process. When you're young, you think you're a genius, you want to get it all in, you think you got a message for the world, and [you have] some sort of weird ego. [It] makes you think—or made me think everything I was going to say was so special that everybody needed to hear every segment of it.

Enhancing Lyrics

Editing can also be done by going over lyrics and adding to them, enhancing their effect in some way. This may involve such techniques as adding more rhymes per line (see chapter 6, p. 104) or including more punch lines (see chapter 3, p. 58).

Rah Digga

It usually takes me 20 to 30 minutes to actually write 16 lines, but I like to give myself another 20, 30 minutes to enhance those lines. When I say enhance, I mean where I'm double rhyming can I triple rhyme, where I'm triple rhyming can I quadruple rhyme. Where I'm just rhyming can I make it a punch line, where there's a punch line can I make it a double punch line—I just like to keep going and going and going. Usually I'll keep tweaking a verse until it's like, OK, it's time to lay it down already.

You can also enhance the lyrics by adjusting the flow so that they fit the beat more precisely.

2Mex, The Visionaries

Sometimes it doesn't fit in that pocket, like you write it but it doesn't fit into the beat that you have. Sometimes you write something without listening to the beat and then you drop it on the beat and it just sounds [wrong, so] I just edit and edit and edit until it does sound good. Sometimes it just takes a syllable change.

Often the enhancement may be something as simple as changing the verse order to make the song more effective.

Bishop Lamont

Sometimes you write a record and it's first verse, second verse, third verse, and then it might be so potent on the third verse that you decide to switch the second verse with the third verse.

And finally, enhancement may consist of making sure all the segments work together as a whole.

Zumbi, Zion I

Sometimes it just doesn't fit with the mode of the rest of the rhyme, so sometimes I got to just play with the phrasing and switch it around. I'll go back and kinda proof the rhyme again once I'm done, then I'll definitely switch certain phrases to maybe better fit the whole idea of the rhyme.

Knowing When to Stop

Another part of being a good MC is knowing when a song is done—when no more editing is needed.

Del the Funky Homosapien

When I'm writing, I'm always ready to chuck whatever I'm doing in favor of coming up with something better. I don't try to marry the idea too soon . . . but I also know when to settle on something and build on it. I'm not a perfectionist to the point where I can't get anything accomplished.

Selecting Which Lyrics to Use

Related to editing is the process of selecting material to release or perform—deciding which of your lyrics you are actually going to use. Wu-Tang Clan affiliate Killah Priest says, "I look back at my old rhyme books and I'll be like, 'Yo! When did I write this?' I use about perhaps 50 percent [and] 50 percent I put away."

Use Most of Your Lyrics

Many MCs make use of most of the lyrics they write. Tech N9ne says that he doesn't "write 50 tracks and choose 12 out of them. Everything is valuable to me." Stressmatic of the Federation comments that "all of them get recorded, because when we're actually sitting there writing, we're writing in the studio, so they'll get recorded." Bishop Lamont explains that he uses most of his lyrics, because if an idea isn't good enough he'll scrap it early on.

Bishop Lamont

Pretty much everything I write I'll use, because if there's some ideas I don't like, they get erased, they don't live, those fetuses get aborted, those things never see the light of day. So pretty much everything gets used, either for myself or I write records for other artists and it's like, this might work for somebody else—I'm pretty much done with this chamber but this might be dope for somebody else.

Artists who have lyrics left over from albums often try to use them in other ways, such as on mixtapes or at shows.

Stat Quo

They go somewhere. I put them on a mixtape or somebody else might want a song, so [in any case] I use them.

Chuck D, Public Enemy

I try to [use everything]. I'm always writing, so there's always going to be something that's going to be unused that I can use for something else.

Don't Use Most of Your Lyrics

Other MCs end up not using a lot of the lyrics they write, for various reasons.

R.A. The Rugged Man

I got a lot of lyrics and a lot of notebooks that never made it to the studio, where I said, yeah, that's a wack rhyme, keep moving.

Andy Cat, Ugly Duckling

Don't be afraid to write something you're not gonna use, [and don't] think that everything you say is all important or that everything you come up with is genius.

A way of creating an album that a lot of MCs use is to record a large number of tracks and then keep the best, rejecting the leftovers.

Big Noyd

I'll just record a lot of songs, and then I'll pick the songs that sounded best to me to make an album.

MURS

I've been recording this Warner Bros. album [*MURS for President*] and it's been the longest I've ever taken with recording a record. I've probably written 120 songs' worth of material and only recorded 60, and of those 60 the world will only ever hear 15.

Keeping the quality control high and selecting only the best lyrics to be released can be a good reason to discard some of your lyrics. Del the Funky Homosapien says, "I've thrown away full notebooks of lyrics before. I'm even more of a perfectionist now."

Archives

Some artists keep an archive of the verses they don't use, instead of just discarding them.

Immortal Technique

There is stuff I have sitting around—there's an emergency 16-bar verse here and there, there's an emergency 27-bar verse somewhere.

Brother J, X Clan

[Because I have so many songs archived,] I don't have to record right now. I can just go back in my library and pull things out that will still be dope.

Fredro Starr, Onyx

I think all rappers have those secret rhymes that never came out. I remember they had a 2Pac book [with] some poems that never came out.

T3, Slum Village

Half we never come out with—that goes in the archives. . . . You may leak one song out just to throw out there.

Selecting Singles

In addition to selecting which songs to release or perform, MCs must also decide what songs to release as singles. MCs are usually known for a handful of specific songs, often their singles, so this decision can define the MC as an artist and make or break an album.

Writing Singles as Regular Songs

Some artists feel that it's best not to write a song thinking that it is going to be a single but instead to write the best songs they can and later pick one to be a single.

Stat Quo

I like [producer] Rick Rubin's thing—when he's in the studio working on a record, he never lets the artist say anything about a single, because sometimes you just jinx the shit. It's like meeting a girl: "Oh, she's gonna be my wife." You jinxed it off the top—she probably ain't gonna be shit.

Dray, Das EFX

[The classic Das EFX single "They Want EFX"] was just like any other song. You don't really know what it's gonna do, so it wasn't like writing it knowing it was going to be a smash. It was just another song—we wrote it, put it away, went about our business, cool feedback from our friends. That's who we played them for at the time, that was our gauge—if our boys like it, then it's straight. It didn't feel special, it didn't feel "Oh, snap"—we had a whole bunch of songs like that one, for the first album, that the world never heard.

will.i.am, Black Eyed Peas

Sometimes [I'll write a song specifically as a single], but that's dangerous, because "Where Is the Love" was not sup- posed to be a single—we didn't think that was a single when we wrote it—so you never know.

Twista

[Writing the hit single "Slow Jamz" with Kanye West and Jamie Foxx]—it was fun. It was fun because a lot of times you don't get to have a concept for a song or vibe to a song before you write it, so I knew when I was writing "Slow Jamz" that I was about to name a lot of different R&B bands and different types of singers in the song. I knew that was like a hot idea, so I just really had fun writing that song, fitting in all of the names. . . . When I was spitting all of those names, it was just fun, so I had a ball working on it—I had no idea [it was going to be a single].

Nelly

You never know until you're done. Sometimes you can go into it if you hear a hot beat and you're like, "Yo, this is a hot beat—this could be a jam," but until you lay it down, you don't really know. Sometimes you can have ideas in your head and it sounds so great, and then when you lay it, it didn't come out the same way. Or sometimes you can do [a song] and you're not really paying attention to it, and before you know it you're just like, holy shit, this shit is crazy.

Knowing a Song Will Be a Single

Alternatively, some MCs realize that a song is good single material as they're writing it.

Gorilla Zoe

You can feel a single when you make it.

Tajai, Souls of Mischief

We wrote [the classic single "93 'Til Infinity"] as an anthem. We had a "91 'Til Infinity"—that's a concept we had been reworking more than once—but when we heard that beat, we were like, oh, we gotta use this shit. That was like the last song we made [for the album].

Pharoahe Monch

I wrote [the hit single "Simon Says"] knowing that it felt like I've never felt before—it felt special. After I came up with the chorus, I wanted to write verses that the whole crowd could say, rather than a flow where people were staring at me like, how does he do that? I wanted [verses] where people could feel like they were part of the song. Like when I listened to "I Can't Live Without My Radio," I felt when I was saying the rhymes, I felt like LL Cool J. [So] I think when [the crowd says] "Y'all know the name . . ." it's empowering—it's not me, it's them.

Twista

When I wrote "Overnight Celebrity," I knew it was going to be a single. When I wrote "Girl Tonite," I knew it was going to be a single. Sometimes you don't know and you're trying to make something hot and then you pick something, but then sometimes, like when I got the "Overnight Celebrity" beat, at the time Kanye was getting real hot and we knew the beat was real hot, so I knew I had to deliver to that beat and make it a single. Same thing with "Girl Tonite"—it was time to deliver for a single, and I had that beat and I thought it was hot.

Having Others Help You Pick Singles

It can be hard to be objective about which song is your best song and which has the most potential as a single, so having other people help you choose can be a big advantage. B-Real explains that often the record label made good choices for singles for Cypress Hill.

B-Real, Cypress Hill

When [the record label] chose "Insane in the Brain," I was pretty much thinking that that *wasn't* going to be a hit—and sure enough, it was a hit, but I had no idea. When they picked "Rock Superstar" to be the single, I thought that was a great album song but I didn't know if it was a single, and it turned out to be a big single for us. Sometimes we get too attached to a lot of our music and when we say this should be the single it's because we're really attached to it, we're not looking outside of ourselves as much as the record company. Back then I don't think I had the ability to step back and see those things. Now I definitely do.

Input from other people during the actual recording process can also lead to a song becoming a single.

Devin the Dude

[The single "What a Job," featuring Snoop Dogg and André 3000 of OutKast] was just a skit and it was just like a brief

message within the album, but when we mixed it, other people from the record company and a few people that I work
with in the studio, they was like, "Man, that oughta be a song,
that oughta be a whole song!" We were debating about who
would get on there, and I was like, maybe Snoop and André
3000, that'd be great, and within a couple of weeks it worked
out.

Evidence, Dilated Peoples

We went into D&D Studios later [to record "Worst Comes to
Worst"], put it down, and DJ Premier was in the other room
with Freddie Foxxx, working on something, and they heard it
and ran into the room. Premier said, "If this isn't your single,
I'm gonna punch y'all in the face in public." So I didn't want
to get socked or have to scrap with Premier, so we made it our
single. We spent a lot of time on the song after we dropped
our lyrics, because then Alchemist went back and added little violin parts and then we got Guru on the little bridge and
then Premier mixed it later. It took a while before the song
was done.

In fact, an artist may not even particularly like a song that turns
out to be a great single. For example, O.C. of Diggin' in the Crates
recalls that his hugely revered single "Time's Up" wasn't a favorite
of his and he had to be talked into releasing it.

O.C., Diggin' in the Crates

I really didn't like the record. I [only] did two verses because I
couldn't finish a third verse for it. I hated that record! It took
so long to write and I love the beat so much I had to prove
I was worthy to rock to it—it was defeating me, man, so it
was a crazy process for that record. Everything else flowed
except for that record, [MC] Serch had to really, really convince me—the record almost didn't happen. I'm glad it did,

at this stage of the game, because I guess it's one of those records that's in hip-hop history books, but [Serch] had to practically go, "Oh, this is it, this is it. You said you wanted something to the left—this is it." And I just felt like everything is off—I didn't think people was gonna like it. The subject matter in the song is what caught people—it's relevant today—so that's why I'm proud of the song now, now that I'm a little wiser and a little older and I look back on it.

11

Writing with Other People

Swords sharpen swords.

◄ Killah Priest, Wu-Tang Clan affiliate ►

The writing process can change when you're collaborating with other people, a frequent occurrence in hip-hop. Artists often find themselves working in a group, doing a guest vocal on someone else's track, asking someone else to guest on their track, ghostwriting lyrics for someone else to perform, or working with a producer on their own lyrics. Many MCs find such collaborations to be an enjoyable experience.

Big Pooh, Little Brother

For me, [collaborating with other artists is easier], because I'm used to being in a group setting, so when you're used to being in a group setting, you're used to having someone else to bounce ideas off of. Doing a group track and actually being in the room or in the studio with that other MC that you're doing the work with, for me, it's second nature.

Working with other artists is an excellent way to improve your skills. It gives you a chance to learn from other talented people.

Bobby Creekwater

As far as [working with] Eminem is concerned, I picked up tips from him about everything, man. He's a workaholic, he's serious, he's very passionate, and it rubs off on you, so it's good to be around him—it takes what I was doing a step further. That could be the best choice an MC or an aspiring artist could make, is to surround themselves with like talent or even better talent.

The process can also encourage the collaborators to bring their most creative work to the table. When artists with complementary styles collaborate, for example, they often bring out the best in one another.

Planet Asia

[On working with Evidence of Dilated Peoples on the album *The Medicine*:] Me and Ev's shit, we're like peanut butter and jelly. We matched perfectly—we're kind of like one and the same when it comes to taste of certain types of hip-hop and sounds. We don't try to be obvious with what we're gonna do—it's like we already feel the same way when it comes to music.

A collaboration may not be the best option in all cases, however. Certain concepts are better suited for solo work, while others are more appropriate for group efforts.

Shock G, Digital Underground

Solo [tracks are] easier for keeping an idea uniform, where it maintains a certain style or point of view, like "Humpty Dance," or "So Many Tears" by 2Pac. Even though we were back to produce another one for him, unlike "I Get Around," Pac kept us off "Tears" because it was specific and focused on his life, just like the "[Humpty] Dance" focused on [my alter ego] Humpty's. But then, collaborations are easier for making something interesting and diverse—more input, more variety, more levels of thought, like "Doowutchyalike" or "Same Song" [with 2Pac].

Writing in a Group

Writing in a group can be a different experience from working on solo records, as you have to take into account the other group members' opinions and vision for each song. It's not necessarily easier or more difficult—just different.

Lord Jamar, Brand Nubian

Everything has its pros and cons. The pros might be that you write less. The cons are that you have to sometimes compromise what the whole thing might be about or something to appease everybody's tastes and stuff like that. It's different but the same.

Advantages of Writing in a Group

One major benefit of writing in a group is that each artist has less to write.

Sheek Louch, D-Block/The LOX

It's way easier [in a group]. Say, like, we're making a LOX album—it's way easier because it's three verses already right there. If I'm by myself, I gotta come up with the hook, I gotta come up with all three verses, the concept. With the group, we're gonna build on an idea, and chances are we're all just gonna bug out over a hook. [With] the verses, I gotta write my 12 or 16 and we feed off it. I hear [their verses] or they hear mine and it's on and popping.

However, having less to write can mean that you have to make your message understood using fewer words and you must ensure that the material you've written is as strong as what the other MCs on the track have written.

Sean Price, Heltah Skeltah

You've got less to write, but at the same time you've gotta still get your point across in a shorter time, so that is a challenge too.

Styles P, D-Block/The LOX

It's easier because it's a group, so you have less work to do, but then you also have to ensure that you're up to par with your partners.

Group work also promotes friendly competition to see who can come up with the best lyrics, which often makes for stronger songs.

Fredro Starr, Onyx

When you're working in a group, it kind of brings out the best in your writing, because in a way everybody is competitive. So if I see Sticky [Fingaz] over here writing some shit, I'll be like, damn, he wrote that, well, let me go and write this shit. If I hear Sticky saying some fucked up shit, I'm like, oh, shit, let me dig deep.

Bootie Brown, The Pharcyde

It's a friendly competition between you and your friends because you all want to shine. You want the song to be good as far as the group, but it wouldn't hurt to have somebody compliment you [on your verse]. [Working with] people that wanna work, that's just the best—when you got people in there that say, "Hey, what do you need me to do? OK, I'll do this," and get it done—that's the situation you want to be in.

Writing Together or Separately

Although one particular MC will usually be responsible for performing each verse, most hip-hop groups prefer to write the verses together or at least bounce ideas off one another.

Imani, The Pharcyde

I'm used to working with partners and having people to bounce off of. When you have four people to make a song, your responsibility is totally different from one person or two people, [though] it was never hard, because nobody put no rules on nothing. You could throw a topic out there and everybody go to their own part of the world and think about it. Sometimes we would actually sit and write, like we'd come up with [a concept, like], "OK, this is what we're going to do"—we sat down and wrote some songs like "Officer" and "Ya Mama."

Dray, Das EFX

I wouldn't say [we would] ghostwrite as far as writing whole verses for each other, but we did [say], "Hey, I have a couple of lines left over, you wanna use these lines? Check this out."

In a lot of groups, the MCs write material for other group members to perform, depending on what works best for the song.

Havoc, Mobb Deep

Oh yeah, for sure, I wrote verses for Prodigy, and he wrote verses for me. We're a family, so it doesn't matter. We don't even consider it ghostwriting—it is what it is.

Big Noyd

I've never had a ghostwriter—no one ever wrote for me—but [in collaborating with Mobb Deep] I've definitely had some times where somebody will help me with a rhyme in my camp. Like where I'll write a rhyme and Prodigy might be like, "Yo, that shit sounds good, it sounds ill, but change this part right here, it'd be iller if you say this," and he may throw a couple of rhymes in and stuff like that.

Tajai, Souls of Mischief

We have [written for each other in the group], or we'll do something like we'll write a verse and write it piece by piece together and all say it and pick the parts where each person's voice sounds better—so it's like co-writing. We wrote everything together, [though] of course you bust off and write certain things separately, but you already know the concept and the hook and how long you're going to rap.

On the other hand, some groups prefer to write separately most of the time—each artist writes his or her own verses, and then they all lay them down on the same beat. Even so, the separate rappers may still be inspired by one another, and they may write around the same theme.

Lord Jamar, Brand Nubian

Within my group, basically we would all just go off on our own and write. We might be in the same room, but we're basically just writing our own stuff—it's not like somebody's giving me a line and I'm giving him a line. But we might get inspired by what another man is saying—he might be writing his stuff and he might be like, "Yo, listen to what I got so far," and then you hear that and you're like, "OK, I gotta make my shit a little sharper"—that's how we might help each other. [With the track "Slow Down,"] we knew what the [concept was]. It was like, all right, talk about this—now go.

Deciding Who Rhymes Where

When you're writing a song in a group, you also have to decide the order in which you're all going to deliver your verses. In some cases, it can be as simple as whoever finishes writing first. In others, whatever is best for the song determines who rhymes where.

Havoc, Mobb Deep

Sometimes it depends on who finishes their rhyme first. Most of the time I'm finished first, so I rhyme first.

Dray, Das EFX

It's a feel [when it comes to who rhymes first], and it's whoever's verse sounds like it should start, whoever feels like they want to start.

Back-and-Forth Vocals

In some group songs, instead of each verse being delivered by a different artist, several MCs will rap back and forth a few words or lines at a time.

Andy Cat, Ugly Duckling

That's one element of rap that's kind of another phase, like group-oriented rapping, stuff like Leaders of the New School, or even going way back, Treacherous Three. That's one of the big parts of the rap crews early on—they had all these routines, it's almost like the equivalent of doo-wop harmony or something for hip-hop.

Back-and-forth parts are often written by one member of the group and then divided up, but in some cases the different parts may be written by various members and then pieced together.

Akil the MC, Jurassic 5

[On the back-and-forth parts], sometimes somebody might write the whole piece and then you just break it up. It depends on how many bars it is. If it's a two-bar thing, then you just write your lines and I'll write my lines and we'll go back and forth like that. But [for] the more intricate word-for-word type of stuff, somebody might write the whole thing and be like, "OK, you say this part, you say this part, I'll say this part, and you say this part like that."

Andy Cat, Ugly Duckling

Dizzy [of Ugly Duckling and I], we rap back and forth a lot and set each other up. [I] might go two lines and he goes two, and so I have to be conscious of where he's gonna start his line and where I'm gonna end. Sometimes [one of us will write a whole part], or there's been some songs where it's really back and forth, where I just said, "I got something for the back-and-forth part." I heard with Beastie Boys, [on] "Paul Revere" and those songs where they're having a conversation between each other, that one person wrote those—it makes sense because it's pretty hard for two people to write every single element of a back-and-forth rhyme.

Some artists create even more complex variations on this collaborative style. The song "Latyrx" by the group Latyrx features not just sections in which the two MCs rap back and forth but also verses in which the MCs perform at the same time and their lyrics line up at certain points.

Lateef, Latyrx

"Latyrx" was a situation where we had the beat, we sat down and we wrote the song together, and we kind of came to the conclusion that we would overlap on certain areas, and we just sat down and wrote—it took us like two days. We were kind of going through it and we'd be like, "OK, right here we'll both say this part and we'll come together right here." We [also] recorded it at the same time. We wrote it together, so we always said the raps together, pretty much. With Latyrx stuff, when we have parts that we're writing that we're both going to be trading off, we write them together for the most part—I'll sit there and write a rhyme, like I'll write a line or two and then we'll break up who's gonna say what, and he'll write a line or two and we'll break up who's gonna say what. It's a very organic process—it really becomes a thing where you can't fucking remember who wrote what.

Compromising

In a group situation, members have to compromise with one another in order to make a song work or to make sure everyone is happy with the direction of the song.

B-Real, Cypress Hill

When you work within a group context, there's gonna be situations like that. Like there's probably rhymes that I've wrote over [DJ Muggs's] beats that he might not have liked as much, might have wanted me to change it, so you go through those compromises. Every now and then there might have been something questionable, either a rhyme I wrote or a beat he gave us, but most of the time, I'd say 90 percent of the time, we were on the same page about the music.

If you want things to go smoothly, respect and incorporate the opinions of all the group members.

Vast Aire, Cannibal Ox

When you're working in a group, you have to take into consideration what the other artist wants to work on. We always rhyme on everything everybody's vibing with.

The more people you have working on a song, however, the harder it can be to get everyone to work together. In big groups it can be useful to have one person in charge to set the direction and to make sure everyone works well together.

Tash, Tha Alkaholiks

I love the chemistry of everybody being there. Me, J-Ro, E-Swift, that's the Alkaholiks right there, and doing stuff with Phil the Agony and Xzibit and King Tee, Defari, Lootpack—I love doing that. But when you got too many people in the room working on one beat and everything, everybody has their own opinion. You can't appease everybody—everybody is not gonna be on the same page at the same time.

Thes One, People Under the Stairs

For People Under the Stairs, we get in the studio and we just vibe and I don't ever feel like there's a control thing, but I know other groups where there is definitely a control situation. And it has to be that way, because sometimes when you have more people involved, if one person doesn't step up and take control of the situation, nothing's gonna get done.

Most MCs agree that ultimately whatever works best for the song is what counts, even if that means compromising some of your own ideas or going in the direction of one particular person's vision.

Guest Verses and Other Short-Term Collaborations

It's common in hip-hop for an MC to do a guest verse, in which he or she writes and performs lyrics for another artist's song. Some

MCs do a lot of guest verses to increase their exposure and to bring their flavor to someone else's track.

Tash, Tha Alkaholiks

I did three hundred and something guest appearances on other people's albums, so that was their vibe and me . . . that was their vibe and their beat and their producer and their chemistry and I just went in there and did them.

Similarly, MCs also participate in *posse cuts*, in which numerous rappers (normally more than four or five) all contribute to a single track, usually doing back-to-back verses, in which the next artist starts rapping immediately after the previous MC. Examples include A Tribe Called Quest's "Scenario," Marley Marl's "The Symphony," Wu-Tang Clan's "Triumph," and the Game's "One Blood (Remix)." Tech N9ne worked on the classic posse cut "The Anthem," from Sway & King Tech's album *This or That.*

Tech N9ne

Oh, man, that was so wonderful when King Tech called me and told me everybody that was gonna be on it—it was like, Eminem, the RZA, Chino XL, Xzibit, KRS-One, Kool G Rap, Jayo Felony, Pharoahe Monch. It goes on for days—there's like nine of us—and then we shot a video. It was wonderful that King Tech and them saw that talent in me to put me with all those heavy hitters—much love to Sway and King Tech for even pulling me in like that. I was the first one to do the verse—I was the first one on that track. I just did me, and when I heard everybody else, I was like, damn, that's dope—it just turned into something wonderful.

With guest verses and similar short-term collaborations, each artist generally writes his or her own material, so the process is often more like doing solo songs than working in a group. The idea is usually for each collaborator to bring the style he or she is known for to that track.

Sheek Louch

[When I request a guest verse from someone,] I like them to bring their element—say when I got Jim Jones on the record, I want Jim Jones to do him, I want Bun B to do that Midwest shit that [he does].

Tash, Tha Alkaholiks

The whole thing that I have trouble with is that when [some] people call me to do a guest appearance and they play a beat, they want me to do the whole song and they're guest appearing on their own shit. They want me to come up with the whole song, the hook, rap on it—then it feels like it's not their song no more. It's like it's my song—it turns into, "Hey, man, I'm doing your job for you." I like working with people like Raekwon, Wu-Tang, Mos Def, Busta Rhymes [where they] call me and say, "We already got the song, we just need a little flavor on it, so we came and got you, Tash, to basically add some spice to the mix, add some West Coast flavor." I like to work with artists that know what they want to do and say what they mean and mean what they say.

Doing guest verses can be slightly different from writing solo material, but whether you're working for yourself or for another artist, it's always crucial to write to the best of your ability.

RBX

If I'm working on my shit I'm gonna spit lava, if I'm working on your shit I'm gonna spit lava, if I'm working on her shit I'm gonna spit lava, if I'm working on their shit . . . lava, lava, lava, lava.

Advantages of Short-Term Collaborations

When you guest on someone's record or have him or her guest on yours, you often feel particularly motivated to match or exceed your collaborator's performance on the track. Just like when you're writing in a group, this friendly competition can make you better at your craft.

Big Daddy Kane

With me, that's all it is—it's friendly competition. Back in the '80s, me and Kool G Rap, we would be on the phone, like one, two o'clock in the morning. I'm like, "Yo, check this verse out I just wrote," and I spit the verse to G, and, you know, he's like, "OK, that's hot, that's hot," and it'd make him do his thing. The next night, G might call me and he's like, "Yo, check this verse out," and he spit his verse and I'm like, "Yeah, that's fire, that's fire," and it'd make me step my game up. That's the friendly competition that we had—when you surrounded by talent, it's gonna keep you on your toes and also it makes the whole thing fun.

Bobby Creekwater

There's always gonna be friendly competition. Every MC wants to aspire to be a great MC, and when in the presence of MCs just as good as yourself, you wanna make sure that you rise to the occasion. It's a good thing—it bring the best out of you. [Making the track "We're Back" (also featuring Eminem, Obie Trice, Stat Quo, and Cashis)] was just like heaven, man. [It's all about] being in the presence of like talent or greater talent. You go in with a bunch of MCs who are really good at what they do, and it gets you in the mood of wanting to rise to the occasion, so for me, that's the best thing in the world— it was a beautiful experience for me. Eminem had already penned out his and we heard his verse and the rest is history.

It was like, wow, because he had went in so hard it was like he left us no choice—we had to do our thing on that one.

Rah Digga

It's always easier to work on somebody else's stuff, because the object is to sound better than them, so it's more fun, it's more challenging, it's more of a sport. The bar is raised when you're rhyming with other people.

Hell Rell, Dipset

If I'm gonna be on a song with Jadakiss and Beanie Sigel, those are two respectable artists in the game, so if I'm gonna be on a song with them, I know I gotta come harder. I just can't say anything, I gotta step outside of myself and judge myself as a fan like, "All right, what do I want to hear from Hell Rell on a Jadakiss track?"

It's important, however, that the competition be friendly rather than personal.

R.A. the Rugged Man

A lot of times you put me on records with rappers [and] I'm not trying to destroy that rapper because I dislike the rapper, but I like destroying rappers because I got that old-school MC in me—where we're not just on a record to do a record . . . let's see who shines the most.

Kool G Rap

I think I tend to step it up a lot more when I'm guest appearing on somebody else's track, because I like to give people their money's worth. A lot of people look at it like G Rap be trying to tear [MCs] up on the features and shit I do, but it don't really be me trying to go after the rapper like he's a target, because I don't really do that. To try to minimize somebody's demeanor or whatever that comes at me to work with them, I wouldn't do that—that's malicious. But I am gonna make sure G Rap sounds good, and I'm competitive, so I'ma come out like a beast.

Working with other MCs on a track can also inspire better work simply because you have other artists around during the creative process.

David Banner

I like having other spirits in the room, period.

Big Daddy Kane

I think the most fun I have is when I'm working with some-one who's a nice MC, because it's inspirational. I come from where you're hearing cats like Kool G Rap, KRS-One, Rakim— you're hearing a lot of rappers that's spitting hard, so it's like you gotta stay on top of your toes because there's a lot of com-petition. If I'm in the studio with someone who's a nice MC, it inspires me to really write. Like, for example, I was on a UGK album and, you know, I respect [Kool] G Rap as a nice MC and I respect Bun B as a nice MC, so knowing I was going to be on a song with the two of those dudes was like I really had to step my pen game up, because I respect those dudes as MCs. I just did something with [the] Game [in early 2008], and when I came to the studio, I'll be honest with you, I was pissy drunk. And then KRS-One put his verse down, and when I heard KRS's verse, I sobered up real quick! And [I] started really writ-ing, because he wasn't playing and I respect KRS as an MC.

Collaborating on the Same Idea

On some collaborative tracks, the MCs write completely separate verses based on whatever they want to write about, while on oth-ers they all write about the same topic. The second option often requires greater willingness to compromise.

DJ Quik

You gotta be a little more open when you collab—you have to be open for camaraderie. You're sharing this record, and sometimes I can be Napoleonistic about it and want to do it my way, tyrant-like, [but you] gotta give up your brain-child sometimes when you share lyrics with somebody.

Collaborating on a single topic can be easier or harder depending on what the topic is and how difficult it is to write about.

Pharoahe Monch

Sometimes the collaborations will be easy. If it's a song about happy, sunny picnic days, you're like, oh, OK. Other times it's like, this song is about the Afro-American struggle in America, and you're like, all right, this is going to take a little more time.

Deciding Who Records First

Some MCs prefer to record their verse (or verses) before the other people on the track so that they can set the tone. Others prefer to record once other artists' vocals are on the track, since they feel inspired to put in more effort if someone else has already recorded something powerful.

B-Real, Cypress Hill

If I'm first and I haven't heard anybody else's stuff, there's a little more pressure, because usually when somebody hears your shit they try to write to blow you out of the water so that they can have the best verse. So what I do is, I think about it in terms of, OK, well, if I didn't hear anything from all these other dudes, then I know I have to set the pace—they're gonna have to do some really raw shit to outdo me. So if that's gonna make the song better, fuck it, I'll set the pace if I don't hear anybody and I'll make them come to me. If you settle for just doing some easy shit, then the [MC] that's coming after you is gonna blow your ass away, so you gotta go in there thinking, "I'm gonna blow this fucking track apart before anybody even gets on it."

Sheek Louch, D-Block/The LOX

I hate it when they just send me the track [without vocals]. I'll be like, "Yo, what's the concept? What's the whole song about?" You can't really give it to [someone] without a verse on there or a concept or what's going on—that's some sucker shit.

Ghostwriting

Ghostwriting is when one artist writes lyrics for another art-ist to perform, or when several people work on one set of lyr-ics. Termanology says of ghostwriting that "it really broadens and opens up your mind, because you're like, wow, I have to write from a whole 'nother perspective. I like it, though—it's a challenge."

Knowing the Artist's Style

One of the main aspects of being a good ghostwriter is know-ing the rapping style of the MC who will be performing the lyrics.

B-Real, Cypress Hill

You gotta be careful not to write your style for them. You have to give them something different so they don't just sound like what you doing—you have to give them something com-pletely customized for them.

For example, on Public Enemy's album *Rebirth of a Nation*, Paris wrote the majority of the lyrics performed by Chuck D. It helped that Paris was familiar with Chuck D's style of writing.

Chuck D

[Paris] kind of wrote in a way that was reminiscent of earlier work that I've done. He had great substance in the writing of the words [and] he laid a guide vocal [for me to learn from]. It's really a total science [how] he put it together—he's almost like a scientist/musician.

Paris

I've only written lyrics for two other artists in my career, Public Enemy and the Conscious Daughters. Both were easy to write for because I knew the styles of each ahead of time.

Big Daddy Kane wrote for other members of the Juice Crew, adapting his writing to fit their personalities.

Big Daddy Kane

For me, ghostwriting for someone else wasn't hard, because doing it in someone else's style, if they have a more simpler style, then it makes my job easier because now I ain't got to think too complicated. For example, writing for Biz, it wasn't really about having hot rhymes, it was about having something funny. And with Shanté, I could try to pretty much put it in her flow, but really with Shanté, she wanted to do what I liked doing, just basically being sarcastic, and she is like the master of sarcasm. So basically I'd be sarcastic like I normally would but just make it to fit a woman.

To master another artist's style, research his or her past work, and get the artist's input into what he or she wants you to write. Once you have the style down, you can add your own twist to take it in a slightly different direction.

Bishop Lamont

When you're trying to write for other people, you have to get to know them or look at their body of work and look at what they've done before—like, where would I go from here? So you just look at all the work they did before—videos, interviews—and then sit down with them and say, "Where are you now and what are you trying to say?" And once you get pretty much a good idea of where [they're] trying to go and what their bottom line is, you can put your extras with it to give them new characteristics, to make it unpredictable to fans who're used to hearing them bust one way or talk about these specific topics—it's a new twist plus what they used to spit.

Writing for a Particular Project

MCs will sometimes be hired to ghostwrite for a particular project. RBX describes how working on *The Chronic* with Dr. Dre was more of a team effort, in which everyone would submit the best work possible for the overall good of the album.

RBX

I wrote some things for Dre. Dre doesn't profess to be no super-duper rap dude—Dre is a super-duper producer, so when we were trying to get some things together, sure, I wrote some things. I wrote "Let Me Ride" . . . in that instance I think I was working on some things and Dre heard it and was like, "Oh, wow, that's hot right there. X, what are you gonna do with that?" And we spoke about it and I was like, "Shit, we're trying to make the project hot—*you* say it and we're gonna do it like that." I don't remember [if I made a guide vocal for him to learn it from]—Dre is sharp, I think it was on a CD or something and he just memorized it and went in and knocked it out. It came out beautiful, but I don't think it took that long [to do the vocals].

Similarly, Pharoahe Monch explains that writing for P. Diddy on his album *Press Play* was like being part of a writing team and that his writing had to fit in with Puffy's vision for the album.

Pharoahe Monch

[With P. Diddy], it was challenging and rewarding at the same time, in that it pushed me in a direction that I was willing to be challenged in. With my own stuff it's like this is what it is— if I'm feeling it, it fits, maybe one or two rewrites, but with his stuff, he pushes artists to begin with. And when you're writing for somebody else, they have their own vision and you want to make sure that everything is matching up, so there were a couple of rewrites on a couple of things. Puff is big on Motown and big on Berry Gordy, Tammi Terrell, Marvin Gaye—[they] would write songs for people, they had a team of writers and producers that would write songs for that artist . . . that is his music model.

Delivering Lyrics Someone Has Ghostwritten for You

Delivering lyrics that another artist has written for you is similar to performing your own vocals, except that the ghostwriter may help you with the flow or delivery.

Shock G, Digital Underground

[On "I Get Around," 2Pac] announced that a messenger from Interscope Records was on his way to the Bay Area to collect the tapes as soon as we finished, and then fly them back down to L.A. in time for the album's scheduled mastering session the next morning. I planned to begin writing a verse afterwards, but as I was putting the final touches on the track and adding all the little live piano accents and whatnot, Pac was walking around with a pad writing verses for me and Money-B. Mun didn't like his and decided to write his own, but I liked what Pac wrote for me, so I rewrote it in my own writing, to read it easier, and rehearsed it once or twice before I laid it. Thanks for the hot verse, Pac! R.I.P.

Producer Writing Input

When they're writing their rhymes, many artists like to receive some input from the producer of the record—usually an idea for a topic or advice on a few lines—which they will take into account alongside their own opinions.

will.i.am, Black Eyed Peas

[As a producer,] yes, [I give writing input to people.] Sometimes I write the whole song, sometimes [it works better like that]. It's all about the songs—if a song needs it, I will come in with something, and if it doesn't, then I'll step back.

Big Pooh, Little Brother

All the producers I work with, they pretty much give me the free will to go about it how I want to go about it. I find that when you're working with a producer that's also a writer, a lot of times that's when they throw in their input.

N.O.R.E.

I insist on the input. When I [make] records with great producers like Swizz Beatz, like Pharrell, like Scott Storch, I always want to hear their input—I always want to hear what they think about it. And then I also have a process where I wipe out everything they say and I do exactly what I feel, and then in the middle is how the record is made.

B-Real, Cypress Hill

I appreciate [input from the producer] because, I mean, it's somebody's opinion, whether they're right or wrong. I appreciate the opinion, and it might give me inspiration to do something different or better or add to what I have. I don't mind the direction—it's part of the creative process. You get suggestions and inspirations.

E-40

I let 'em [give me input], because I'm open minded, I'm not a stubborn rapper, I don't think I know it all. I listen to the producers in my surroundings, and if you listen, you get further.

Different producers have different ways of working. Some will want to have input on the ideas and content, or the flow and delivery, and some may want to simply change the odd word or line here and there.

Royce Da 5′9″

Pharrell, he'll even give you a flow to use. That's kind of a talent [for the MC], just to stick to somebody else's flow—that's fun to do. Preem [DJ Premier] is pretty instrumental in that he won't really tell you what to rap about, but he'll tell you change this line and do this different. Puff will tell you change lines—I mean the real big producers, they just try to be more involved. And you want to take their input, because they've accomplished way more than you, so you want to listen to what they're saying.

Fredro Starr, Onyx

Jam Master Jay [of Run-DMC] was our real first producer we ever really had [on Onyx's first album, *Bacdafucup*], and his influence was definitely, definitely respected. His opinion was respected and he was like a mentor. Coming from Jam Master Jay and Run-DMC, we took what he said at value, so if he said, "Yo, Fredro, I think that you should change that up," or "Come at it this way," I took that into consideration and I used it to my advantage. I think *Bacdafucup* was probably the most well-received album we had, and I think Jam Master Jay was a big part of that. So yeah, I listen to producers.

More Input

MCs generally appreciate it when a producer offers more substantial input, since it means they'll have two creative minds working on the song instead of just one.

Lateef, Latyrx

I work with a lot of producers, and I've found that a lot of that kind of negotiation can make for stronger songs if a producer has an idea or concept or direction he wants to take the song. I think that makes for the best songs, actually—if you can make a song that's like a synthesis of both personalities, I think you can come up with a strong song.

Pusha-T, Clipse

Usually it's a collaborative effort, like there's just so many times I come in the studio and it's just the beat playing and [producer Pharrell of the Neptunes] is like, "Damn, man, I feel like the hook should be [like] this, but I just don't got the words, I don't got the words for it," but he has the cadence like, "Here's how the cadence go," and then I'm like, OK, [and I'll write the words to fit that cadence].

Sheek Louch, D-Block/The LOX

With [producer] Red Spyda, when he came to me with "Good Love," my single, when he told me about the song . . . let it breathe and pause right here and do this and that—it was dope us working hand in hand.

However, even MCs who are always open to the input of producers don't necessarily follow all their advice. Planet Asia says,

"It depends on who I'm working with. I always take advice and criticism—I love it all—though if I don't feel like their opinion is right, I won't do it."

Less Input

Some MCs, on the other hand, prefer to keep producer input to a minimum.

Tech N9ne

Most of [the producers on my records], I have never met. Some of these producers we got in Denmark, Berlin [in] Germany, and we've never met them. They just send me [the beats] and I know how I want my album—they just feed them to me, and then when they hear them, they're like, "Wow, I can't believe you did that on that beat—I never would have heard that on that."

Bishop Lamont

[Dr.] Dre, he just does some amazing beats and you gotta come with some amazing shit over it. If he's not feeling something, he's gonna let you know, but he's gonna let you do what you do—he's not gonna be over your shoulder. [He won't give a lot of writing input] unless it's, like, really conceptual records that I'm writing for him or he has in mind for me and him. Other than that he'll be like, "Yo, I got magic beats, you tell me what you think should go over it"—and we'll go from there.

RBX

If you're working with Dr. Dre, Dre gives you an idea and he expects us as professionals to translate what he said into a hit. So when you're dealing with producers such as Dre and

Timbaland and those cats, they might have an input on a certain topic, but for the most part they rely on the person who's rhyming to know what the fuck they're doing and to do it.

Sometimes collaborations between MCs and producers simply work better if they do their work separately.

Vinnie Paz, Jedi Mind Tricks

[With Jedi Mind Tricks and the group's producer, Stoupe the Enemy of Mankind,] we really stay out of each other's way with that kind of stuff. When you're doing it as long as we have, and we feel that we have something really good, we don't really fuck with the way that we do things. We sort of feel that it's been successful, so if it ain't broke, don't fix it.

Producer-Supplied Hooks

As mentioned in chapter 10 (see p. 192), producers can have a particularly big impact on the writing of a track if they give an artist a beat that already has a hook on it. Since the hook will usually have some sort of content or theme to it, this can shape the rest of the lyrics.

Styles P, D-Block/The LOX

If you got something with a hook already in that's crazy, then obviously that's what it's gonna be. If the hook's already there and it makes sense, then, yeah, that would be a lot of input, I would say, if that was to happen.

Twista

[On working with producers Kanye West and Pharrell of the Neptunes:] Kanye will do the beat and then he'll be spitting a hook or like half of a hook—that always helps me—like he did that with me with "Overnight Celebrity," so I really didn't have to do a lot of work on that one because he helped me. Same with Pharrell when he did "Lavish." I love it when a producer comes with something along with the beat—it makes your job just that much easier.

Royce Da 5'9"

I normally only let producers put hooks on shit if I really trust their judgment. Like when I worked with Pharrell [of the Neptunes] in the past, most of the beats he gave me, he already had hooks written. And I trust his ear and his judgment, so I just went with it and wrote the verses. But that's like the easy way out—I [normally] like to challenge myself to come up with the hook and come up with the concept.

◀ IV ▶

Delivery

12

Vocal Techniques

Take it into the studio and take time to perfect your breath, your phrasing, your cadence . . . everything up on the track.

◄ **Zumbi, Zion I** ►

Until you deliver your lyrics in a recording or a live performance, they are just words on the page or in your head. If you don't have a strong grasp of how to deliver them well, listeners will not be interested in the flows you have come up with or the content you're trying to convey. To develop an effective and interesting vocal delivery, you must master several basic vocal techniques.

Breath Control

Breath control allows you to say your rhymes without running out of breath and to adjust the volume and strength of your vocals. If you're not in control of your breathing and you don't get enough air when you're performing your lyrics, then either you won't be able to complete your rhymes or they won't come out the way you intended.

Planet Asia

You have to have your breath control down pat—that's what the whole thing about MCing is.

Steele, Smif N Wessun

[In the supergroup Boot Camp Clik, we're] definitely hard on each other when it comes to breath control, and we've learned from others before us that to be the best MC you possibly can, you have to have good breath control.

KRS-One is a master of breath control, using strong, forceful vocals on all of his tracks—even recording two songs entitled "Breath Control" and "Breath Control II" on Boogie Down Productions' albums *Ghetto Music: The Blueprint of Hip Hop* and *Edutainment*.

O.C., Diggin' in the Crates

Probably the first thing I learned in MCing is breath control, I learned that from KRS. I seen him do a show one time—I seen him rock for two hours that night. He had his hype man or whatever, but for the most part I never seen nothing like that. Like, damn, this dude sounds like his records or better, so I learned that from Kris.

The more complicated your verse is, the more breath control you'll need to pull the song off live. For example, Papoose's popular concept track "Alphabetical Slaughter" goes through all the letters of the alphabet and is harder to perform correctly than a lot of simpler hip-hop tracks.

Papoose

When you're performing your songs and you spit the alphabet, all 26 letters, live, without taking a breath . . . it takes experience. So definitely, it takes some skills, but if you're just a happy-go-lucky type of dude—"I went to the store, *ungh*"—that shit is nothing, but some of the shit I be spitting, it takes breath control.

It's also important to know the limits of your own breath control, so that you don't overstretch yourself on a track.

Zumbi, Zion I

I know when I'm trying to push my breath to the point where it's gonna sound exasperated on a record. It's kinda just knowing what I can do.

How to Improve Your Breath Control

There are several obvious ways of improving your breath control. Akir advises "trying to spit as long as you can without taking a breath," which over time will increase the amount of air you can take in with each breath. As Bobby Creekwater says, "It comes natural. It's like with time and doing it long enough, all of that shit comes natural to you."

Akir also suggests finding "a way to take a breath without making a breath known," which will allow you to take more breaths throughout a verse.

Zumbi, Zion I

Some MCs have like that breathless phrasing where they can spit like almost a minute and a half straight without breathing. I don't know if I'm like that, but I know how to make it *sound* like that by taking breaths, just being relaxed.

Diaphragm Exercises

The breath control needed in MCing is similar to the breath control singing and acting require, so MCs use the same techniques and exercises singers and actors use to project their vocals through their breathing.

K-Os

Singing helps with that, and because I was singing before I was rapping, I think that I already figured that out a little bit.

Akir

Some of my actor friends have put me onto different exercises you can do. I work with diaphragm exercises at times. I lost my voice one time at a show—I had a 30-minute set, I was just finishing the first verse and the first hook of the first song and my voice completely went out, and the rest of the show I did basically from my diaphragm. So I think that's a part of what actually makes people professional artists, both recording artists and performing artists, is to be able to do those exercises so that when things happen, you know how to rock.

Singers and actors practice *diaphragmatic breathing*, using their diaphragm (a sheet of muscle under the lungs) to control their breathing. To breathe in this way, expand your stomach rather than your chest when you breathe in—this fills your lungs more completely, letting you take in more air to strengthen your vocals. To become better at this method of breathing, simply practice inhaling by expanding your stomach and taking slow, deep breaths.

Performing Live as Practice for Breath Control

Performing live is an excellent way to practice and improve your breath control, because it forces you to deliver verses correctly all in one go—there are no retakes when you are performing live. Live shows also require more movement than recording in the studio, which in turn requires more breath.

E-40

When you're doing concerts, you're moving around and that's when you gotta catch your breath in between. I'm a pretty heavyset dude, but I'm not sloppy. I carry my weight well, and when I'm up onstage, I make my presence be felt. My lyrics—you can hear them clear, and that just comes from experience.

Del the Funky Homosapien

Performances in the worst conditions is what has given me better breath control—what doesn't kill you makes you stronger.

Pusha-T, Clipse

[There are] different skills when I'm performing live, [such as] breath control and just knowing how to pace yourself really well [so you don't run out of breath and energy early in a show.]

MCs who regularly perform live find that not only does their breath control improve, but they become more relaxed and comfortable onstage as well.

Zumbi, Zion I

Just from touring for the last five to six years, almost straight through, there's definitely been shows where I can feel that I'm very attuned to what I'm doing now, I don't stress as much, I can breathe.

A lot of MCs also recommend regular cardiovascular workouts so that you won't be out of breath and you'll generally be able to perform more effectively.

Joell Ortiz

The shows and working out every day have helped my breath control.

MURS

I think you need to be in shape. I personally run like a mile and a half to two miles a day just so I can be in shape to run back and forth on the stage—I jump up a lot and just do all types of punk rock shit and swing the microphone. My breath control and my cardio is up, so I don't sound out of breath. I think that's an important skill to have.

Enunciation

Enunciation refers to how accurately and clearly words are said. You have to have good enunciation to be able to pronounce all the separate syllables fluidly and quickly enough to stay in time with the beat. Writing great lyrics with a great flow means nothing if you are stumbling over the words, they are not in time, and no one can tell what you're saying.

Big Daddy Kane

If you say the rhyme to the track and when you're listening back, it sounds like something is mumbled to you . . . if it sounds like that to *you*, then imagine how it's going to sound to everybody else if you can't recognize your own shit.

MCs are often praised for how sharply and clearly they say every syllable in a rhyme—so that the listener can make out every word. For example, Slick Rick and Eminem are considered masters of enunciation.

O.C., Diggin' in the Crates

The Great Adventures of Slick Rick is one of the greatest albums ever, and the stuff he was just saying on there and how it was so clear, I've yet to see that [again]. The [clear] syllable dude was Slick Rick for me.

Cashis

Eminem enunciates his words really, really well. [With] me being from Chicago, I have a Midwestern drawl [when I speak], but when I rap I have to enunciate the words better, because I want to get to that perfection level where he's at. That's [one of the] things that makes Em so special, because he can do voice-overs, he can make his voice sound like a cartoon, he can do whatever he wants in the record, and he enunciates it perfectly so that you still understand it and it sounds insane—that's something that I've definitely picked up from him.

Enunciation is especially important if you plan on rapping fast, because if syllables have to be said more quickly, there is a greater risk that you will mumble or mispronounce them.

2Mex, The Visionaries

I was rapping fast ever since I started rapping, because I came from that school of fast, jazz rapping, so I wanted to rap as fast as I could but at the same time be as coherent as possible. [Enunciation] for me now, it's not as hard, because I've been doing it for so long, but it took a while to develop.

How to Improve Your Enunciation

The most straightforward way to improve your enunciation is to repeat lyrics over and over until you can say them fluidly with no mistakes, with every syllable under your control. Gift of Gab of Blackalicious, known for his strong enunciation and fast rapping style, says, "It doesn't take real long. It's just a matter of going over it, repeating it, repeating it, repeating it—just getting comfortable with what you've just written." If the flow is particularly dense and fast, it pays to practice more than usual.

Zumbi, Zion I

If I'm trying to go outside of my box and [rap very fast] like Twista, I'm gonna practice it so it sounds good.

Twista

[I practice the lyrics a lot], definitely—depending on the rap pattern. Some of the patterns are so loose that usually, if I'm not rapping fast, it's so easy to me that I don't have to practice them a lot, but if I'm rapping fast I practice—not even to memorize it but to give my mouth the experience of repeating the words over and over so I can do it with a little less effort.

Akir

Sometimes what I'll do, especially if it's a very condensed rhyme, I'll try to spit it really, really fast, over and over and over and over again, and see if I can get all the words out properly enunciated while I'm doing that. Enunciation is something that I try to work on, so I might take a line and just repeat it over and over again.

Stressmatic of the Federation says that good enunciation also comes from simply "a lot of recording—once you record a lot, you get used to it." While you're recording, it's also helpful if someone involved in the process tells you when you need to go back and record a lyric with clearer enunciation.

Sheek Louch, D-Block/The LOX

You and your engineer should be tight with it. He should be telling you, "You know what, slow up, get that a little clearer, they need to hear that part right there."

Vocal Style

When you deliver your lyrics, you can adjust your voice in many different ways to create a particular vocal style. You can alter the pitch of your voice and make your delivery more or less melodic. You can adjust how muffled, clear, or nasal your vocals are. You can control your voice's volume and how smooth or harsh it is. An outstanding and unique vocal style can help you to stand out from other MCs.

Schoolly D

I've been doing this for 25 years, and I can do it for another 25 years, because my voice and my style is so distinct.

Cashis

DMX has a great, great voice where he can just speak to you and you understand exactly what he's saying.

Chuck D, Public Enemy

I [think it's important to have a distinct voice], but I can only talk for myself, because I do. If you have a distinct voice and vocal style, it really doesn't matter what language you speak in, you'll command attention. [Someone who doesn't have a great voice,] they can become a great writer, they can even become a great performer, but it might take that much more work to actually get a point across than somebody with just a great voice.

One of the main points of vocal style, according to Akir, is "not being monotone, having a certain level of expression in the recording, which is something that a lot of people don't really take into consideration." He adds that "some people just have it naturally, but part of being a recording artist is to be able to bring that expression out and that feeling on the actual recording." This natural vocal expressiveness can often be the sign of a particularly talented artist.

Brother J, X Clan

That inner voice of talent tells you where to lift your voice up at and where to drop it and where to ride and bounce and play at. That's not a joke, that separates Gladys Knight from "I sing well in the shower"—it's two different worlds. Someone who does it on [that] level . . . it's like the heavens come through their throat, man—that's some powerful thing.

Chuck D of Public Enemy has a powerful, resonant voice that is often acclaimed as one of the most distinct and impressive in hip-hop. His vocal style was inspired not only by other rappers but by sports announcers as well.

Chuck D, Public Enemy

I liked the guys with the great voices, guys like Melle Mel—I thought they were unbelievable. I wanted to become a sports-caster, so the use of my voice actually came about talking about play-by-play announcing in baseball and basketball.

RBX, too, is noted for the strength of his delivery, which is aided by the natural gruffness and color of his voice. His nickname, "The Narrator," reflects how his lyrics are made more vivid through his vocal style.

Another artist with a unique and instantly recognizable vocal style is B-Real of Cypress Hill. Compared with many other rappers, his delivery is more nasal (more of the sound is produced in the nose) and sometimes more melodic.

B-Real, Cypress Hill

You want to be able to stand out from the others and just be distinct, period. A lot of shit sounds the same, so when you got something that can separate you from everybody else, you gotta use it to your advantage.

Devin the Dude is known for his laid-back, smooth, relaxed, and often very melodic vocal style.

Devin the Dude

I like to listen to groups like the Bar-Kays, and groups like Funkadelic and older solo artists like Stevie Wonder or Donny Hathaway, they have distinctive voices. When you hear those voices, you be like, "Oh, that's like an instrument almost." And I just wanted to get my own voice, to make it a certain instrument, so that when people hear it, they go, "Oh, that's . . . the new XJ-9000," ha-ha. I think every voice is like some sort of an instrument—and that's why the price of features go up so much, because of the "instrument" involved.

The type of vocal style you use can say a lot about who you are as an artist, and it can also play into preconceived notions that people have regarding particular styles. This may be either a positive or a negative thing.

David Banner

I feel like southern rappers are just as lyrical as anybody else in the world, but because of our southern drawl we don't get much credit for it. I don't think that's fair—Bun B is one of the best lyricists ever, André 3000 [of OutKast] is one of the best lyricists ever, Scarface is one of the best lyricists ever. Listen to Bun B on a song called "Murder" on the UGK album *Ridin' Dirty*. . . . André 3000 never kicked a wack verse in his life.

Some artists find one style and stick with it, especially if it is popular and successful, while others switch up their techniques for variety, either within the same verse or from song to song. Steele of Smif N Wessun explains how he likes to try various ways of delivering his rhymes:

Steele, Smif N Wessun

I love music, I have a high respect for the instruments of music, and I think that one of the most underrated instru-

ments in music is the vocalist—I'm intrigued by trying different shit. I think that some people find themselves and they
sit there and that's where they at, but then others just continue to do things and flex and bend and do a lot of shit—I
like to do my thing like that.

Yukmouth explains that he changes his voice frequently on
choruses but not very often on verses: "I change my voice up for
the hook [and] do all types of shit, people won't even know it's me,
but as far as my rap game, my voice gonna stay the same."

Sometimes MCs will change their whole style of delivery over
time, either due to personal preference or to keep up with the
new vocal styles that are continually emerging, so that they don't
sound dated.

Andy Cat, Ugly Duckling

When I first started trying to rap, messing around with it in
the '80s, I can remember being in the fifth grade and saying
to my friend, "OK, let me do my rapping voice," and the rap
was like, "Hey, party people in the place to be"—[using] those
sort of [old-school] voices. That was the thing to do, like Kool
Moe Dee's "Wild Wild West," or Kurtis Blow—that's how rappers sounded. It wasn't until later on where the voices really
changed up [with] groups like De La Soul, where you just
had very nontraditional-sounding guys rapping starting to
come in. And then in the '90s with the Wu-Tang and all those
sort of more guttural and ghetto [sounding MCs]—that stuff
started to come around as well.

A lot of MCs formulate exactly how they will use their voice before
they record a track; others prefer to do it more spontaneously.

Termanology

I usually know exactly how I want it to sound. As soon as I go in there, I know what bars I'm gonna sing, what bars I'm gonna rap, which ones I'm gonna scream, which ones I'll stay low.

Mr. Lif

To a large extent, [I have the delivery worked out beforehand], but then you get in there and it's kind of a process of trial and error. Sometimes there's an inflection that I had planned to put on a word that might not be quite the right approach—you always have to refine that and that's why you have to do several takes, to really crystallize it.

Melodies and Matching the Pitch of the Beat

As part of their vocal style, many hip-hop artists like to include elements of melody—they'll sing some of their lyrics instead of rapping them.

Speech, Arrested Development

[For the hit single "Tennessee,"] I just wanted to come up with something unique, and I had just started to discover rhyming and putting it into more of a melodic style. I had never heard it in hip-hop, really, especially for the whole song. Afrika Bambaataa and the Soul Sonic Force would put melody in rhyme, a lot of old-school cats . . . Funky 4 + 1 would put melodies in rhyme, but it would just be for one line of the rhyme. And for me, I saw a whole new opportunity to add more emotion to what I was saying when I started to put more melody to it, and so "Tennessee" was one of the first songs that I did that. . . . "Raining Revolution" was the first.

Artists often mimic melodies that they hear on the track they're rapping over—a synthesizer line, for example. They also create their own melodies that fit over the music. (As Cage says, "I think that's the songwriting thing right there—using your voice as another instrument. Do you match the melodies in the music or do you create your [own] thing?") Steele of Smif N Wessun explains how he comes up with an original melody that is not part of the beat already: "Sometimes I might hum it—I might just have a melody in my head and I might hum it out until I find words to it."

Adding melodic sections can require a slightly different writing style, because lyrics that work well rapped may not work well sung, and vice versa.

K-Os

[Writing lyrics to be sung is different from writing rap lyrics]—there's a cadence difference, and some things don't sound [right]. . . . Like "onomatopoeia," that word, no matter how many times you sing it, it's just not a really sexy word to sing, but if you say it in a rap, you get to fit it somewhere. A word like that is a wicked rap word because it's got so much movement.

Royce Da 5'9"

If I try to do a melodic flow, I'll go in there and [sometimes] forget the melody just because I don't retain melodies that well, not 16 bars' worth of them, because I'm not a singer. If I'm doing a hook, I can retain 8 [bars], but if I want to do 8 bars' worth of one melody and then switch up to a different melody in the verse in order to do [another 8 bars], I might forget. If I do forget, then my only option is to rap the words instead of putting melodies with them and then it's like, shit,

I wouldn't write a regular rap like I would write a melodic rap, so I end up just scrapping it and just starting fresh again.

Using melody adds another dimension to your vocal style and can make your songs more interesting and varied, as Myka 9 of Freestyle Fellowship points out when describing Cee-Lo of Goodie Mob and Gnarls Barkley: "I like Goodie Mob—cats like Cee-Lo are really, really tight and diverse because they incorporate melodic skill as well."

Melody and pitch can play a big part in getting people to remember your lyrics, by giving them some sort of tune they can latch on to. Tech N9ne has a distinct way of saying his own name that grabs your attention—he raises the pitch on the "N9ne" part of his name, and this makes it far more memorable than if he kept it at a regular pitch.

Tech N9ne

I always loved pitch. A lot of rappers are bland, but Tech N9ne, I love pitch. Like I could easily tell you my name . . . what's your name? "Tech N9ne," but you'll remember "Tech *N9nnnNne*!" It's all in the pitch—that makes people remember it.

Creating memorable melodies is a powerful way to increase a song's longevity, a technique that many hip-hop artists have used to good effect. A melodic, easy-to-remember chorus can be especially effective.

Andy Cat, Ugly Duckling

[It's good to use melody sometimes], especially like Slick Rick with "Hey Young World," and Snoop will do it sometimes too, half-singing. Even Eminem, he'll do that stuff once in a while, probably more in choruses than in rap verses, or sometimes in a certain part of a rap verse he'll do it. For most people melody is a lot more catchy than just rhythm, and every big, great hit song over the last 50 years usually has melody. So I think a lot of people who are interested in songwriting are dabbling with melody, especially in the choruses—we've definitely done that sometimes.

Even if you're not fully singing or half-singing sections of the song, it is often useful to match your rapping voice to the general pitch of the beat, so that the overall track becomes more tuneful.

MURS

Most of the time [the lyrics I write are] based on the music, because you want something, a harmony or a melody, that's in sync with the beat you're writing to.

Myka 9, Freestyle Fellowship

I like to rap somewhat in pitch and in tune—I might write a rap that might end up being a song that I sing, because I like to sing too, or something that I sung, I [might make] into a rap chorus—it all depends on the vibe of the scenario.

Other MCs do not entirely match the tune of the beat they're rapping over, but they may alter their voice in some other way to suit that particular track.

Yukmouth

[On] "Puffin Lah," I really took it on some loony shit and changed my voice—I styled [my voice] with the beat. That's like some real shit, like not normal rap shit, strictly style— that shows that I'm [an MC] that knows how to work styles.

If the pitch of your voice is an especially bad match for the pitch of the beat, your rapping can sound unintentionally grating. This often comes from not knowing which notes or pitches work harmoniously with one another. Groups of notes that work together musically are called *keys*, and the notes in one of these groups are said to be "in the same key." If you listen to a recording of your vocals over the beat, you can often hear when you're off-key, as your voice will not seem to "fit" with the other instruments on the track. By altering your pitch until you no longer hear this discord, you can often produce vocals that are more on-key.

Bishop Lamont

There's a few that's on the same page with understanding rapping in key—[some] cats be sounding so garbage over their beats because they don't realize keys, they don't understand tones [pitches]. You have to approach it the same way you approach an R&B record—that's why motherfuckers be shouting over records that they shouldn't be shouting over, they be sounding all raspy over shit they shouldn't sound raspy over. They have no understanding of keys and tones and adjusting to complement the beat.

Musicians also adjust their melody and pitch to reflect the content and emotions of their songs, giving the listener a clearer picture of what they're trying to convey. Pharoahe Monch explains that MCs do this with their voices just as jazz musicians have done it with their instruments for many decades.

Pharoahe Monch

With a sax or a horn up in the higher range of pitches, you can sound like a bird or you can sound frustrated, [and] in the lower ranges, you could sound aggravated or fat or jolly, like an elephant, and jazz musicians used this because most of their works are instrumentation. So if John Coltrane is doing a piece called "Africa," and he wants to convey to the listener how beautiful he thinks elephants are, it'd probably be in the lower range. And how fast he thinks a cheetah is or how beautiful a cheetah is it'd probably be [in the mid to higher ranges] and with very quick rhythms, painting a picture. You'll notice that from song to song—my voice is different on "Hypnotical Gases" and "Prisoners of War" than it is on "Chicken," and my voice is different on "Simon Says" than it is on "Behind Closed Doors" or "Desire."

Sometimes, depending on the beat, you may want to change the pitch of your voice simply to be heard more effectively over the other elements on the track. For example, if you give your vocals too much bass on a track in which there is a lot of bass already in the mix, then those pitches could conflict with and obscure the vocals.

Esoteric

Some beats I can get on top of—my voice is a unique voice in terms of its pitch—[and] sometimes I try to make it a little bassier, but I can't get on top of the beat that way. There are certain beats where I come in and have a force over the beat, and there's other beats that I feel I'm getting drowned out by. It all depends on a way a song is mixed, the instruments being played, the degree of bass and volume on the drums, or whatever.

Syncopation

Syncopation is a form of vocal styling in which an MC delivers the lyrics very slightly before or after the beat, rather than exactly on the beat. This difference is so slight that it would not change how the flow looks in the flow diagram from the previous chapters—instead, it is something that can only be felt when saying the lyrics over the track. This technique is similar to the "swing" that jazz musicians use in their music.

Shock G, Digital Underground

My friend Saafir, a West Coast underground champion, once told me he gets his word patterns from jazz horn players like Charlie Parker and John Coltrane, [and] he swings his words around the beat rather than on it.

If the vocals fall before the beat, it sounds like the verse is rushing along, and this gives the lines more urgency. Eminem occasionally does this to make a rap sound more on edge. If the vocals are slightly behind the beat, they sound more laid-back and casual. Snoop Dogg sometimes uses this technique to give his raps a nonchalant, relaxed feel, as does Evidence of Dilated Peoples.

Evidence, Dilated Peoples

I have a slow flow—I always rhyme behind the beat. A lot of rappers nail the drums [hitting the beat exactly], and that's a beautiful thing if you have that talent. . . . It's also a talent to know how to stay behind the rhythm—it's something a lot of people don't know how to do. A lot of the people who nail the drums literally can't stay behind the beat.

Presence/Swagger

Your presence and attitude on the microphone also can be important elements of your vocal style. Some rappers don't necessarily have the greatest content or flow, or the most precise delivery, but they give themselves an edge by conveying their personality and charisma through their delivery.

Thes One, People Under the Stairs

Biz [Markie] has a ton of classic songs, more than most people, and it wasn't about how dope his rhyme was, it was about the way that it fit over the beat and his attitude and his approach—for a lack of a better term, his *swagger*. . . . Sometimes it means more than the rhyme.

Guerilla Black says, "The swagger—that's one of the big things right now," which can be seen in the rise of Lil Wayne, who is often commended for the swagger he has on his records. By injecting your delivery with this kind of personality, you can add more life and intrigue to ordinary words and phrases and make even a well-written verse more entertaining.

Bootie Brown, The Pharcyde

Presence on the microphone is everything. It's like Guru [of Gang Starr] said—the voice, it's the voice. That has a lot to do with it because when you hear somebody say "yeah" and then you hear Lil Jon say "YEEEAH!" it's totally different. It's like Flavor Flav saying "booyyeee!"—it's presence. I think presence has a lot to do with the whole situation.

Guerilla Black

I want my swagger to be where you remember it so [that] what I'm saying is actually cutting through. I could have all of the crazy wordplay and all of the crazy punch lines, but the way I'm saying it is gonna make the difference.

Recording to Develop Your Style

With today's technology, recording yourself is relatively straight-forward—as Brother Ali puts it, "Every kid that has a computer basically has a home recording studio." Many MCs recommend recording a lot to develop your own vocal style. This lets you hear exactly how you sound on a track so you can tell what you need to do to improve your voice or change the way you're using it until you're happy with how it sounds.

Devin the Dude

I think you have to develop [your vocal style], and it comes [from] however much experience you have in the booth and how much you hear your voice after you record it. You kinda pick out certain things you want to change to develop a style—a lot of styles are incorporated in what I do.

Brother Ali

I think people should record themselves, if you're able to do that, and really use it as a way to develop what you're doing. When we record the rough versions of songs, we record those at [producer] Ant's house on an old cassette four-track, and that's when we work that kind of stuff out—we'll just try playing with the delivery of things.

By recording your vocals, you get a much better idea of how you sound than when you rap out loud to yourself. This is because when you rap out loud, you hear your own voice through the vibrations in your body in addition to the vibrations in the air, which makes it sound different to you than it does to everyone else. You're also concentrating on delivering the vocals, so it's difficult to listen to them at the same time.

Big Pooh, Little Brother

You don't know how you sound and how you're coming across until after you record it and you listen to it—then you can get a proper gauge on the way you're saying it. It's one thing when you just write and you say it out loud, but you really can't hear yourself because you're really trying to say the words, so you need to record so you can go back and check what you were doing.

Recording yourself is a great way to hone your delivery skills and experiment with how you're going to say your rhymes, but it can also help you recognize when you're drifting too much in the direction of one of your favorite rappers and copying his or her vocal style. This is a common issue for MCs, as they tend to mimic whoever they happen to like.

Andy Cat, Ugly Duckling

I know I tried a couple of different voice tones, especially early on, because I liked Q-Tip so much, and Guru. So sometimes I'll hear a recording and I'll be like, "Oh, man, I was definitely trying to Q-Tip that one." So try a few things, because you can't help but do that sometimes—you meet guys who love Eminem and it's hard to help doing what [he does] if that's where you learned your style from, [and] you definitely wanna get past that.

Taking Care of Your Voice

Because your voice is your instrument for delivering your rhymes to people, it is important to look after it. You can damage your voice by straining it and not properly resting it, so be careful to avoid these tendencies when recording or performing live.

Pusha-T, Clipse

Making sure you don't scream [is important]. I'm about to be on the road for this month—I'm in Europe for a month—and I'm trying my damnedest to come home with a voice. If I can come home with a voice, homeboy, I'm on.

Touring can take its toll on the vocal cords, and using your voice correctly is important to keeping it in good working order.

Immortal Technique

Obviously my voice is a little deeper now from [my first album, *Revolutionary*] *Vol. 1*, or even a tiny bit more raspy from [*Revolutionary*] *Vol. 2*, and it's because I do a hundred shows a year at least—so it takes a toll. I started taking voice lessons because of shit like that, because it's just making my voice real gruff—I try to keep it like so I can actually speak to people audibly.

Many up-and-coming MCs don't pay proper attention to maintaining their voices. Vinnie Paz of Jedi Mind Tricks, known for his guttural vocals, explains that "the process of taking care of your voice is a whole art in and of itself. There are a lot of younger MCs, you see them do one show and their voice will be blown out."

13

In the Studio

*I love creating a new song—when I go to the studio
and I'm about to create a new baby.*
◄ Dray, Das EFX ►

The studio is where your vocals are recorded—where your content, flow, and delivery all come together to make an actual hip-hop track for you and others to listen to. A "studio" can range from an expensive professional recording facility to a home computer with a microphone. Even the most basic recording opportunities define you as an artist, and recording regularly can improve every aspect of your MCing.

Esoteric

When I took the idea of wanting to be an MC, that's really pretty much all I did. I would come home from school and I had this little tape recorder, real primitive-looking tape recorder—you just throw the cassette in—and I would make an instrumental just looping up somebody's beat on a cassette—[called] a *pause tape*. I would just rap over that and I'd do that pretty much every day after school until the night—write lyrics and deliver them over the beat. I mean, I made a lot of shitty recordings, a lot of shitty songs, but all that helped to shape me into who I am today and what I'm doing today.

C-Murder

They gotta get in the booth and keep laying songs and laying songs—that's the only way you're gonna get to be a good MC. Laying in that booth is different from just rapping to your homies—you gotta get in there and lay a lot of songs, and then you're gonna get your style and your flow together.

Recording is a vital step in your development as an MC, because you need recordings of your songs if you want to share your music with others, sell records, or even convince people to come to your shows. As Buckshot of Black Moon says, "Without hearing a record, you don't wanna see the group live. You gotta hear the record first in order to go, 'Hey, I wanna go and see that live.'"

Reading or Memorizing the Lyrics

Reading the Lyrics

When recording a song, an artist may choose to either read the lyrics or perform them from memory. Many MCs find that reading the lyrics works best for them. Some say that if you take the time to memorize a song, you may lose some of the enthusiasm you felt for the lyrics when you first wrote them. B-Real of Cypress Hill says, "Sometimes when you do it off the jump, it's fresh and it's got a certain energy to it. For me, when I memorize it too much, it seems robotic." Others simply enjoy reading the lyrics as part of their creative process. Steele of Smif N Wessun says, "Most of the time I read them from the paper, even when I know them. I think everybody has their methods—that's just one of the methods that I like."

If you don't have a great memory, or if you write and record an especially large number of songs, then reading the lyrics may be particularly helpful.

Del the Funky Homosapien

My memory is shot from all the dizzying travels that I've been on and the terrible episodes I've experienced in my life. So memorizing lyrics is kind of a task for me—I can memorize them good enough to look at the paper and recite them on the mic with flavor, but not without the sheet in front of me. Also, I write so many rhymes I couldn't possibly remember them all.

Finally, the demands of the recording process can often mean that reading the lyrics is an MC's best or only option.

Fredro Starr, Onyx

You might be on your way to the studio [and you] gotta get a record done, so sometimes you might go in just with your book.

Speech, Arrested Development

I think the reason I read them is because I play more than one role. A lot of cats that I work with that are MCs will memorize theirs, but they only MC, they don't produce. I produce music as well, so for me that's a long process—there's just too much to do, so I just think [memorizing] is a luxury that I can't afford to do sometimes.

Memorizing the Lyrics

Alternatively, there are MCs who prefer to memorize the lyrics before they record them. Wise Intelligent of Poor Righteous

Teachers says that it's something he learned as standard practice: "I come from that school where you had to have it in your head— you had to have your rhymes in your head and just spit it."

One of the main advantages of memorizing a song is that you can often be more creative with the delivery, because you aren't focused on simply trying to get the rhyme out correctly. (Some MCs go so far as to memorize not just the words but how they're delivered as well.)

Big Daddy Kane

I think that when you have the lyrics memorized it's a little better, because you're not concentrating on reading the words and you can concentrate on the cadence, so it makes it a lot easier if you just want to play with it and deliver the words a little differently.

One Be Lo, Binary Star

I think that it's important to memorize the lyrics. When I'm in the booth and I know the verse, it's all about styling, it's all about feeling—I can just say it how I feel it. If I don't got the verse memorized, I'm spending more time and energy remembering what to say instead of how to say it. I coach a lot of MCs in the booth, so many people are caught up in "What am I gonna say," but *how* you're gonna say it is just as important. So I don't just memorize what I'm saying, I memorize how I'm gonna say it so it's easier for me to play around with it.

Other MCs memorize their lyrics because they feel that listeners can hear when they're reading or because they themselves can hear it even if no one else can.

K-Os

Sometimes I hear a rapper and I can hear when they're reading off paper.

Tajai, Souls of Mischief

You can hear your page flip—you can tell you're reading it. Other people can't, but you can tell you're reading when you're reading.

Memorizing also means that you automatically get better at saying the rhyme, because you have to practice a lot in order to memorize it. And studio sessions may be quicker and less frustrating if you turn up with your lyrics memorized and ready to deliver.

Mr. Lif

There's a raw essence when you already know the rhyme. You only get better at delivering it when you know it like the back of your hand.

Tash, Tha Alkaholiks

Some songs I've got in my head, I've known for weeks, so when I get there, push the button—the whole studio session takes an hour and we're gone.

A lot of artists don't memorize the lyrics 100 percent of the time but prefer to if the situation allows. For instance, Glasses Malone says, "I try to. Sometimes I don't get a chance like I'd like to, but most of the time I try to. That's what I find the best—when I know all of my words."

Half-Memorizing the Lyrics

Many artists like to have the lyrics half-memorized—they still take a written form of the lyrics with them into the studio, but it's just a reference in case there are parts they can't fully remember. This can make for a smoother recording session.

Royce Da 5′9″

Even when I'm spitting it off my paper, I'm kind of going off the mind, because for the most part I got it memorized—I'm not reading it word for word when I'm spitting it in the booth. It's like giving a speech: I'm looking at one area of the paper, and then I move to another area of the paper while I'm rapping, just so I can keep my spot.

El Da Sensei

If I can memorize at least to a point where I know how the pronunciation is gonna sound on certain words, and put emphasis on certain sentences or words, phrases, I'll be at a point where I can complete the song faster, because I actually kept saying it to myself to get used to it.

In fact, no matter how completely you've memorized your lyrics, taking the written rhyme with you when you're recording is still a good idea. As David Banner says, "Even if I memorized it, I still have the paper there just in case, because you're in a studio, you're recording. Time is still money. You don't have time to be playing—just get it."

Ways to Memorize the Lyrics

If you write your lyrics down on paper, the main way to memorize them is simply to repeat them over and over again, either while you write them or as you perform them.

Vast Aire, Cannibal Ox

The way I write is . . . I write a line, say it, write the next line, then say everything again, so from doing that, I learn my rhymes quickly. By the time the rhyme is fully written on the page, it's all in my mind, so the page is a reference by that time.

Vinnie Paz, Jedi Mind Tricks

In the beginning I would write these rhymes and I would still
be on the street battling people [with those rhymes], so I had
like everything memorized. So back in the day, like the early
'90s, I didn't really even have use for the rhyme book after a
certain amount [of time], because these are the rhymes that
you would battle people with.

Breaking the lyrics down into more manageable sections also
helps. El Da Sensei says, "I try to practice bracket by bracket, like
the whole [first] verse, [then the whole second] verse."

If you write your lyrics in your head, then you won't need to
make a separate effort to memorize them, since the technique
forces you to memorize them while you are writing them. Esoteric
says that by writing his lyrics this way, "the cadence, the flow, and
the rhyme patterns are already in my head."

Practicing the Vocals

Whether or not you choose to memorize your vocals, the majority
of MCs say it is important to practice them at least several times
before recording so that you can deliver them smoothly. Even if
you have limited time before you record the vocals, Devin the
Dude says, "It's a matter of going over it, constantly, constantly, as
much as you can before you actually go inside the booth."

Some MCs practice delivering the rhymes while they're writing them, so by the time the whole song is complete, they have
already practiced saying the words many times.

Dray, Das EFX

When I'm writing a song, by the time it's done and you hear
it, I've rehearsed those rhymes about at least three hundred
times. While I'm writing the verses, I'm rehearsing them, so

by the time I get to the studio, I'll have already said that one verse hundreds of times.

Practicing the vocals a lot has several advantages. Wordsworth says, "After you say a verse so many times, you realize the flexibility of the flow and the way to say it." MC Serch agrees that getting a good vocal take "comes through rehearsal and practice," and says that he'll practice the vocals "a couple of hundred times" because "you just don't want to waste time in the studio—you really just want to go in and do what you are there to do. Get it popping and get it done."

Practicing the lyrics is also a simple way to memorize or half-memorize them. As mentioned in the previous section, they will automatically stay in your memory if you repeat them many times.

Big Pooh, Little Brother

I read right off the BlackBerry [in the recording session]. I don't memorize the rhyme before I record it, but I have repeated it enough times to where now I'm just using the written words as a guide. Like if you're doing a speech, you could have your note cards, just using them as a guide—that's how I use the BlackBerry now. I've repeated the rhymes so many times that now you can't tell if I'm reading it or if I've memorized it.

Other artists, however, don't spend much time practicing their lyrics. They believe the song comes out better when it hasn't been over-rehearsed.

2Mex, The Visionaries

I've just maybe read it like 10 times, tried it 5 times, and then I'm like, "I'm ready—let's do it," and then you just figure it out because it's fresh. As soon as I finish writing, then I want to walk in and knock it out, like within five minutes.

Q-Tip, A Tribe Called Quest

I just say it a few times and I know the idea of what I'm saying—you connect to the spirit of what you're saying. People can have the words memorized and spit them back to you without a glitch but [with] no emotion or no feeling.

The more you get used to writing and recording verses, the easier the process becomes, so an experienced artist simply may not need to spend as much time practicing a verse. Gift of Gab of Blackalicious says, "It's just a matter of saying it a couple of times to myself. I can memorize a rhyme pretty fast because I've been doing this for so long."

Deciding Where to Breathe

Before or during recording, decide where you're going to breathe within the verses so that you don't run out of breath.

2Mex, The Visionaries

I know when to take that little breath that's gonna make it seem like you didn't take a breath.

Shock G, Digital Underground

I walk around and test-bust it loud and live, to make sure I can breathe it.

Many MCs work out the breathing spaces before they record the vocals. They may insert places to breathe into the lyrics as they write them—see chapter 7, p. 128, for information on how to use rests to create breathing spaces.

Havoc, Mobb Deep

You have to have a time where you gotta take a breath, so you gotta write the rhyme accordingly. If you don't, the rhyme won't sound right.

Tech N9ne

I write my songs to perform, [and] the little breaths allow me to say it. People go crazy, like, "How did he do that?"—but that breath did it. I take big breaths on "Einstein." It's written to be able to perform that shit—there's breaths planted there so you can get it across.

Other MCs don't decide when to breathe until the actual recording process begins. Some suggest that as you go through each song, you write down the places you plan to breathe.

Thes One, People Under the Stairs

The paper provides you kind of like a map through the verse so you know where you're gonna take breaths.

Masta Ace

I don't decide ahead of time, but as I'm laying it down, I may find a spot where [it's like,] wow, that's gonna be kinda tricky, so I need to make sure before I hit that line [that] I take a really, really quick, deep breath and then I have to spit all of this together before I can breathe again. I figure that kinda stuff out as I'm in the booth trying to do it.

Still other artists prefer not to actively think about where to breathe at all—they let it work itself out as they go. For some of them, thinking about it may even affect their natural delivery.

Wildchild, Lootpack

I don't really try to think about it too much—you just gotta feel it.

Stressmatic, The Federation

I don't really think about it—if I thought about it, I'd probably be [out of breath all the time].

Knowing where to breathe in a verse and how to take those
breaths correctly can also be honed by performing live. As El Da
Sensei says, "That also comes from being a seasoned MC."

Guide Vocals

A guide vocal is a rough version of the vocals that you record and
then take away from the studio to listen to. You use this recording to help you memorize your lyrics and/or to look for places
where you could improve your delivery, and then you go back
into the studio and record a new version. This process could
be repeated several times until you get the vocal take that you
want.

The Lady of Rage

I do that with everything. I lay it down, I take it home, I listen
to it, I'm like, "I should have said this that way" or "I didn't
take a breath right here." I analyze it and then I do it over.

If an MC does an initial take and is not happy with it, often
he or she will decide to turn that take into a guide vocal. B-Real
of Cypress Hill says, "Sometimes what I'll do, if I don't feel like I
kicked it 100 percent, I'll listen to what I've put down, memorize
it, and then come back and redo it."

One of the easiest ways to commit a song to memory is to use
the written lyrics to record a guide vocal and then listen to the
recording to memorize the song. By hearing the lyrics and rapping
along, they stay in your memory more effectively than if you're
trying to memorize them from the paper alone.

Masta Ace

Typically what I do is, I go in the booth, I have the paper, I spit it off the paper, I listen back to it over the course of a couple of weeks—that's how I memorize my songs, by listening to them over and over—then once I've memorized it, I go back in the booth and I re-record it, memorized.

Recording over Several Takes or in One Take

Recording over Several Takes (Punch-Ins)

Many times, a hip-hop song is not recorded all in one take. Instead, many MCs use punch-ins, a technique in which they record part of the vocal track, then stop, and then "punch in" the rest of the track. Most MCs at least record each verse separately, and some like to punch in line by line, or every four lines, or just to fix mistakes in a vocal take.

Gorilla Zoe

I do as much as I can in one take and then I punch in—it's the art of recording, it's like drawing a picture . . . recording *artist.*

Gift of Gab, Blackalicious

You can nail four lines exactly like you wanted to and it's like, "OK, well, these other lines could be better compared to these other four lines," so you go back. I like doing it like that because I like to be able to focus on four bars or eight bars at a time and then making sure that I got those eight bars out exactly like I wanted them, and then move on.

Punching In to Correct Mistakes

Punch-ins are most commonly used to correct mistakes—when an MC has gone all the way through a verse and is happy with most of it but wants to fix just a few words or lines.

Cormega

I like to do punch-ins if I mess up—[then] you gotta do a punch-in.

40 Cal, Dipset

I'll do punch-ins because I play with a lot of flows, so all the words might not be clear. I might listen to it later and be like, "Damn, I mispronounced that word a little bit."

Punching In as an Effect

Many artists also use punch-ins as a way to add vocal effects to particular lines. For instance, a line may sound more powerful if it's punched in than if it's delivered as part of a longer take.

Fredro Starr, Onyx

I worked with Big Pun, one of the greats, and he punches every two lines. He was giving you so much energy out of every line, so he punched every line—he had his own technique. I heard [Ol'] Dirty Bastard just rhymed and they chopped his shit up and put it together—there's so many different ways to record your vocals.

Similarly, if you've written a line with a particular vocal effect in mind, it may be easier to pull it off as a punch-in than to switch between vocal styles in a single take.

Pharoahe Monch

[With] certain songs, it's better if you punch in, depending on how you write the record. It could be a song where you literally scream the first line and then cry the second line and whisper the third line, and so on and so forth, and just to get the proper inflection on those pieces, you might want to retake some things—just like a film, like, "Cut! Let's do this crying part all over again."

Slick Rick is a master of such punch-ins. Often in his story rhymes he will use different voices for different characters, and the change between characters is emphasized by using punch-ins. As Tajai of Souls of Mischief describes, "That's cool, [when you're] doing it like Slick Rick, going on top of yourself, where you're rapping like you're two people."

Punching In for Radio Edits

If a song has profanity in it, then often the MC records a special version called a radio edit, in which the strong language is toned down so the song can be broadcast on the radio. The MCs may use punch-ins to record the toned-down portions—as Cashis says, "I only do punch-ins on radio edits, because I don't feel like re-rapping the whole song. I'll just rap the part that needs to be taken out to be played on the radio."

Making Punch-Ins Seamless

When a song contains punch-ins, MCs usually like to make sure it sounds as much as possible like one continuous take, especially if the punch-ins are just to correct a mistake. Havoc of Mobb Deep says, "After a while, if it's taking too long, I'll punch in, but I'll try to make the punch as unnoticeable as possible." If a punch-in is done well, it's very difficult to spot it. As Wordsworth says, "I do punch-ins, man, don't nobody know the difference. I can say I did it in one take—would you know?"

If punch-ins aren't up to a certain standard, however, then careful listeners (particularly other MCs) can often pick them out.

Guerilla Black

Sometimes people don't know. You could listen to their album and a lot of people don't know because they're not in the studio—they don't know anything about it. But I be hearing [people's] punches all the time.

Recording a seamless punch-in is easier now than it was in the past, thanks to technological advances. Of course, results will depend on the quality of the recording equipment and software you use.

Tajai, Souls of Mischief

We used to record on tape, [but] with digital it's like you could do it in punch-ins and the shit can come out better than if you did it in one take, because you're never gonna run out of breath.

Del the Funky Homosapien

My software I use [Ableton Live] allows very simple punching, and it works seamlessly.

In addition to the programs and hardware you're using, the skill of the studio engineers you're working with also contributes to the quality of your punch-ins.

Bootie Brown, The Pharcyde

[It] depends on the engineer behind the boards. If you're

working with a producer, they can say, "Hey, you know what, we need to keep this part, because the way you said it is tight, now do this" . . . they can tell you how to piece your rhymes together. If you don't have that real super engineer, there's always gonna be little breaks with punch-ins—it's gonna be slightly off. Somebody who knows the difference can tell the difference. Though depending on the rhymer, depending on what you're talking about, [it can work]. I heard Big Pun did line by line—I heard he did four bars at the most. He had to have a hell of a super engineer!

Recording in One Take

Alternatively, many artists prefer to avoid punch-ins by recording a whole verse, or a whole song, in one take.

AZ

I wouldn't say I never did a punch-in, but the majority of the time I try not to punch in—I'd rather do the verse over than have to punch in.

Wise Intelligent, Poor Righteous Teachers

I've done punch-ins but I prefer all in one take because that's the school I come from—I come from an era when there was no automation, really. We wasn't really using automated boards when we recorded our first three albums—that didn't happen until we recorded the *New World Order* album. So, Poor Righteous Teachers, we were a one-take crew, and not just one take but one take for a whole song too.

Some artists see one-take recording as a rite of passage. They believe that an MC should be allowed to use punch-ins only once he or she has mastered the ability to record vocals in one take without making mistakes.

Sean Price, Heltah Skeltah

In [the supergroup] Boot Camp [Clik,] you gotta earn the right to punch in, and what I mean by that is, when I did *Nocturnal*, I never punched in nothing. Like if I wanted to punch in, Buckshot would be so disappointed in me, like, "Aw, man, come on, man, don't punch in, man—you wrote it, say it . . . *you wrote it, say it.*" And I did the whole album like that. On *Magnum Force*, we did it like that too. We punch in now, but at Boot Camp you gotta earn that right. You just can't come [as a] rookie and just be like, "Punch this in, punch that in"—no, you gotta earn that right.

Making It Easier to Perform Live

Recording a song all in one take is extremely useful if you're preparing to perform it live, since you'll have to say it in one go for the live performance.

Thes One, People Under the Stairs

For any MC I'm engineering for, I try to encourage [him or her] to get it down in one take. If you can't say it, then don't put it in a song—it's kind of a bad look if you can't do it live.

Rah Digga

I don't punch at all, never did. I feel like if you can't say it all in one shot in the booth, how are you going to do it onstage?

A Better Take

If you record a vocal all in one take, you can often achieve better results than if you piece the track together from different takes. Some artists believe that relying on punch-ins robs songs of their emotion and energy.

Ill Bill

I prefer it better if it's all in one take. I just feel it sounds more natural.

Styles P, D-Block/The LOX

The thing a lot of our fans love is the lyrics and the passion inside of it. I don't think I could give you the passion and that "uhh" feeling if I was to punch. I feel like I'm trying to go "*aarrgh!*" at you. . . . If I punch in, you can't punch a "*aarrgh*"—impossible.

A single take may also include small mistakes that would be eliminated via punch-ins, but if these imperfections are allowed to remain, they can sometimes add color and interest to the track.

Hell Rell, Dipset

It sounds better in one take. It's the emotion and the highs and lows in the voice—I like to hear the emotion in the artist's voice, I like to hear a voice crack sometimes here and there, because it's like . . . true, raw.

Finally, recording in a single take allows for a vocal consistency that is hard to beat when you're punching in—especially if you are doing varied things with your voice in the song. Chuck D of Public Enemy says, "I really don't like to punch in—with the amount of inflections I put into a rhyme, it definitely sounds like it's consistent [in one take]."

Number of Takes

The number of takes an MC must record to complete a verse or song differs from artist to artist and from verse to verse. David Banner says, "Sometimes I can get it the first time, [but] I've done as many as 80 takes on one verse before."

Some MCs prefer to get the vocals recorded in only a few takes. (AZ says he'll get it in "one shot or two shots . . . three if I'm drunk.") They often feel that the first take is generally the freshest and the best.

Thes One, People Under the Stairs

In my experience as an engineer, and as a producer and a rapper, the first take is usually the best take. So even if someone is just testing the mic, I usually have the tape rolling because that first take, it usually has all the excitement and the passion that the later takes could end up missing.

Even when an artist likes to do it in one take, he or she will often record a second or third just in case. As Rah Digga explains, "Most of the time I can do it in the first take, but I always do a second one for safety."

On the other hand, some MCs prefer to take their time and do several takes—like the members of D-Block/The LOX.

Styles P, D-Block/The LOX

I never rush recording, I don't believe in that. I'm the exact opposite—I do it a thousand times until it's right, if I have to.

Sheek Louch, D-Block/The LOX

When you own your own studio, ain't no "I only got this amount of hours, then I gotta get out because this other artist is coming in"—ain't none of that. I don't like to record nothing quickly.

Multiple takes are often needed because you listen to a track later and decide you want to redo it, as Termanology notes: "Sometimes you're in the booth and you're mad tired at three in the morning—you might be able to spit it better the next day when you got some energy and breakfast in you."

Doubling Up and Ad-Libs

Doubling up vocals (sometimes called *overdubbing*, *double track-ing*, or *stacking* vocals) is when an artist records another layer of vocals over an existing take, to make the lyrics sound fuller and stronger. Ad-libs are improvised comments and words that are mixed into the background of a track to add more interest.

Some MCs prefer not to double up their vocals at all—Chuck D of Public Enemy says, "I prefer a single track"—while some like to record complete doubles of their verses and choruses.

Cashis

I don't have the loudest voice, [so] I layer my voice. I stack my vocals a lot so that my voice sounds big—it gets mixed well on the record so that you can hear everything that I do. I do a lot of stacks—I do 8 vocal tracks for the verses and I do 11 vocal tracks for the chorus, and then I do 2 ad-lib tracks through the whole record. Each artist, you do it differently—Eminem does stacks and I do a lot of stacks.

In between those two extremes is a common doubling-up tech-nique: instead of stacking whole verses, an MC will repeat certain key words and phrases in the lyrics to emphasize them.

Thes One, People Under the Stairs

After you lay the verse, you hear certain words—you want to overdub those, so you underline them, and then you go back in the booth and say the words that are underlined.

Twista

I do a lot of ad-libs, double-ups—some people double up the whole flow, which is dope. I feel like Jadakiss is the originator of the full double-flow style. But me, like the regular way you do it, you kinda accent the last words of each bar—that's the way I do it the most.

Further Editing the Lyrics

While many MCs go through a rigorous editing phase when they write their lyrics (see chapter 10, p. 197), there are also those who will do further editing during or after the recording of the song. After listening to the actual recording many times, they may have new ideas that didn't occur to them during the writing process.

Havoc, Mobb Deep

Sometimes you gotta live with a song, and after you live with it, sleep with it, you might see a different vision for it.

Andy Cat, Ugly Duckling

[Sometimes] in the process, you're recording and you're listening back, you may be like, "Let me change that."

Fredro Starr, Onyx

I look back in my rap books right now and I'll look at the old "Throw Ya Gunz" rhymes and "Slam" rhymes [and] my books are totally different from the records that come out. You could write a record and then change it, like you'll record it and then you'll change certain things about the record. I like to go in the studio and hear it, and if I don't like it, I change it up.

Zumbi, Zion I

Sometimes it sounds good when I'm saying it in my head, [and then] when I take it to the mic, there's maybe too many syllables, or it's jumbling over, it's not locking to the beat the way I thought it would, so I have to edit it once again.

Some MCs will simply change the lyrics on the spot, without rewriting the actual lines on paper. Others like to have the written rhymes with them when they record so that they can physically edit them as they find things they want to change.

Zumbi, Zion I

A lot of the editing is actually just in the performance. I don't even change it on paper, [I] just kinda learn the flow of the rhyme and I'll leave out certain words to make it sound better.

MC Serch

Sometimes when I write and then I go in and record it, there are those occasions where it doesn't lay right. So I'll have to do an edit, and I have the rhyme right there so I can edit out the words and feel how it's gonna be phrased and sit into a pattern.

Rejecting Lyrics

Occasionally you may want to reject a whole verse, chorus, or song once you hear it back on the recording. Some lyrics may look great on paper but simply don't work when you've recorded them, so don't feel that you have to use everything just because you've recorded it.

Masta Ace

That happens all the time—that's part of the creative process when you're putting together a record or an album. You write something down and at the moment it sounds really dope, and then you get in the booth, and you're spitting it and you can just feel that it's not right, and you go back to the drawing board. I've laid verses down where I was like ashamed of that verse, like I don't like that verse at all, like erase it, and you gotta make sure the engineer erases it, because you don't wanna hear it again.

Tajai of Souls of Mischief warns that it pays to take your time and prepare yourself to reject things if they don't work, because a record will potentially stay around much longer than it took to record it: "We're not trying to just bust out of there, because it lasts a lot longer than your recording session."

Producer Vocal Direction

Just as many artists appreciate it when producers offer writing advice (see chapter 11, p. 231), most MCs are open to producers giving them input and feedback on their delivery as well, especially if the producer is known for making great records.

Pusha-T, Clipse
[The Neptunes (Pharrell Williams and Chad Hugo)], they're producers—that's the difference between them and other people. Certain people are just beat-makers—other people are producers. They definitely give a good amount of vocal coaching insight.

Stressmatic, The Federation
On the Federation projects it's basically just Rick Rock [producing] all the way, so he's the one that gives the input like, "You should spit it like this." It's really helpful because he's worked with a lot of artists [he's produced for Snoop Dogg, E-40, Jay-Z, and G-Unit, among others] and he knows what it should sound like and what it's not supposed to sound like.

Dr. Dre and DJ Premier, two of hip-hop's most lauded producers, are known not only for giving a lot of vocal direction but also for going as far as stopping an MC in the middle of a verse if they feel that artist isn't delivering it to the best of his or her ability.

The Lady of Rage
That's what I like—Dre and Premier, they both do that. If I'm laying down my lyrics and maybe I didn't put enough into

it or didn't say it right, they'll cut me off, they won't let me go to the end of the rhyme. They'll say, "Nah, nah, nah, do that again," or "Do that better," or "Say it like this," and I like that—that doesn't offend me or bother me.

Devin the Dude

When I worked with Dr. Dre [on his album *2001*], he wanted a lot of input in it. He was real particular about it, about the way I said this or "Bring the bridge back in again"—certain ways like that he wanted to orchestrate it. Which was cool— at the time I wasn't really used to that, [but] it was real cool, and I was very surprised and very fortunate to see some of the work ethics that he used.

A producer who is an experienced MC and recording artist can also be a valuable source of vocal advice, because he or she will have firsthand knowledge of your role in the recording process. Shady Records artist Stat Quo says that Eminem will give him input, not necessarily into the writing of the rhymes but "actually the recording of it, how to pronounce things—[Eminem] definitely puts his input in there."

While most MCs are open to producer input, it will usually depend on the producer and the type of advice that is being given.

Hell Rell, Dipset

If I respect their vision, I'll let them give me some input, like, nah, Hell Rell, I should say the hook like this, because it matches with the beat, or whatever, and if it sounds hot I'll pretty much go with it. I'm used to constructive criticism. I won't let just anybody tell me what to do, but certain produc- ers, I respect their opinion and their craft—I'll let them give input.

Ill Bill

I think if the producer is responsible for the music on the track, it's fair to take some direction from him, if that direction is there. It's on a case-by-case basis—I'm not necessarily gonna take direction from some dude that might be a new jack that has a hot beat that I'm fucking with—it doesn't mean I'm gonna let him direct me on the track—but if it's DJ Premier, I'm gonna listen to anything he has to say.

14

Performing Live

Ability to connect with the audience, confidence, rehearsal,
ability to improvise—everything. It all comes into play right
there—it's make or break, sink or swim time.
◄ Evidence, Dilated Peoples ►

Performing live, whether it's for a few people in the same room as you, an audience in a club, or a crowd at a big concert, is considered an important aspect of being a great MC. In fact, live performance is closely associated with the term *MC* itself (from *master of ceremonies*, a person who hosts or presents live events).

Thes One, People Under the Stairs

Being onstage—that's the part where the MC comes out, I think, the actual, real definition of the MC. Because shit happens onstage, and your ability to roll with the punches and to keep going, or to start freestyling or whatever, that's beyond what you're capable of doing in the comfort of a studio.

Evidence, Dilated Peoples

[Performing live is where either] rappers turn into MCs [or they don't]. This is where the separation really begins.

For many MCs, performing live is also one of the best parts about being an artist.

Planet Asia

I love to perform—that's my favorite part because you really see what the song is worth.

Buckshot, Black Moon

Performing live—never could beat that. Hip-hop is all about performing live.

Giving the fans a good live show is an essential part of a successful hip-hop career. If you have great live performance skills, fans and other artists take notice.

Kool G Rap

[The song] "Men at Work" was hard to perform, and that's why I never really liked to perform it that much—because your breath control gotta be crazy. But somebody sent me a clip of the Roots—they was onstage and they performed "Men at Work," and [Black Thought] did all three fucking verses and I couldn't believe it—he killed that shit and he had the crowd going crazy.

Joell Ortiz

If you have a shitty show and a hit record, you're fucked—when people spend their money, they want a fucking show. If you calling yourself an MC, you better be prepared to give those people what they paid for.

Del the Funky Homosapien

[Performance is] more important than having good records. Performances is the main way to glorify your paper route, as my dude E-40 would say. If you can't come off as good, or hopefully better, live, you won't make it for too long. It seems like you're fake or something if you sound good on record with Auto-Tune and all of that but onstage you sing horrible.

It just seems like it's only for the record and the money when it's like that.

Performing live can also add an extra dimension to your music and help you connect with fans in a more direct way than through a record.

MC Serch

I always had a little bit of a following in the mid-'80s—I always had a following of people that had heard about me and liked what I was doing, liked my style, and would follow me club to club. For me [back then], performance was much more important than recording, because at the time I felt like I wasn't selling a lot of records. I felt like I was impacting and influencing more people while I was performing live rather than through hearing my records.

Big Pooh, Little Brother

[Performing live] is very important. That's where you get your fan interaction—that's where people come to be part of the experience that you provide. It's one thing to listen to a record, but if you come to see an artist perform, it's supposed to be a different experience—it's supposed to raise how they feel about you, it's supposed to accentuate how they feel about you when they come to see you perform live. A lot of times people may hear a Little Brother record, then when they come to see us live, they'll be like, "Wow, I get it now—I thought one way when I just heard you on record, but when I came out here to see you perform live, you gave me a whole 'nother feeling" . . . and I think that's important.

Mastering live performance does not happen overnight. No one steps onstage and is instantly the best at it.

B-Real, Cypress Hill

All of us, when we first start, when we get on the mic for the first time and we had no practice at it, you don't sound that great and it takes you a minute to get comfortable to being onstage and having your voice in control, your breath in control, and performing the song right—all that shit takes time.

It may be helpful to start small and gain experience, testing out your songs in different live situations, honing your craft as you go.

B-Real, Cypress Hill

You want to try to perform [your songs], even if it's not to nobody—maybe it's just you in your room on your little system that you might have, or if you have the chance to go to clubs and get on the mic and push out your songs like that.

Keep in mind, however, that advice on performance doesn't apply across the board. Different MCs have different styles of performing, so a "good" live performance can be difficult to gauge. You have to find out what techniques work best for you. As long as the audience leaves your show happy, then you've done your job.

Shock G, Digital Underground

For the record, a good performance doesn't require any specific behavior—it only means that your audience is left happy and satisfied. Let's take, for instance, Jay-Z, P. Diddy, LL Cool J, and 2Pac: 2Pac moved around onstage with a drink in one hand, voice cracking, and gasping for breath the entire time. LL Cool J moves around onstage substance-free and with plenty of breath, but also sweaty and with no shirt. Diddy wears a nice shirt onstage, a suit even, but still moves around and even does extensive dance routines. While Jay-Z also dresses neatly, barely moves, rarely breaks a sweat, and instead uses smoothness and clever wordplay to keep the audience interested and entertained. All of them [are] totally different onstage, but still move the crowd, and all make great records in my opinion. Acts like Biggie or Wu-Tang just stand there and bust, with all their homies and entourage onstage, not giving a fuck. But they know their audiences don't wanna see them dance—they just wanna see and hear them.

Confidence and Showmanship

The first crucial ingredient of a live show is confidence and show-manship onstage. This helps you connect with the audience and get your message across more effectively.

Chuck D, Public Enemy

Projection, conviction, belief in what you're saying, confi-dence—[the best performance is] if you're talking to a crowd of non-believers and at the end of your musical statement you have them understanding what you're trying to say.

Tech N9ne

If you've ever seen a Tech N9ne show, you see a lot of the things we do are in unison. That comes from dancing, being a b-boy—you'll see me doing pop moves. You have to be a performer, man. That's why we sell out all our shows—it's because we give them a show. You have to have showman-ship, and that comes from me being a dancer and being onstage all my life.

For this reason, compared with recording rhymes in the studio, performing live requires an extra level of what Shock G of Digital Underground describes as "nerve, self confidence, and gall."

Rah Digga

You gotta look strong and confident onstage—you gotta make people believe that you are the freshest person on the planet.

Big Pooh, Little Brother

You have to be a showman. It's easy when you're in the booth
by yourself to perform to nobody and do multiple takes of a
verse—if you mess up, you can go back and fix it and make it
sound perfect and not have no breath control in the booth.
But when you get up on that stage, you have to know what
you're doing. You have to be able to look into the eyes of the
people who came to see you perform—you have to be able
to control what's going on onstage, and know that this is your
show. So it's a whole different set of skills.

Using the Mic and PA System

Another key element to performing live is knowing how to handle
the mic, and also being aware of the importance of a good live
PA system (the *public address system*—the mixer, amplifier, and
speakers used to play the music and vocals).

C-Murder

Of course [you need a] perfect sound system. If you ain't got
the right sound system, you're in trouble.

Royce Da 5'9"

A great sound system, a good soundman—these are elements to a good show.

Proper breath control (see chapter 12, p. 239) and what Akil the
MC of Jurassic 5 calls "clarity on the mic" are also important.

MC Serch

It's a much different process [than in the studio]. Being live
with a microphone and a PA system and being an MC, and
wanting to get your message across—it becomes difficult

because when you're doing the spoken word over beats, and you're rhyming over a beat live, it's very easy for the mic to get muffled and for your voice to become muffled. So really, it's quite a skill to have your breath control and be able to be sustained and clear so that people can hear your lyrics. A lot of the time I'd like to go onstage live and kind of flow with the crowd and maybe come off the head a little bit, and it's difficult if you have a bad PA system. So having really good mics was always important to me, and not cupping the mic—being able to have people hear you clearly was very important.

Rocking the Crowd

According to most hip-hop artists, a third essential is getting the crowd hyped up, energized, and engaged by your performance.

Sheek Louch, D-Block/The LOX

[It should look like] you're not just trying to get that show over with—you're rocking.

Hell Rell, Dipset

If the crowd is just standing there looking at you like you're crazy, then you gotta do something—do some type of hand movements or yell out to the crowd and get them aroused.

A big part of rocking the crowd is simply bringing the proper attitude to your performance and letting go of your inhibitions.

Vast Aire, Cannibal Ox

I love to perform and getting the crowd amped and seeing their response to the music. You gotta engage the crowd sort of like a comedian does—you gotta be personal with them.

You gotta show the crowd that you're here to rock, and if they're here to rock, then let's rock. You gotta believe in what you make—if you believe in what you make, then your show will just come together.

Esoteric

[Performing live is] all about rocking a party. [In] the beginning, before there were videos, before there was access to recording studios, that's how it started. Rocking the crowd, keeping people entertained that way, that's first and foremost—you gotta be able to rock a crowd and deliver your rhymes and have a stage presence. There are a lot of MCs that are dope, but if they're in front of the crowd, it goes away—to get up onstage you really have to have no inhibitions. [Then] you're gonna be a more successful performer and I think that's important, that you can engage the crowd.

Energy

Another good way to engage the crowd in your performance is to make sure you keep a high level of energy. If you don't have energy onstage, the audience won't have energy either.

Rah Digga

They gotta feel your energy and if they see you feeling it, they're going to feel it. If you're just standing there and you're not giving them any type of flair, then they're just going to stand there too.

The energy level of your performance is one of the biggest ways that performing live can differ from recording in the studio.

Vinnie Paz, Jedi Mind Tricks

When you're a group that focuses as much on energy as we do, it's a huge difference [between being in the studio and performing live]. Maybe if you talk to people who make more laid-back music, it's not much difference, but for us, [it's] going from a relaxed studio session and then going to a thousand people in a mosh pit.

Part of that energy can come from the music itself.

Fredro Starr, Onyx

Our energy in our music is so crazy. When "Slam" comes on, I have seen no record in the history of rap that destroys a fucking crowd worse than "Slam"—I haven't seen it yet. When that record comes on, everybody is dead. I feel sorry for somebody coming after us.

Many MCs also talk about how they like to feed off the energy that the fans give them.

Sheek Louch, D-Block/The LOX

The energy from a fan that loves your music and paid their money to come see you, and they're singing all your lines with you, it's dope. I like that energy.

Steele, Smif N Wessun

At a show, you feel the energy of everything and you're absorbing that, and when you get on that mic, you just explode.

Movement Onstage

Many hip-hop artists feel it's necessary to move around a lot onstage, not only to rock the crowd and keep the energy high but simply to be more visually entertaining as well.

Big Daddy Kane

[It's good to master] general stage movement, like you know

how to work the stage. You understand that there is a stage left and a stage right—people on the right side don't feel cheated because you stood on the center of the stage the whole show. You didn't bring a whole entourage of mother-fuckers that's trying to get shine and [the audience] can't even see the person that's singing the song.

David Banner

I'm not just standing onstage. I'm crowd diving—I do any-thing to make people feel [captivated], whether it's praying onstage, whatever it is. It's the best feeling to have people cap-tivated. If you want to be a better performer, run, work out.

Royce Da 5'9"

You just go out there and you just work, man, and at the end of the show you should be sweating. It should look like peo-ple got their money's worth—that's a good show to me. Busta Rhymes [does that]—the Up in Smoke Tour was probably the best hip-hop show I've seen. The Glow in the Dark Tour—I've seen clips of that—Kanye's doing his thing on that. The people that's really out there working, man. Usher got a real good show—he get out there and work his ass off. I like those kind of shows.

Your movement onstage can even reflect the content of your lyrics, helping the audience to connect better with your music.

Cashis

You have to be animated. If I say I'm running down the block or the police is looking for me or I'm putting my middle fin-ger up—I'm doing that to the crowd when I'm rapping the record. I'm acting like I'm running from the law—I get lost in the song and they see that and they feed off that energy. And even if that wasn't one of their favorite records, they're gonna go back and they're gonna enjoy that record now, because they're like, "Wow, did you just see that?"

Interacting with the Crowd

Most MCs suggest that interacting with the crowd on some level also builds a greater connection with fans and makes the show more entertaining.

Crooked I

[It's good to have] interaction with the crowd, letting them know that you're up there for them, providing a service for them—it's not all about you.

Big Daddy Kane

You have to interact with the crowd—making eye contact with a chick in the audience, snatch somebody's hat off [and] put it on your head, stuff like that—where they know that you recognize them.

Fredro Starr, Onyx

I know how to talk to the people—Run-DMC taught me so much, just going to their shows and Jam Master Jay telling me, "Yo, man, you gotta talk to the crowd, you gotta make the crowd feel you, they gotta love you, man, they gotta understand you before you even say anything."

Strong interactive elements like crowd surfing or having the crowd complete phrases are a great way to make the audience a part of the show.

Rock, Heltah Skeltah

Ain't nothing like the addiction, the rush of going, "When I say Heltah, y'all say Skeltah," and I go "Heltah," and y'all go "Skeltah." If I do that shit a hundred times, if I go "Heltaaaaaaaaaaah," they gonna go "Skeltaaaaaaaaaaaah." If I jump in the motherfucking crowd, they're gonna carry me around like a blunt. I'm 6'5"—they gonna pass me around, and then if I just point with one finger back towards the stage, they gonna pass me back towards the stage, and they're gonna throw me onstage in time for my verse. There's no comparison to that power right there. . . . And I'm gonna land on my feet, because I'm fresh like that.

Another way to add interactivity is to learn about the cities you're performing in so that you can tailor a show to those specific venues.

MURS

You have to interact with the crowd more—if you're in their city, you have to be observant. If you're driving to the venue, [you should] see something unique about that city, so your show is different—you're not doing the same thing in every city.

Being Spontaneous, Improvising, and Freestyling

If an artist finds a way to make his or her show feel spontaneous, audiences are more likely to find it exciting and memorable. Tash of Tha Alkaholiks says, "Don't do things that are typical. Every time we do a show, nobody knows what to expect. Be spontaneous and in the moment."

One great way to add spontaneity to a live show is to freestyle certain portions of your performance (see chapter 9, p. 181). You can either perform separate freestyle verses or improvise new lyrics to parts of your regular songs.

Cashis

[I freestyle at shows]—most of my shows I do that. When I have the opportunity to, usually at the end of the show, I'll be walking off the set and then I'll come back and be like, what up? And it'll be with no beat and I'll just freestyle something about wherever I'm at and [about] the people in the crowd—the fans enjoy it because they know it's a real free-style. It [adds a lot], because it's like you got something that I won't remember and you'll remember only part of what you heard and I can't duplicate that in another state or at another venue. So they can hear that and walk away with something special—everyone that was there that night has something that no one else can ever receive again.

If you're good at freestyling, you'll also be able to adapt to the surprises that inevitably arise during live performances. Regardless of what happens during the show, you'll be able to continue rapping.

Akir

I'm always practicing freestyle sessions with different artists that I hang out with—that's a very valuable skill because at any time you can lose your state of focus during a perfor-mance—something might happen in the crowd that changes the mood of the whole thing—so you always have to be able to have those skills to back you up if something happens.

Improvisational ability is particularly important when you yourself make a mistake, since you have to keep going and correct it on the fly.

O.C., Diggin' in the Crates

You know [that] in the studio you can stop. It ain't like you being onstage—you can't go through a record onstage and stop and say, "Yo, I need a punch."

MURS

Your improvisation has to be up—that's how you get the crowd involved. . . . If you slip and fall, you have to be able to come back and be witty.

Making a mistake and having to adjust can even make a show more interesting, if you respond with a memorable improvisation.

One Be Lo, Binary Star

When something is live, there's a lot of room for opportunity—you can make a mistake live, and the illest part about making a mistake live is because it ain't about the way you make a mistake, it's the way you correct it that makes it good or bad. You could drop a bottle onstage and then spontaneously you can talk about it, and now it's funny and it's not like, "Ah, man, this dude is clumsy."

Adding Something Extra

Some artists like to run through all their best-known songs and try to perform them in a similar way to how they sound on record, and this strategy often works well. But other artists prefer to change the songs up and give the audience extra things that they haven't heard on the record—a surprise or bonus for coming to the show.

Royce Da 5'9"

[It's good] being able to trick the crowd so that they don't know what's coming next—surprises in live hip-hop shows are always good.

Big Daddy Kane

I feel like you have to give somebody something extra—you shouldn't just come to a show and perform your hit songs and bounce, because if that's the case then they could have just stayed at home and listened to the album. Give them something extra, give them a freestyle or two, maybe some dancing if you want to take it there—I don't know how b-boy you get—your DJ got a solo where he doing some fancy scratching, whatever the case may be, throwing some T-shirts in the crowd, just something extra other than what they hear on the song all the time. Even if you're doing a song, you take the last four lines of a verse and switch it to something else, just something extra where there was some type of twist where they felt like they got something different than what they got on the album.

MCs sometimes use a combination of these two techniques. They feel that some songs work best the way they are on the record but that other songs can be changed in order to make them fresher and more interesting.

Schoolly D

Certain songs you have to present [like on the record], like when I do "Gucci Time," "PSK," and "Saturday Night"—those songs gotta sound like the record. Other songs can sound more like a freestyle, so [it's] knowing what songs should sound like what and making the audience feel like it's something definitely special. If I'm doing something with a live band, certain songs I can do—like "Saturday Night" and "Gucci Time" I can do—but [for] "PSK" it's best to use the original music.

Working with a Hype Man, DJ, or Group

It can be good to have someone else with you onstage, whether it's the DJ, your hype man (a person who does backup rapping and ad-libs and helps to get the crowd excited—like Flavor Flav of Public Enemy), or, if you're in a group, the other members of the group. If you're a solo artist without any support onstage, you have to put in more effort to keep the audience engaged.

Akil the MC, Jurassic 5

It's a lot easier [performing in a group]—there's more people to concentrate on for the audience. If it's just you, up there by yourself, or just you and the DJ, [then] it's just you—you have to be something that people want to look at, [but if you're in] a group, people have more to concentrate on. If you [as an audience member] don't like this person, then you can find somebody else you may like to focus your attention on. If you're up there by yourself, you have to be exceptionally good.

Other performers can help you keep the energy up, jump in to let you catch your breath, and otherwise back you up and make sure everything goes smoothly.

Royce Da 5'9"

I got a real good hype man, my brother Kid Vicious. Like, he can almost hear when I'm about to run out of breath, and he's always there—he ain't never let me down. If I had to go onstage by myself, then at least my DJ would have to help do some ad-libs. Like, a lot of my verses be so constant with the flow [that] I'd need somebody to help me do the hype man thing—I got a good hype man, so it always works.

Lateef, Latyrx

When you're doing it live, you're probably gonna have to figure out how to get a breath, because you're moving around— you [could be] in the fifth song of the set, [and] you're gonna have to have somebody say something somewhere to give you a breath, or just change your flow however you need to, to take that breath. Usually it's just a matter of getting somebody to hit some line or some word in a line—that's all you really need—so you just have your DJ or background singers to say the word.

Learning from Other Artists' Performances

A good way to develop your live performance style is to study other artists who you think are great at performing—either fellow MCs or performers in other musical genres.

Joell Ortiz

Older MCs respected the craft more and their shows were nuts. I study old KRS-One, LL Cool J, and Run-DMC show videotapes.

MURS

I go to a lot of punk shows and hard-core shows, and I've seen Tito Puente, Sergio Mendes—I go everywhere and just try to incorporate elements of other music into performances.

You may even want to watch several shows by an artist you admire and take notes on what he or she does.

Glasses Malone

Lupe [Fiasco] is one of those new guys who has a great show. I've watched his show three or four times, and I always take notes of the different things he'll do, like, he has a really ill stage show. He has a certain way he does everything—he has a certain way he reacts with the crowd. It's a combination of things—the DJ, maybe dropping things on the right words. He always has the crowd into it.

Rehearsing

The majority of MCs do some form of rehearsal before a live show, though preferences vary—as Immortal Technique puts it, "I definitely do rehearse, but not, like, religiously." It is helpful to try out your performance in front of some sort of crowd in order to see what reactions you get and adjust your performance accordingly.

Big Noyd

I try to rehearse in front of a crowd, even if it ain't a crowd of fans, even if it's just my homies or whatever. I can tell from their reactions what parts I should change or what parts I should put more energy into.

Rehearsal can also ensure that you have the timing down and that every aspect of the performance and every performer works together well.

Schoolly D

I really depend on everybody knowing their part. It's just like football: if I'm the quarterback, I'm throwing the ball and you're the wide receiver—it's like we've gotta be so on [that] by the time game time is, when I throw that football, you just gotta be there. So I practice the timing, I practice being in shape to jump around, dance around. We just go through the songs and the song list, and I allow the DJ or the backing band to add their creativity.

Tajai, Souls of Mischief

Our shittiest shows are when we do a song and then talk, a song and talk. That basically means we haven't practiced the show—we're just performing songs. A real show, you want to do it to where if somebody is watching a DVD of it, they're not gonna fast-forward through all your little talking parts and shit.

At the same time, many hip-hop artists don't like to rehearse to the point that the performance seems too forced and overproduced—they like to keep some elements of it raw.

RBX

I don't really like that contrived, super-duper, overpracticed, shined-down, polished-out, dancey, staying-on-cue type of shit—that's not my thing. I like it when you get up there and be who you are, as opposed to coming up with an image and a dance twist move.

How much rehearsal is appropriate may depend on the type of show you're doing as well.

Royce Da 5'9"

I normally don't rehearse for club dates—I only rehearse when I'm out on the road. Like when I was on the Usher tour, we rehearsed, when I was on the Nelly tour, we rehearsed— we rehearse for real shows, but when we're doing club dates and shit like that, me and [Kid] Vicious, we don't need no kind of rehearsal. We go out there, [and] even if we hadn't been out there in a minute, we go out there and it's like second nature to us.

Learning the Lyrics

When the time comes for you to perform songs live, you may have to go back and memorize them, either because you didn't do so during the writing or recording process (see chapter 13, p. 264) or because you need to refresh your memory.

Ill Bill

You better memorize it! What are you gonna do if you don't memorize it? It depends on the song—if it's been three years since I've performed the song or if I've never performed it. I've recorded songs that I've never performed live until two or three years later, and I guess, yeah, I have to go back and study it and make sure I remember it. Just because you know a song doesn't mean you necessarily remember every single word and will be able to deliver it properly in a live situation, so yeah, that's happened before—that I've had to go back and relearn the lyrics.

Most MCs don't find memorizing lyrics for performance particularly difficult. C-Murder says, "Once I listen to them a couple of times, it's in my head." Pusha-T of Clipse says that it's an enjoyable process for him, and that comes from making music he loves: "That's easy—I love what I say, I love what I do, I love my record."

Gift of Gab, Blackalicious

People act like [memorizing it] is such a difficult thing, like how do you memorize all of that? But look at all your favorite songs—how did you memorize them? Just by listening to them, because the more you hear it, the more it becomes in sync in your mind. Everybody does it, because everybody listens to music, and everybody has a song that they can sing all the words to just based off of loving the song so much and listening to it.

Making sure you know the lyrics is especially important when you add a new song that you are unfamiliar with to a live set.

B-Real, Cypress Hill

It's the newer songs that you have to get used to. When you do the old songs, they're in your head—they ain't going anywhere unless you take a 10-year hiatus. Mainly it's the new songs that you have to get used to when you make a new album.

Rah Digga

A lot of times I do need to drill myself with the iPod before I go onstage if I'm performing something new that I just recorded. But it's not hard to learn.

There may be occasions when you forget some of the lyr-ics onstage, even if you've rehearsed them many times. This is another instance in which it is helpful to have another performer with you. As Dray of Das EFX says, "That's what's good about hav-ing a partner—at times he can remember the lines." He adds that if the fans know your lyrics, you can have them take over for a few bars—just "look into the crowd and they'll help you!" And once you're onstage and into the song, the lyrics will often come back to you if you've practiced them enough.

Evidence, Dilated Peoples

Fortunately we rehearse, so I'm not caught out there—and a lot of times you'll forget the rhyme, but then as soon as you get onstage and your adrenaline starts kicking, somehow the rhyme just comes back to you. Weirdest shit.

Most artists don't have their entire catalog memorized, only the songs they are currently performing and the selected older songs they've done many times. It's just not practical to have every song memorized.

Thes One, People Under the Stairs

Those [particular older] songs I know like the back of my hand, but if someone wanted us to do some random song off some random album, I definitely would not be able to do it—I can't remember all those lyrics.

R.A. the Rugged Man

Cats will be at my concerts like, "Yo, could you do that 'Give It Up' shit that you did with J-Live?" I'm like, I don't know it. . . . I did the tour with Jedi Mind Tricks, [and] they wanted me to do the shit I did, the "Uncommon Valor" shit—I'm like, motherfuckers, the shit is 44 bars! I was like, give me a couple of days on the train or something to try to memorize it. I've been doing this for goddamn over 20 years now. I've been doing it since I was 11, 12, years old, and I got, what, five hundred fucking songs? I got probably one million rhymes, so I bet you there's kids out there that know way more of my lyrics than I do.

Final Words

I think that hip-hop should always change and evolve and that's what makes it hip-hop. I love the new MCs, I love the old MCs, I love hip-hop, period. I'm a big fan of hip-hop.

◄ N.O.R.E. ►

Papoose

If you look at any profession . . . sports, it's about skills—whoever got the best skills, that's who the best is, not who got the most money. When Allen Iverson and Kobe Bryant go on the court, it ain't about who got the most money in their bank account, it's about who gets busy on the motherfucking court. You don't even care about how much money they got, you care about how they're gonna perform. I got money, so don't get that twisted, but it's about how you perform on that mic.

Crooked I

Try to elevate your mind, no matter how that may be. For some people it could be reading books, for other people it could be meditating, for other people it could be being hands-on with whatever they want to learn about. Expand your mind, because a dumb MC is not gonna be tight. You have to have some sort of sharpness to you if you want to be a hot MC. I don't care [what type of rapper you are], you still gotta be sharp.

E-40

Treat rap as if it's a real occupation, because at the end of the day, it is. Don't take it for a joke. If you wanna play around with it, that's up to you, but with me, and a lot of other people, when I go out to do something, I'm serious about it. If you're gonna do it, do it right. Shouldn't be no half-stepping—put 100 percent in it. Be diligent, do your homework, stay focused, don't be sleeping, don't be all tardy and lame, be up on game. And surround [yourself] with people who want to see you win, surround yourself with people that have a goal, that wanna be something—that's what's up.

The Lady of Rage

It's gonna be a hard field to break into, especially a female, it's gonna be hard for her. So you definitely gonna have to come with it, and there's gonna be some hard knocks, so prepare to fight for it if that's what you want.

Phife Dawg, A Tribe Called Quest

Make sure you really don't have a problem honoring your craft. You really gotta love it—you really gotta be in tune and in love with it in order to make it. And even sometimes some of those people don't make it, but as long as you know you love it, you're doing the right thing.

Sean Price, Heltah Skeltah

I think it's getting back to lyrics, man, and that's good. I'm ready for that—I can rhyme. Redman, he can rhyme, Jadakiss, he can rhyme—it's gonna get back to them [MCs] who spit real hard-body lyrics, lyrics that count—Talib Kweli and all of them, they spit bodies. I like those dudes.

Rock, Heltah Skeltah

If you want to be better at MCing, keep it real with yourself. Don't catch yourself saying no shit that you would call somebody else corny for saying.

Buckshot, Black Moon

Hip-hop has changed, but hip-hop is great, man—hip-hop to me is a beautiful, beautiful thing and in a beautiful place because it's surviving, longer than a lot of music has. Every time there's a new young generation, there's a new form to give them that's still hip-hop.

Myka 9, Freestyle Fellowship

I would say that for MCs and people out there that are interested in it, [MCing] is really good therapeutically. Whether you ever put a record out or not, it's a good pastime.

Shock G, Digital Underground

Don't try to fit in—break all the rules and go left, young Jedi. The fans and listeners will appreciate you more. Doowutchyalike, writewutchyalike, and be free! Think HUGE—don't plan to add another leaf to the tree of hip-hop, instead start your own branch. Shit, plant your own tree, even. Everybody who does, and who means it, and who sticks to it, eventually wins.

Pusha-T, Clipse

Being better at MCing? Be yourself. If you can be yourself and feel like you're fresh, dog, you gonna be the man—you're gonna be light-years ahead of everybody else because a lot of these people ain't being their self.

Sheek Louch, D-Block/The LOX

Don't sign anything until you get it checked out all the way— take it from me.

Esoteric

Don't try to be the next whoever—be the first you. That's a lot easier said than done, of course, because when I started rhyming, I was trying to sound like King Tee, or whoever the fuck was in my tape deck at that time.

MC Shan

I just feel lucky to be one of those that fell into grooves of the wax and 20 years later still have people mentioning my name and interested in what I'm doing and things like that. So I feel lucky. I hope somebody else has the same luck I do.

Tash, Tha Alkaholiks

It starts in your heart—MCing, rapping, come from the heart. Be yourself on the microphone—if you're from Saudi Arabia, and you could teach me something through your rhymes about Saudi Arabia, I'm willing to listen, I'm willing to sit there and give you a fair shot, man.

Mighty Casey

I'm not the world's best basketball player—I never made the NBA—but I still play basketball for fun. A lot of people just rap for fun.

Guerilla Black

The longer you're on your craft, the more you sacrifice for your craft, the hotter your craft will be. It's about the time you're gonna put into it, just like a baby—you have to put time into your baby and then you know how they're raised. Put in time, quality time, sit down and teach your kids, show them this, show them that, take your time with your kid—that's how I look at rhyming.

RBX

Practice, practice, fucking practice, practice, practice, practice, and practice, then you go practice some more.

Interviewed Artists

The following is a list of all the artists who have been interviewed exclusively for *How to Rap*, with brief descriptions of each, in alphabetical order.

A Tribe Called Quest (Q-Tip and Phife Dawg)

One of the most influential groups in hip-hop, A Tribe Called Quest have sold over four million records as a group, and their members have also released successful solo albums. They have had three albums in the Top 10 of the Billboard Top 200 albums chart and are respected critically for their first three classic albums. They have collaborated with, and produced for, artists such as Mobb Deep, Jay-Z, Kanye West, Pharrell Williams, Nas, Busta Rhymes, the Beastie Boys, Black Eyed Peas, DJ Shadow, De La Soul, the Roots, Common, Mos Def, Janet Jackson, Mariah Carey, R.E.M., the Chemical Brothers, and Whitney Houston.

Aesop Rock

A critically acclaimed MC on the Definitive Jux record label, Aesop Rock is one of the most notable figures in hip-hop's underground. He has collaborated with many other underground artists and groups, including MF Doom, Vast Aire, Mr. Lif, MURS, Rjd2, Blockhead, Zion I, Cage, El-P, and Percee P.

Akil the MC, Jurassic 5

The alternative hip-hop group Jurassic 5 is one of the most popular acts to emerge from the independent scene. They have several critically acclaimed albums and have collaborated with Linkin Park, Nelly Furtado, Dave Matthews Band, Dilated Peoples, and Blackalicious, among others. They formally disbanded in 2007, but their members still tour and have released solo material.

Akir

Akir is a well-respected underground rapper known for his intricate lyrics and politically aware content, as well as his close association with acclaimed rapper Immortal Technique.

AMG

AMG is known for several classic West Coast singles such as "Bitch Betta Have My Money" and "Tha Booty Up," as well as "Can U Werk Wit Dat" with DJ Quik. He is also noted for his humorous and explicit lyrics.

Andy Cat, Ugly Duckling

The members of Californian independent hip-hip group Ugly Duckling are known for their humorous and intelligent lyrics, as well as the old-school influences that inform their sound—they have released several acclaimed albums and EPs and are one of the most prominent underground hip-hop groups.

AZ

AZ has had four albums in the Top 30 of the Billboard Top 200 albums chart, is Grammy nominated, and is known for his complex lyrics. He has guest rapped on several key releases by Nas, including *Illmatic* (one million sold), *It Was Written* (two million), and *Stillmatic* (one million). He was also a member of the supergroup the Firm, with Nas and Dr. Dre; their debut, *The Album*, has sold over half a million copies.

B-Real, Cypress Hill

Cypress Hill is one of the most well-known and acclaimed West Coast groups in hip-hop. They have sold over nine million records and are known for their first three classic albums and signature songs, such as "Insane in the Brain," "Dr. Greenthumb," and "Rap Superstar." They have worked with Eminem, Wu-Tang Clan, OutKast, Dr. Dre, and N.O.R.E., among many others.

Big Daddy Kane

One of the most influential and well-respected MCs ever, Big Daddy Kane is often featured in the top 10 of many "greatest MCs of all time" lists, including lists by MTV and Kool Moe Dee. He has collaborated with Jay-Z (who was Big Daddy Kane's hype man), Busta Rhymes, Public Enemy, 2Pac, Big L, UGK, Q-Tip, Jurassic 5, and others.

Big Noyd

A close affiliate of Mobb Deep who is featured on many of the group's albums, including the classics *The Infamous* and *Juvenile Hell*, Big Noyd is known for his agile flow and hard-core lyricism. He has also featured on tracks alongside Nas and Rakim.

Big Pooh, Little Brother

Josh Dehonney

Little Brother is one of the most critically acclaimed underground hip-hop groups, known for conscious lyrics and concept albums. Their first two albums were produced by Grammy Award–winning producer 9th Wonder, who was previously part of the group and has also produced for such artists as Mary J. Blige, Jay-Z, and Destiny's Child. They have also collaborated with such artists as Lil Wayne and MURS.

Bishop Lamont

A protégé of Dr. Dre (whose previous protégés include Eminem, 50 Cent, and Snoop Dogg), he has collaborated with many of the biggest names in hip-hop, such as Busta Rhymes, Dr. Dre, and Warren G, among others. He is known for his often humorous and confrontational lyrics.

Bobby Creekwater

One of a select number of rappers signed to Eminem's Shady Records label, Bobby Creekwater is a popular southern MC who has released several acclaimed mixtapes, and who was featured on Eminem's 2006 Shady Records mixtape LP *The Re-Up*, which has sold over one million copies.

Boot Camp Clik (Sean Price and Rock, Heltah Skeltah; Buckshot, Black Moon; Steele, Smif N Wessun)

Legendary Boot Camp Clik groups Black Moon, Heltah Skeltah, and Smif N Wessun have all released classic hip-hop albums, have sold over three million records together, and continue to release highly respected records. They are known for their intricate yet rugged flows and have worked with numerous renowned artists such as 2Pac, Busta Rhymes, and M.O.P.

Bootie Brown, The Pharcyde

See "The Pharcyde."

Brother Ali

Signed to the acclaimed label Rhymesayers, Brother Ali is known for his intelligent lyrics, agile flow, and expressive voice, and he has released several critically revered underground albums, often featuring production from Atmosphere producer Ant. His lyrics regularly include political themes and socially conscious subjects.

Brother J, X Clan

Devin DeHaven, courtesy Suburban Noize Records

X Clan is a conscious hip-hop group whose debut album, *To the East, Blackwards*, is considered a classic and was included in *The Source* magazine's 100 Best Rap Albums. They have collaborated with Jurassic 5, KRS-One, and Jacoby Shaddix of the rock band Papa Roach.

Buckshot, Black Moon

Robert Adam Mayer

See "Boot Camp Clik."

C-Murder

C-Murder is a southern rapper who is also the brother of Master P and Silkk the Shocker. His first three albums reached #3, #2, and #9 on the Billboard Top 200 albums chart, and he has collaborated with many other artists, including Akon, Ludacris, Master P, Mystikal, Silkk the Shocker, M.O.P., Snoop Dogg, Kurupt, Nate Dogg, and Fat Joe.

Cage

Cage is part of the respected Definitive Jux label and is known for his poetic and intelligent lyrics, as well as his earlier horror-core albums. He has also collaborated with many esteemed underground artists, including Aesop Rock, El-P, and Necro.

Cappadonna, Wu-Tang Clan affiliate

Very closely aligned with Wu-Tang Clan, one of the most successful and widely recognized groups in hip-hop, Cappadonna has appeared on several classic Wu-Tang albums—being especially heavily featured on *Wu-Tang Forever*, which sold over eight million copies—as well as on two of Wu-Tang's most praised LPs—Raekwon's *Only Built 4 Cuban Linx* (over one million sold) and Ghostface Killah's *Ironman* (over one million sold)—and many other Wu-Tang releases. His classic debut LP, *The Pillage*, sold over half a million copies.

Cashis

A protégé of Eminem, Cashis was featured heavily on Eminem's 2006 Shady Records mixtape LP, *The Re-Up*, which has sold over one million copies, and his *The County Hound EP* was well received, reaching #1 on the Billboard Top Heatseekers chart. He has appeared on tracks with Eminem, 50 Cent, Stat Quo, Obie Trice, Lloyd Banks, and others.

Chuck D, Public Enemy

Sarah Edwards

Public Enemy is one of the most influential groups, in hip-hop and outside of it, of all time, often included in "best" and "greatest" lists by *Rolling Stone*, *The Source*, *XXL*, MTV, VH1, and others. Chuck D is known for his insightful, confrontational, and often politically oriented lyrics, as well as for having one of the most recognizable voices in music. They have sold around five million records, and their album *It Takes a Nation of Millions to Hold Us Back* is often referred to in publications such as *NME*, *Vibe*, and *Q* as the greatest hip-hop album ever.

Cormega

Cormega is a critically acclaimed MC, known for his intricate and sincere lyrics, who has released a number of notable albums. He has also collaborated with many of the most distinguished lyricists in the genre, including Nas, AZ, and Ghostface Killah.

Crooked I

Crooked I is a West Coast artist known for his exceptional MCing skills and lyrical dexterity. He has collaborated with, among others, Luniz, Akon, Joell Ortiz, Joe Budden, and Royce Da 5'9", and has released numerous acclaimed mixtapes and freestyles.

D-Block/The LOX (Styles P and Sheek Louch)

Styles P and Sheek Louch have sold over two million records combined and as part of the group D-Block (formerly known as the LOX) along with group member Jadakiss, with their two albums reaching #3 and #5 on the Billboard Top 200 albums chart. They are renowned for their raw and intelligent style and have collaborated with Jennifer Lopez, Mariah Carey, Akon, the Notorious B.I.G., P. Diddy, Bun B, Jim Jones, the Game, Fat Joe, DMX, and others.

David Banner

David Banner is a southern MC who has sold over one million records and has had several hit singles, including "Play," which reached #7 on the Billboard Hot 100 singles chart in 2005. He has worked with many of the biggest names in hip-hop, including Snoop Dogg, Akon, and Lil Wayne, all of whom were featured on his 2007 song "9mm." He is also known as a philanthropist and actor, having starred alongside Samuel L. Jackson and Christina Ricci in the film *Black Snake Moan.*

Del the Funky Homosapien

Scott Stewart

Del is an esteemed West Coast rapper, is a member of the Hieroglyphics crew, is Ice Cube's cousin, and is known for his distinct style, intelligent lyrics, and classic catalog. He was also featured on the self-titled debut album of Gorillaz, with Damon Albarn of Blur, and rapped on the group's hit single "Clint Eastwood."

Devin the Dude

Devin the Dude is a cult favorite who regularly collaborates with the biggest names in hip-hop, such as Snoop Dogg, Jay-Z, Dr. Dre, Lil Wayne, Ice Cube, André 3000 of OutKast, Scarface, Xzibit, the Roots, Lil Jon, De La Soul, Chamillionaire, and Nas. He is also famous for his guest appearance on Dr. Dre's classic *2001* album (10 million copies sold), which led to him being part of the Up in Smoke Tour with Eminem, Dr. Dre, Snoop Dogg, Xzibit, and Ice Cube.

Dipset (40 Cal and Hell Rell)

40 Cal and Hell Rell are both part of the Diplomats (Dipset) crew. 40 Cal is known for his battling and freestyling abilities and was featured on the show *Fight Klub* on MTV2, and both have appeared on numerous popular Diplomats records that have collectively sold in the millions.

DJ Quik

West Coast favorite DJ Quik has sold over two and a half million records and has collaborated and produced records for 2Pac, Snoop Dogg, Jay-Z, Dr. Dre, Ludacris, Janet Jackson, Whitney Houston, Xzibit, Eazy-E, and many others. He has released a number of acclaimed albums over his long career, including his classic debut, *Quik Is the Name*, which was in *The Source* magazine's 100 Best Rap Albums.

Dray, Das EFX

Dray is one-half of Das EFX, known for their lyrical creativity and the influential vocal style they pioneered in the early 1990s. Their debut album, *Dead Serious*, is a hip-hop classic, included in *The Source* magazine's 100 Best Rap Albums, and their first three albums reached #16, #20, and #22 on the Billboard Top 200 albums chart—they have sold over one and a half million records.

E-40

E-40 has sold well over three million records; has had six albums in the Top 20 of Billboard Top 200 albums chart, including a #3 in 2006; and has had several hit singles, such as "Tell Me When to Go" and "U and Dat." E-40 is known for his agile flow and expressive delivery. He appeared on 2Pac's *All Eyez on Me* LP, which sold nine million copies, and has worked with Ice Cube, Bone Thugs-N-Harmony, and Too $hort.

El Da Sensei

Josh Dehonney

Underground MC and part of New Jersey–based Artifacts—whose debut album, *Between a Rock and a Hard Place*, was an underground favorite—El Da Sensei is also known for his intelligent lyrics and raw, uncompromising approach. He has worked with Brand Nubian, Pharoahe Monch, J-Live, O.C. of Diggin' in the Crates, and Sean Price, among others.

Esoteric

Diana Levine

Esoteric is one-half of the well-respected underground duo 7L & Esoteric. They have worked with many other hip-hop artists, such as Inspectah Deck of Wu-Tang Clan, Jedi Mind Tricks, Apathy, Celph Titled, and Outerspace, and are also members of the underground hip-hop supergroups the Demigodz and Army of the Pharaohs.

Evidence, Dilated Peoples

One of the most notable groups to come out of hip-hop's independent scene, Dilated Peoples have released several acclaimed albums and have collaborated with Cypress Hill, Kanye West, Devin the Dude, Aceyalone, Planet Asia, the Alchemist, DJ Premier, the Roots, Gang Starr, the Beatnuts, Tha Alkaholiks, and others.

40 Cal, Dipset

See "Dipset."

Fredro Starr, Onyx

Fredro Starr is a rapper in the group Onyx, who have released several classic albums, as well as selling over two million records—they are best known for their hit single "Slam." They have had three albums in the Top 25 of the Billboard Top 200 albums chart, and their debut album, *Bacdafucup*, was selected as one of *The Source* magazine's 100 Best Rap Albums. Fredro has also had two acclaimed solo albums and is an actor who has starred in major films such as *Clockers, Sunset Park, Ride, Light It Up*, and *Save the Last Dance* and appeared in TV roles on such shows as *Moesha, The Wire, NYPD Blue, Law & Order, Blade: The Series*, and *Promised Land*.

Gift of Gab, Blackalicious

Gift of Gab is the MC in the group Blackalicious, on Quannum Records. They are noted for their intelligent and intricate lyrics and music, have worked with revered producer DJ Shadow, and are one of the most popular groups in the independent hip-hop scene. Gift of Gab is also known for his tongue-twisting flow.

Glasses Malone

West Coast rapper Glasses Malone has released several acclaimed mix-tapes and was signed to Sony for $1.7 million before moving to Cash Money Records. He has worked with Lil Wayne, Akon, Mack 10, the Game, Bishop Lamont, and Crooked I, among others.

Gorilla Zoe

Gorilla Zoe is a southern rapper who is part of the group Boyz N Da Hood, signed to P. Diddy's Bad Boy Records. His debut album, *Welcome to the Zoo*, made it to #18 on the Billboard Top 200 albums chart, and he has collaborated with artists such as Yung Joc, Lil Wayne, Rick Ross, Shawty Lo, and Sha Money XL.

Guerilla Black

Guerilla Black is a West Coast rapper from Compton, California, who is often noted for his similarity in style and appearance to deceased hip-hop legend the Notorious B.I.G. His acclaimed debut album, *Guerilla City*, reached #20 on the Billboard Top 200 albums chart, and he has also released several well-received mixtapes.

Havoc, Mobb Deep

Mobb Deep is one of the most critically acclaimed hard-core East Coast hip-hop groups, selling over three million records as a group as well as bringing out well-received solo records—their 2006 group album reached #3 on the Billboard Top 200 albums chart. Havoc is also a producer who has worked with many of the biggest names in hip-hop, including 50 Cent, Nas, the Notorious B.I.G., the Game, and LL Cool J. Mobb Deep is also now a part of 50 Cent's G-Unit camp.

Hell Rell, Dipset

See "Dipset."

Ill Bill

Mike McRath

Ill Bill is a hard-core MC who is part of underground favorites Non Phixion. He is known for the political nature of his lyrics, has released acclaimed albums, and is part of the group La Coka Nostra, along with Everlast, Danny Boy, and DJ Lethal, all of House of Pain. He has also worked with Vinnie Paz, B-Real, Immortal Technique, Tech N9ne, and Raekwon, among others.

Imani, The Pharcyde

See "The Pharcyde."

Immortal Technique

Carey Stuart

Immortal Technique is an acclaimed MC and political activist with confrontational lyrics often dealing with political themes. He has collaborated with a number of other MCs, including Crooked I, Pharoahe Monch, Akir, Chino XL, Ras Kass, and Jean Grae.

Joell Ortiz

Joell Ortiz was signed to Dr. Dre's Aftermath record label, having been previously featured in the Unsigned Hype column of *The Source* magazine, and was also selected as Chairman's Choice in *XXL* magazine. He is known for his complex lyricism, and he has collaborated with many of hip-hop's greatest talents, including Big Daddy Kane, KRS-One, and Kool G Rap.

Killah Priest, Wu-Tang Clan affiliate

Killah Priest is one of the most respected rappers associated with the Wu-Tang Clan since his appearance on GZA's album *Liquid Swords* (over 500,000 copies sold), which included Killah Priest's classic solo track "B.I.B.L.E." He is also featured on GZA's *Beneath the Surface* (over 500,000 sold), and on Ol' Dirty Bastard's *Return to the 36 Chambers* (over 500,000 sold). His debut album, *Heavy Mental*, is considered a hip-hop classic and reached #24 on the Billboard Top 200 albums chart.

Kool G Rap

Kool G Rap is one of the most influential MCs of all time, with Eminem, Jay-Z, Big Pun, R.A. the Rugged Man, and many others citing him among their influences. He is frequently on "greatest MCs of all time" lists, and is featured in the Top 15 of Kool Moe Dee's book *There's a God on the Mic: The True 50 Greatest MCs*. His techniques are evident in many of the most acclaimed MCs' lyrics, and he has appeared on tracks with numerous artists, including Eminem, Nas, AZ, Mobb Deep, Busta Rhymes, Big L, Ghostface Killah, and Canibus.

K-Os

K-Os is a Canadian rapper known for his conscious lyrics and for incorporating various styles of music such as funk, rock, and reggae. All his albums have been well received, and *Atlantis: Hymns for Disco* debuted at #1 on the Canadian charts. He has also collaborated with the Chemical Brothers (on the track "Get Yourself High") and others.

The Lady of Rage

Considered one of the most skillful female MCs, the Lady of Rage has appeared on some of the most highly rated West Coast albums, such as Dr. Dre's *The Chronic* (three million sold), Snoop Dogg's *Doggystyle* (four million), Tha Dogg Pound's *Dogg Food* (two million), and the soundtrack album for the film *Above the Rim* (two million). She is known for her mastery of flow and her hard-core lyrics.

Lateef, Latyrx

Lateef is half of the acclaimed duo Latyrx (along with Lyrics Born) as well as a member of the Quannum collective along with Blackalicious, DJ Shadow, and others. Lateef featured on Fatboy Slim's hit singles "That Old Pair of Jeans" and "Wonderful Night," and he has also appeared on two of DJ Shadow's singles.

Lord Jamar, Brand Nubian

Alternative hip-hop group Brand Nubian are known for their socially conscious lyrics and classic albums. Their debut album, *One for All*, received the highest rating possible in *The Source* magazine and was included in the magazine's 100 Best Rap Albums. Group member Lord Jamar is also an actor, best known for his role of Supreme Allah on the TV series *Oz*. He has also appeared on *The Sopranos, Law & Order: Special Victims Unit*, and *Third Watch*.

Masta Ace

A highly respected MC with a long career, Masta Ace has consistently put out acclaimed releases from the 1980s to the present day. He is frequently on "greatest MCs of all time" lists, and is featured in Kool Moe Dee's book *There's a God on the Mic: The True 50 Greatest MCs*. He is part of the Juice Crew, the famous late-1980s hip-hop collective, along with several other of the most highly rated MCs in hip-hop history.

MC Serch

As part of the group 3rd Bass, MC Serch sold over one million records as well as releasing *The Cactus Album*, which was included in *The Source* magazine's 100 Best Rap Albums. He was also closely involved in the careers of Nas, O.C., and Non Phixion and hosted the VH1 reality series *Ego Trip's The (White) Rapper Show*.

MC Shan

MC Shan is part of the legendary late-1980s hip-hop collective the Juice Crew. *The Source* magazine ranked his 1988 debut, *Down by Law*, as one of the 100 Best Rap Albums of all time, and he is featured in Kool Moe Dee's book *There's a God on the Mic: The True 50 Greatest MCs*.

Mighty Casey

Mighty Casey is an underground artist from Boston, best known for his humorous lyrics and his song "White Girls," which was in rotation on cable network BET and was also used in the film *White Chicks*, a popular comedy by the Wayans brothers.

Mr. Lif

Mr. Lif is an MC on renowned record label Definitive Jux and is known for the political content and intelligence in his lyrics. He is also a member of the hip-hop group the Perceptionists (with Akrobatik) and has released several acclaimed albums and EPs.

MURS

Signed to Warner Bros. Records, MURS is known for his insightful and intelligent lyrics. He is also part of the Definitive Jux record label, which includes some of the most notable independent hip-hop artists. He is a member of several hip-hop collectives, such as Living Legends, Felt, and 3 Melancholy

Gypsys, and has worked with Snoop Dogg, DJ Quik, and will.i.am of Black Eyed Peas.

Myka 9, Freestyle Fellowship

Daniel Solomon

Myka 9 is part of the influential underground Californian group Freestyle Fellowship, known for their expert freestyling techniques and incorporating elements of jazz into their music. Their early albums are considered hip-hop classics, and they continue to put out highly acclaimed and boundary-pushing material.

Nelly

Grammy Award–winner Nelly has sold over 20 million records, as well as numerous Top 10 hits, including four that reached #1 on the Billboard Hot 100 chart and three #1 albums on the Billboard Top 200 albums chart. He has worked with T.I., Lil Wayne, Snoop Dogg, LL Cool J, Akon, Chuck D, the Neptunes, Fat Joe, Remy Ma, Mobb Deep, and Missy Elliot, among others.

N.O.R.E.

N.O.R.E. has sold over a million records, has had three albums in the Top 10 of the Billboard Top 200 albums chart, and is known for working with top hit-makers such as the Neptunes and Swizz Beatz as well as Kanye West, Missy Elliot, Nas, Ice T, Nelly, Ja Rule, Kelis, Fat Joe, and Busta Rhymes. He is also one-half of respected hard-core hip-hop duo Capone-N-Noreaga.

O.C., Diggin' in the Crates

O.C. is part of the Diggin' in the Crates (DITC) crew and is known for his widely acclaimed debut album, *Word . . . Life,* and for commanding great respect as an MC, especially from fellow rappers and long-time hip-hop fans. He has worked with Pharoahe Monch, Lord Finesse, Fat Joe, Big L, Buckwild, Sadat X, Chubb Rock, Jeru the Damaja, and others.

Omar Cruz

Omar Cruz is a West Coast MC signed jointly to major labels Interscope and Geffen Records. His street album, *The Cruzifixion,* received the highest possible rating from *Scratch* magazine. He has worked with some of the most esteemed hip-hop producers, such as Cool & Dre, Hi-Tek, Nottz, and DJ Khalil, and collaborated with West Coast favorites the Game and WC.

One Be Lo, Binary Star

Part of the group Binary Star, One Be Lo is known for his conscious and intelligent lyrics, and for Binary Star's debut album, *Water World,* which is highly regarded among fans of underground hip-hop. One Be Lo has also released a number of acclaimed solo albums.

Papoose

Papoose was signed to Jive Records for $1.5 million after a bidding war between top mainstream labels. He has a wide fan base, thanks to numerous mixtapes and collaborations with many of the top artists in hip-hop, and has a reputation as a complex lyricist. He has worked with Snoop Dogg, Busta Rhymes, Dr. Dre, and Kanye West, among others.

Paris

Paris is a West Coast MC known for his complex, intelligent, and confrontationally political lyrics. He has released a number of acclaimed albums over his career and has worked with Dead Prez, Public Enemy, Kam, MC Ren, Immortal Technique, and others—he also ghostwrote and produced the Public Enemy album *Rebirth of a Nation*.

Pharoahe Monch

One of hip-hop's most well-respected MCs, Pharoahe Monch is known for his complex lyricism and mastery of flow. He has released acclaimed solo albums, as well as classic LPs as part of the group Organized Konfusion, and has worked with Q-Tip, Mos Def, Nate Dogg, De La Soul, Kool G Rap, O.C. of DITC, Talib Kweli, DJ Quik, Ras Kass, Canibus, Macy Gray, and many others.

Phife Dawg, A Tribe Called Quest

See "A Tribe Called Quest."

Pigeon John

Pigeon John is an L.A. rapper who is also part of the group L.A. Symphony. He is signed to the Quannum label along with Blackalicious, Lyrics Born, Lateef, and Lifesavas. Known for his often humorous and positive lyrics, he has released numerous well-respected albums.

Planet Asia

Shemp "The Photo Doctor"

Planet Asia is a Grammy-nominated underground rapper who has been awarded the Independent Album of the Year award twice by *The Source* magazine. He has collaborated with artists such as Linkin Park, Talib Kweli, Bun B, and Ghostface Killah, among others, and is known for his versatility and intelligent lyrics.

Pusha-T, Clipse

Clipse have two widely acclaimed albums entirely produced by the Neptunes, including their hit single "Grindin." They have sold over 750,000 records, with their two albums reaching #4 and #14 on the Billboard Top

200 albums chart. *XXL* gave their 2006 album *Hell Hath No Fury* its highest review rating, only the sixth album to receive the rating in the magazine's history. They have collaborated with Justin Timberlake (on his hit single "Like I Love You"), Kelis, Nelly, the Game, Fabolous, and Faith Evans, among others.

Q-Tip, A Tribe Called Quest

See "A Tribe Called Quest"

R.A. the Rugged Man

One of the most skillful lyricists in hip-hop, R.A. the Rugged Man has worked with legends such as the Notorious B.I.G., Mobb Deep, Tragedy Khadafi, and Wu-Tang Clan. He was also a contributor to *Ego Trip's Book of Rap Lists* and *Ego Trip's Big Book of Racism*, and has written articles for popular magazines such as *Vibe, King,* and *The Source.*

Rah Digga

Formerly part of Busta Rhymes's Flipmode Squad, Rah Digga is one of hip-hop's most skilled female MCs, appearing on the Fugees' *The Score* (six million sold) and numerous Busta Rhymes albums. She also released an acclaimed solo album, *Dirty Harriet,* which went to #18 on the Billboard Top 200 albums chart.

Rampage, Flipmode Squad

Part of Busta Rhymes's Flipmode Squad, Rampage has appeared on six Busta Rhymes albums (combined sales of over five million). He was featured on Craig Mack's "Flava in Ya Ear Remix," widely regarded as one of the greatest posse cuts in hip-hop history, as well as on Busta Rhymes's classic single "Woo Hah!! Got You All in Check." He has also released several successful solo albums.

RBX

RBX has had memorable guest appearances on some of hip-hop's most influential and lauded albums, such as Eminem's *The Marshall Mathers LP* (nine million sold), Snoop Dogg's *Doggystyle* (four million), and Dr. Dre's *The Chronic* (three million)—he also ghostwrote Dre's Grammy-winning hit single "Let Me Ride" and has released several well-respected solo LPs.

Remy Ma

Remy Ma is one of the most popular and acclaimed female MCs and is a former member of Fat Joe's Terror Squad. She is Grammy nominated, and in 2004 she rapped on Terror Squad's "Lean Back" single, a #1 hit on the Billboard Hot 100 chart.

Rock, Heltah Skeltah

See "Boot Camp Clik."

Alexander Richter

Royce Da 5'9"

Well-respected lyricist Royce Da 5'9" was part of the duo Bad Meets Evil with long-time friend Eminem and has ghostwritten for Dr. Dre and P. Diddy. He is known for his intricate flow and wordplay, has released several well-received albums and mixtapes, and has also collaborated with DJ Premier, the Neptunes, Clipse, and Twista, among others.

Schoolly D

Otto van den Toorn

Schoolly D is an influential MC who debuted in the mid-1980s and is often credited with inventing gangsta rap. He has a number of classic tracks that have been sampled and referenced by countless other hip hop artists, such as "P.S.K. What Does It Mean?" "Gucci Time," and "Saturday Night," and his album *Saturday Night—The Album* was included in *The Source* magazine's 100 Best Rap Albums. He also wrote the theme music for the popular TV show *Aqua Teen Hunger Force*.

Sean Price, Heltah Skeltah

See "Boot Camp Clik."

Alexander Richter

Sheek Louch, D-Block/The LOX

See "D-Block/The LOX."

Shock G, Digital Underground

Heather Christianson

Shock G is the lead rapper of Digital Underground, who have sold over three and a half million records and released several classic albums, with their debut album, *Sex Packets*, being included in *The Source* magazine's 100 Best Rap Albums list. They are also noted for launching the career of 2Pac, who was a dancer and roadie for the band. Shock G produced numerous tracks for 2Pac during his career.

Speech, Arrested Development

Speech is the lead rapper of Arrested Development, a progressive hip-hop group whose classic debut, *3 Years, 5 Months & 2 Days in the Life of . . .*, won them two Grammys, and who have sold over five million records. Their song "Tennessee" is part of the Rock and Roll Hall of Fame's 500 Songs That Shaped Rock and Roll list.

Spider Loc

Spider Loc is a West Coast rapper who is part of 50 Cent's G-Unit clique. He has collaborated on tracks with 50 Cent, Lloyd Banks, and Young Buck, including the 2005 film soundtrack *Get Rich or Die Tryin'* (over one million copies sold).

Stat Quo

Stat Quo is a southern MC who was signed jointly to Eminem and Dr. Dre's record labels—Shady and Aftermath, respectively. He has appeared on various Eminem projects, such as the *Encore* album and *The Re-Up*, and has worked extensively with Dr. Dre, as well as collaborating with Young Buck, 50 Cent, Obie Trice, Cashis, Bobby Creekwater, Rah Digga, and others.

Steele, Smif N Wessun

Todd C. Westphal
(Toddwestphal.com)

See "Boot Camp Clik."

Stressmatic, The Federation

The Federation is a popular Bay Area hip-hop group on Warner Bros. Records produced exclusively by Rick Rock, who has produced for other artists such as 2Pac, Jay-Z, Busta Rhymes, Method Man, and Will Smith. As a group they have collaborated with Snoop Dogg, Travis Barker of rock band blink-182, E-40, and others.

Styles P, D-Block/The LOX

See "D-Block/The LOX."

T3, Slum Village

Slum Village is an acclaimed Detroit hip-hop group who had a hit single with "Selfish," produced by Kanye West and featuring John Legend. They are also known for working extensively with the late J Dilla, who was originally part of the group and is regarded as one of the best hip-hop producers of all time.

Tajai, Souls of Mischief

Souls of Mischief is part of the Hieroglyphics crew, along with Del the Funky Homosapien and others. They are noted for their classic debut album, *93 'Til Infinity*, which was included in *The Source* magazine's 100 Best Rap Albums, as well as for consistently releasing quality material as individual solo artists and as a group.

Tash, Tha Alkaholiks

Tha Alkaholiks, one of the most notable groups on the West Coast, have had a series of respected albums as a group and as solo artists and are known for their humorous and skilled hard-core rhymes. They are also part of the Likwit Crew—with King Tee, Xzibit, Lootpack, and others—and have worked with Bishop Lamont, Busta Rhymes, Kurupt, Raekwon, B-Real, OutKast, and Q-Tip, among others.

Tech N9ne

Joshua Hoffine

Tech N9ne is known for his mastery of flow and intricate lyricism, and for being able to rap incredibly fast in a variety of complex rhythms. He has released numerous acclaimed albums and has appeared on tracks alongside Eminem, Kool G Rap, Pharoahe Monch, the RZA, KRS-One, Yukmouth, Brotha Lynch Hung, Ill Bill, Twista, Ice Cube, Scarface, X Clan, and many others.

Termanology

Known for his complex lyricism, Termanology has collaborated with many of the biggest names in hip-hop, including Nas, Royce Da 5'9", Papoose,

M.O.P., Bun B, and Terror Squad. He also has the backing and production of legendary hip-hop producer DJ Premier, who has produced for Jay-Z, Snoop Dogg, Nas, the Notorious B.I.G., AZ, and Christina Aguilera.

The Pharcyde (Bootie Brown and Imani)

The Pharcyde is a West Coast group known for their canonical debut album, *Bizarre Ride II the Pharcyde*, which sold over 500,000 copies, as well as their conscious and often humorous content. Bootie Brown also rapped on a single from the album *Demon Days* by Gorillaz, an album which sold over 2 million copies.

Thes One, People Under the Stairs

West Coast group People Under the Stairs is one of the most prominent underground hip-hop groups. They have put out a number of acclaimed albums and EPs, and are known for their conscious, positive content and dense, intricate production, which recalls hip-hop's golden age.

Twista

Twista, known as one of the fastest rappers ever, has sold over three million records. He had a #1 single on the Billboard Hot 100 chart with "Slow Jamz," as well as the hits "Girl Tonite" and "Overnight Celebrity." He has worked with Kanye West, the Neptunes, Jamie Foxx, T-Pain, R. Kelly, Mariah Carey, Trick Daddy, Cam'ron, and many others.

2Mex, The Visionaries

2Mex is part of the group the Visionaries, known for their positive lyrics and intricate rhymes. Their music has been featured in Warner Bros.' box-office hit *Oceans Twelve* and the MTV feature film *Volcano High*, and they have collaborated with numerous distinguished hip-hop artists and groups, including Brand Nubian, RBX, Dilated Peoples, and Brother J of X Clan.

Vast Aire, Cannibal Ox

Cannibal Ox is an underground hip-hop group whose debut album, *The Cold Vein*, produced by El-P, is one of the most acclaimed releases in independent rap. Vast Aire has worked with numerous other underground favorites, including Aesop Rock, C-Rayz Walz, and Cage.

Vinnie Paz, Jedi Mind Tricks

Mike McRath

Philadelphia hip-hop group Jedi Mind Tricks are known for their hard-core and intelligent approach and have collaborated with many of the most respected MCs in the genre, including Kool G Rap, Sean Price, Killah Priest, GZA, R.A. the Rugged Man, Tragedy Khadafi, Ras Kass, Canibus, Percee P, and Ill Bill.

Vursatyl, Lifesavas

Vursatyl is one-third of the group Lifesavas—known for their positive and introspective lyrics and intricate flows. They are signed to popular independent label Quannum, and they have collaborated with several notable artists such as DJ Shadow, Dead Prez, and Blackalicious.

Wildchild, Lootpack

Wildchild is part of the group Lootpack, who are signed to one of the most well-regarded independent hip-hop labels, Stones Throw. They are also famous for being produced by Madlib, who is considered one of the most creative producers in the genre and is known for his work with artists such as De La Soul, Ghostface Killah of Wu-Tang Clan, the Alkaholiks, and MF Doom.

will.i.am, Black Eyed Peas

Black Eyed Peas have sold over 20 million records and are known for positive, conscious lyrics, such as on the hit single "Where Is the Love?" Will.i.am has produced and collaborated with many artists, including the Game, Common, Talib Kweli, Busta Rhymes, Nas, Flo Rida, and Michael Jackson. He also supported the presidential campaign of Barack Obama, releasing the song "Yes We Can" and performing at Obama's inaugural concert.

Wise Intelligent, Poor Righteous Teachers

Known for its conscious lyrics, the debut album of Poor Righteous Teachers, *Holy Intellect*, was included in *The Source* magazine's 100 Best Rap Albums and is considered a hip-hop classic. They continually release acclaimed albums and have collaborated with the Fugees and KRS-One, among others.

Wordsworth

Pawel Fabjanski

A well-respected underground rapper from Brooklyn, Wordsworth appeared on A Tribe Called Quest's *The Love Movement* and on Mos Def and Talib Kweli's album *Black Star*. He was also involved in MTV's comedy sketch series *Lyricist Lounge* and is part of supergroup eMC, with Masta Ace, Punchline, and Strick.

Yukmouth

Yukmouth is a member of the group Luniz, whose debut album, *Operation Stackola*, sold over a million copies, and is known for the smash hit "I Got 5 on It." He has also sold over a million records as a solo artist, with his solo debut, *Thugged Out: The Albulation*, selling over 500,000 records, and he is known for his extensive list of collaborations with such fellow West Coast artists as the Game, E-40, and Shock G.

Zumbi, Zion I

Zion I is a renowned underground group, known for their intelligent, positive, and socially conscious lyrics. They have collaborated with other notable artists such as Talib Kweli, Aesop Rock, Del the Funky Homosapien, Gift of Gab, and others, and they have released a number of acclaimed albums.

Index